Children in Chinese Art

Published with the support

of the School of Hawaiian,

Asian, and Pacific Studies,

University of Hawai'i

Children in Chinese Art

Edited by
Ann Barrott Wicks

University of Hawai'i Press
Honolulu

LIBRARY OF CONGRESS CATALOGING-IN-PUBLICATION DATA
Children in Chinese art / edited by Ann Barrott Wicks.
p. cm.
Includes bibliographical references and index.
ISBN 0-8248-2359-1 (cloth : alk. paper)
1. Children in art. 2. Art, Chinese—Ming-Qing dynasties, 1368–1912.
I. Wicks, Ann Elizabeth Barrott.

N7343.5 .C464 2002
700'.452054'0951—dc21 2001053509

University of Hawai'i Press books are printed on acid-free paper and meet the guidelines for permanence and durability of the Council on Library Resources.

Designed by Diane Gleba Hall
Printed by Friesens Corporation

07 06 05 04 03 02 6 5 4 3 2 1

Contents

Acknowledgments

More than ten years ago, I approached Ellen Avril, who was at that time assistant curator of Asian art at the Cincinnati Art Museum, about the possibility of organizing an exhibition of Chinese representations of children. Ellen was more than enthusiastic, and we began work almost immediately. A year later, our carefully researched proposal was readily supported by the exhibition committee of the Cincinnati Art Museum, under the direction of Millard Rogers. An exhibition-planning grant from the National Endowment for the Humanities (NEH) allowed us to gather a team of experts who met in Cincinnati for three days in June 1993 to discuss and further develop our ideas about the exhibition. The grant also funded travel to collections of Chinese art in North America, Europe, and Asia for primary research, followed by a second meeting of the consultants to plan the exhibition.

During 1993 and 1994, Ellen Avril and I studied depictions of children in more than fifty public and private collections. Nora Shih accompanied us to study collections on the West and East Coasts, in Hawai'i, and in Asia. Diana Tenckhoff went with us to see art in the Midwest and in Toronto. We were delighted with the friendly and interested response we received in each locale, and the willingness of museums and collectors to lend art to the show. In Honolulu, we met with Patricia Crosby, senior editor at the University of Hawai'i Press, who agreed to copublish the exhibition catalog.

The implementation of the exhibition unfortunately coincided with a period of decreased national funding for the arts, as well as a leadership change at the Cincinnati Art Museum. It was a great disappointment when the new director of the Cincinnati Art Museum canceled the exhibition. We cannot adequately apologize to the museums in China, Europe, and Taiwan with which we had negotiated contracts, the museums that were scheduled to host the additional venues, the catalog essay authors whose finished work we could not publish, and the anticipated symposium speakers whose plans were so abruptly changed. Nonetheless we do apologize, and thank them for their gracious acceptance of the circumstances.

This volume of essays evolved from research done for the proposed exhibition and symposium. Some of the illustrations included were among those previously planned for the museum show. The book, however, is not an attempt to reproduce what would have been the exhibition catalog. The emphasis has changed from visual presentation to an examination of the social context of the works. I am grateful to Patricia Crosby of the University of Hawai'i Press for her willingness to consider publishing a volume of essays. I appreciate her support, patience, and editorial expertise.

NEH consultants to the proposed museum project, to whom Ellen and I owe many thanks for their enthusiastic support, their time, and their knowledgeable suggestions, are Richard Barnhart, art history, Yale University; Terese Tse Bartholomew, art history, Asian Art Museum of San Francisco; Anne Behnke Kinney, history, University of Virginia; Anne El-Omami, art education, Cincinnati Art Museum; Miriam Levering, religion, University of Tennessee at Knoxville; Stephen Little, art history, Chicago Art Institute; Catherine Pease, literature, Western Washington University; Diana Tenckhoff, art history, University of Oregon; Nora Ling-yun Shih, art history, New York; Ann Waltner, history, University of Minnesota; and Zhou Xiuqin, museum studies, University of Pennsylvania.

I would also like to thank the many following museum curators and personnel for their time, expertise, and kindness. Each of them contributed something to the outcome of this book. In China: Ma Chengyuan, Wang Qingzheng, and Zhong Yinlan of the *Shanghai Museum*; Yang Xin, Shan Guoqiang, and Xia Jinping of the *Palace Museum*, Beijing; Liang Baiquan, Xu Huping, Zhang Pusheng, Zhou Guangyi, and Huang Ping of the *Nanjing Museum*; Chen Jun of the *Suzhou Museum*; Chen Ruinong of the *Wuxi Municipal Museum*; Ren Zhilu, Tao Zhenggang, Wang Xiaorong, Zhang Xishun, and Gao Ke of the *Museum of Shanxi Province, Taiyuan*, and *Shanxi Provincial Cultural Relics Bureau*; Cui Jin, Liu Guozhan, and Zhang Shulan of the *Tianjin Museum of Fine Arts*; Cai Changkui of the *Tianjin Folk Customs Museum*; Lü Changsheng and Zhou Baozhong of the *Museum of Chinese History*, Beijing; Philip Y. C. Mak of the *Tsui Museum of Art*, Hong Kong; Christina Chu of the *Hong Kong Museum of Art*; Wang Limei of the *State Bureau of Cultural Relics*, Beijing. In Taiwan: Chin Hsiao-yi, Lin Po-t'ing, and Chang Lin-sheng of the *National Palace Museum*, Taipei; Shi Shou-chien of the *Graduate Institute of Art History*, National Taiwan University, Taipei. In Japan: Yutaka Mino, Asaka Hiroshi, Suzuki Yukito, and Ishikawa Tomohiko of the *Osaka Municipal Museum of Art*;

Nishigami Minoru and Kawahara Masahiko of the *Kyoto National Museum*; Fujita Shinya of the *Museum Yamato Bunkakan*; Kohno Keiko of the *Sumitomo Collection*; Koike Tomio, Yamamoto Yasukazu, and Sato Toyozo of the *Tokugawa Art Museum*; Minato Nobuyuki, Nishioka Yasuhiro, and Imai Atsushi of the *Tokyo National Museum*; Ebine Toshio of the *Tokyo National University of Fine Arts and Music*. In Europe: Jessica Harrison-Hall, Anne Farrer, and Joe Cribb of the *British Museum*, London; the *Percival David Foundation*, London; Regina Krahl and Craig Clunas of the *Barlow Collection*; Peter Hardie of the *Bristol Museums and Art Gallery*; Jean-Paul Desroches, Laure Feugere, Věra Linhartová, and Anne Marie Amon of the *Musée National des Arts Asiatiques Guimet*, Paris; Lucie Borotová and Ladislav Kesner, the *National Gallery*, Prague; Willibald Veit, Uta Rahman-Steinert, Herbert Butz, and Waldemar Porzezinski of the *Museum für Ostasiatische Kunst*, Berlin; Jan Wirgin, Mette-marie Siggstedt, and Louise Virgin of the *Museum of Far Eastern Antiquities*, Stockholm; Vladimir A. Nabatchikov, Guenrikh P. Popov, Andrey Anikeyev, Natalia A. Kanevskaya, and Vladimir E. Voitov of the *State Oriental Museum*, Moscow; G. Vilinbakhov, Maria L. Ptchelina (Rudova), and Tatiana B. Arapova of the *Hermitage Museum*, St. Petersburg. In North America: Jim Robinson of the *Indianapolis Museum of Art*; Li Jian and the now deceased Clarence Kelley of the *Dayton Art Institute*; Maxwell K. Hearn of the *Metropolitan Museum*, New York; Wu Tung of the *Museum of Fine Arts*, Boston; Shen C. Y. Fu and Jan Stuart of the *Freer and Sackler Galleries of Art*, Washington, D.C.; Patricia Berger and Terese Bartholomew of the *Asian Art Museum of San Francisco*; Sheila Keppel and James Cahill of the *University Art Museum*, Berkeley; Michael Knight of the *Seattle Art Museum*; Stephen Little and Julia White of the *Honolulu Academy of Arts*; Stephen Little and Elinor Pearlstein of the *Chicago Art Institute*; Bennet Bronson and Chui-mei Ho of the *Field Museum of Natural History*, Chicago; Steven D. Owyoung of the *Saint Louis Art Museum*; Yang Xiaoneng of the *Nelson-Atkins Museum of Art*; Barbara Stephen, Doris Dohrenwend, Hsu Chin-hsiung, Patty Proctor, and Ka Bo Tsang of the *Royal Ontario Museum*, Toronto; Mark Carr-Rollitt of the *Museum for Textiles*, Toronto; Diana Tenckhoff of the *University of Oregon Museum of Art*; Claudia Brown of the *Phoenix Art Museum*.

We owe thanks to numerous private collectors and dealers who allowed us to study works in their collections and kept us informed of new pieces on the market. Among these are Wango H. C. Weng, New Hampshire; Howard and Maryanne Rogers, Kamakura; Paul Moss, London; Valery Garrett, Hong Kong; Dr. S. Y. Yip, Hong Kong; John Fong, Pennsylvania; John Singer, London; and Sam Fogg, London.

I would like to acknowledge support received from Miami University for this book. A grant from the Committee on Faculty Research paid for computer equipment and Chinese word-processing software necessary to the project. The Fine Arts Development Fund for Academic Excellence, the School of Fine Arts Special Projects Fund, and the Office for the Advancement of Teaching and Scholarship provided money for photographs. In addition, I was given a four-month professional leave to finish the final editing of the book.

Very special thanks are reserved for Ellen Avril, currently Curator of Asian Art at the Johnson Museum, Cornell University, with whom I traveled widely and worked closely for the first fifteen years of our careers in Chinese art, she at the museum and I at the university. I am grateful for her intelligent insights, her museum expertise, the many hours she spent on grant writing and trip planning, her good humor while traveling; I greatly value her friendship.

Finally, I must thank my husband, Robert Wicks, and my children, Christopher, David, and Elizabeth, for their patience during the hectic months in which I traveled to museums throughout the world. It was invaluable experience for me, and I am grateful they allowed me to draw on our family's resources of energy, time, and money to gain that experience.

Periods in Chinese History

Neolithic Period	from ca. 7000 B.C.	ca. 2100–1600 B.C.	*Xia Dynasty*
Shang Dynasty	ca. 1600–1050 B.C.		
Zhou Dynasty	ca. 1050–221 B.C.	ca. 1050–770 B.C.	*Western Zhou*
		ca. 770–475 B.C.	*Spring and Autumn Annals*
		ca. 475–221 B.C.	*Warring States*
Qin Dynasty	221–206 B.C.		
Han Dynasty	206 B.C.–A.D. 220		
Three Kingdoms	220–265		
Six Dynasties	265–589	265–317	*Western Jin*
		317–420	*Eastern Jin*
		317–589	*Southern Dynasties*
Northern Dynasties	386–581	386–535	*Northern Wei*
		534–550	*Eastern Wei*
		535–556	*Western Wei*
		550–577	*Northern Qi*
		557–581	*Northern Zhou*

Periods in Chinese History

Sui Dynasty	581–618		
Tang Dynasty	618–906		
Five Dynasties	907–960		
Liao Dynasty	907–1125		
Song Dynasty	960–1279	960–1279	*Northern Song*
		1127–1279	*Southern Song*
Jin Dynasty	1115–1234		
Yuan Dynasty	1279–1368		
Ming Dynasty	1368–1644		
Qing Dynasty	1644–1911		
Republican Period	1912–1949		
People's Republic	1949–present		

Children in Chinese Art

1

Introduction: Children in Chinese Art

Ann Barrott Wicks

and Ellen B. Avril

Depictions of children have had a prominent place in Chinese art since the Song period (960–1279). The number of works commissioned at all levels of society indicates that child imagery was exceptionally meaningful to generations of people across China. Yet one would be hard-pressed to find in the carefully preserved historical documents of imperial China any significant discussion of children in art. Neither has contemporary scholarship given the subject much coverage, despite the rich materials available for research. Very little has been published in the way of serious study of the iconography or meaning of images of children. This volume begins to fill that gap by bringing to the forefront of scholarship themes and motifs that have crossed social boundaries for centuries but have been overlooked in scholarly treatises on Chinese art.

That attention is now given specifically to depictions of the child in Chinese art is as much a comment on our own times as the disregard of the subject is a comment on the past. Children in contemporary middle-class American society command respect nearly equal to adults. The changing power structure in many American families has shifted to give mothers a voice more equal to fathers. With fewer models of obedience to authority in the family (i.e., mother to father), children have also found a voice. Combined with Americans' emphasis on democracy and the rights of special interest groups, shared family power has given rise to an especially strong focus on children. In this context, the study of children and their place in society is naturally appealing.

While not comprehensive in coverage of the subject, the essays in this book introduce and elucidate many of the issues surrounding child imagery in China.

Figure 1.1 Four human figures, one in the form of a child. Eastern Zhou, fourth century B.C., Zhongshan state. Brown and black jade plaques; 2.5 x 1.2 cm (child). Institute of Cultural Relics, Hebei province. After Jessica Rawson, ed., *Mysteries of Ancient China: New Discoveries from the Early Dynasties* (New York: G. Braziller, 1996), pl. 75.

These issues include the pervasive use of pictures of children for didactic reinforcement of social values as well as the amuletic function of these artworks to encourage the birth of sons. The objectives of this volume are to (1) establish the study of child imagery as a viable pursuit in the field of Chinese art history, (2) begin to document the historical development of the iconography of the child in Chinese art, (3) explore multiple aspects of style and meaning through the analysis of specific works of art, and (4) make available to interested readers recent historical research of the art. Together the essays provide a unique means to explore aspects of Chinese private life through visual representations of ideas about gender, family roles, and social goals.

Early Representations of Children

Possibly the earliest identifiable representation of a child in Chinese art is a small jade plaque dating from the fourth century B.C., excavated from the royal Zhongshan tombs in Hebei province (fig. 1.1). Found along with similar jade plaques of three female adults, the child is depicted frontally, wearing a skirt with an unusual checkered pattern that matches the clothing of the adults. The child's facial features are not distinguished from those of the adults; the short stature and hairstyle are the only indications that the figure is indeed a child. The head appears to be shaved except for a small tuft of hair, or topknot, in a style that was common for young boys throughout most of China's long history; thus the child is presumably male. The function of the four jade figures is unknown.

Representations of children are found in more significant numbers in the context of Han dynasty (206 B.C.–A.D. 220) tomb decoration and furnishings, yet still represent a trivial percentage within the corpus of Han figurative art. In general, these images are

Figure 1.2 Lamp in the form of an adult holding a child. Han, first or second century. Red earthenware with greenish lead glaze. Shanghai Museum.

related to the instruction of the descendants of the deceased in their familial duties. Made for didactic purposes, they rarely describe the playful gestures or endearing characteristics associated with children in later periods. The negligibility of childhood demonstrated by the infrequent portrayals of children is consistent with the attitude toward children that is reflected in Han burial practices, as revealed in studies by Anne Behnke Kinney and K. E. Brashier.[1] Prescriptive texts suggest that mortuary rites were not performed until a child was at least eight *sui* (Chinese years), and even then in an abbreviated version. Anne Kinney observed that the *qi* (spirit/vitality) of a child was thought to be weak, even to the point that the ghost of a drowned child was not capable of seeking revenge as adult ghosts would.

One type of child motif found among Han tomb ceramics is the green-glazed pottery lamp in the form of an adult holding a childlike figure in its lap (fig. 1.2). These curious pieces may represent a shaman holding a child who impersonates an ancestor in sacrificial rites. As described by Michael J. Carr, ancient burial practices in which the deceased man's grandson acted as his representative in receiving the funeral sacrifices are outlined in the *Liji* (Book of rites).[2] If the grandson was too young, someone would be assigned to carry him.

In addition to the ceramic pieces, a few children are incidentally depicted in illustrations of historical and didactic tales painted or carved in relief on Han tomb tiles. In a study of the Wu Liang family shrines, Wu Hung has identified several boys among the figures who decorate the stone sarcophagi.[3] For the most part, these boys are participants in well-known stories of virtue and social responsibility. Their portrayals clearly were used to instruct children and others in their filial duties to the patriline, appropriate reminders carved in stone at the ancestral burial grounds. There is one exception to the use of legendary children: an actual boy identified as Ah Qu, who died at the age of five. His portrayal is accompanied by a memorial inscription written by his parents, who express grief at his loss, as well as considerable anxiety over the child's helplessness in the next life.[4]

These Han images can be recognized as children mainly by their reduced size, which is also an indication of their relatively unimportant status. What distinguishes the children from servants or other adults of lesser importance is minimal. Indeed, none of the Han relief figures is easily distinguished by age using purely visual clues; the context and the inscriptions are more reliable factors. There is, however, the barely visible beginning of what one might call an iconography of the child, abbreviated pictorial conventions that indicate figures are children. Some of the children are pictured with topknots instead of hats. Others hold a simple toy. In terms of facial expression or body composition, however, the child figure is no different from that of a miniature adult. While this may be due simply to the stylized representation of all figures at the Wu family shrines, it is also consistent with Han Confucian writings that extol the appearance of mature traits in gifted children in contrast to the ordinary child's tendency to engage in aimless play.[5] Children who acted with adult seriousness and wisdom were upheld as models; thus, there would perhaps be little incentive to portray a naturalistic child.

The attitude that adult behavior in children was praiseworthy persisted through the centuries in China, but after the Han period, it was applied mainly to exceptional individuals, with fewer references to children as a group. Julia Murray discusses in her essay the Chinese adaptation of illustrations of the life of one such individual, Shakyamuni Buddha, and traces the influence of those works on pictorial biographies of other cultural heroes, namely Houji, Lü Dongbin, and Confucius. Meanwhile, child imagery began to change as early as the third century to more naturalistic renditions of children. In her essay, Terese Bartholomew introduces possibly the earliest rendition of auspicious children: a group of children at play, unaccompanied by adults, painted on a lacquer dish from the Three Kingdoms period (220–265).[6] In the center of the dish, two boys, naked except for short aprons, play at *wufeng*, a type of martial art. The boys are in the dynamic position of one leg bent and the opposite foot jutting forward that later became a popular pose for East Asian Buddhist guardian figures (and eventually heroes in Japanese Kabuki theater and prints). Facing each other and holding martial arts sticks, they are shown outdoors with a mountain in the background. The inner border features a design of fish and lotus vines; the outer rim of the dish has a pattern of clouds and dragons.

Was the changing—and, later, proliferation of—imagery of the child influenced by the widening circle of philosophical ideas that expanded rapidly in the third century? While we should be cautious in linking general theories to specific visual expression, both Buddhism and Neo-Daoism contributed positive ideas about childhood and childlike attributes that were missing in the Han period. It is possible that this affirmation of childlikeness reinforced artistic tendencies toward more depictions of children, particularly infants and toddlers. Isabelle Robinet and Livia Kohn have written about the contemplation of the Taiyi, the sovereign of the interior gods according to Shangqing (Supreme Purity) Daoism, as an infant.[7] This third-century school of mystical Daoism taught the visualization of the "world within the body," a universe made up of the entire cosmos and inhabited by all the gods who represent the visible and accessible aspects of the omnipresent Dao. The Taiyi was called "the essence of the embryo, the master of transformations" and was centered in the brain.[8] Through meditative identification with the Taiyi, the adept visualized his own rebirth, from the time of conception, through the nine months of gestation, and into a new life. Various passages of the *Huangting waijing jing* (Outer radiance scripture of the yellow court), the oldest of the "Yellow Court Scriptures," compiled in the third century, refer to the adept's need to visualize the infant within. Excerpts from Livia Kohn's translation:

> The Yellow Court is in the head. It encompasses three palaces known as the Hall of Light, the Grotto Chamber, and the Cinnabar Field. Enter between the eyebrows toward the back of the head. . . .
>
> . . . The Yellow Court is paired with the Grotto Chamber. Together they bring forth an infant god, who is their resident perfected. Always visualize him! Be careful not to lose the image.
>
> The infant turns into a Perfected in the Hall of Light. Then he is called Master Cinnabar. Here, to know the perfected means to concentrate on the Hall of Light as its residence. . . .
>
> . . . In the Hall of Light, the infant and the Master are like lord and minister. Further behind, in the Grotto Chamber, they are like father and mother. In the Cinnabar Field, they are like husband and wife. . . .
>
> . . . The Yellow Court is the eyes. The father and mother of the Tao both nourish the immortal embryo. . . .
>
> . . . Concentrate and visualize mother and child in the spleen. See how they enter the spleen from the stomach, wearing red. . . .
>
> . . . Constantly visualize the infant in the heart. He is clad in red garments, finely ornamented and resides in the middle Cinnabar Field. All exhaustion and bad fortune, all sloth and agitation, through him are made to go. . . .
>
> . . . With all your might, concentrate on the god in the heart and visualize him without interruption. When you can always see the infant within, you will be free from all sickness and disease.[9]

By the eighth century, woodblock versions of Daoist scriptures had pictures to illustrate various exercises. The *Neiguan jing* (Scripture of inner observation), which explains that meditating on the infant within is a means to restore one's original purity, includes a drawing of an infant at the center of an elaborate constellation titled *Neijing tu* (Chart of the world in the body).[10] The mythical founder of Daoism himself was called Laozi, or "Old Child." This is a paradoxical reinforcement of both mystical Daoism's emphasis on the cultivation of the infant within and the more Confucian recognition of genius in children who have adult characteristics.

The Development of Child Imagery in the Tang (618–906) and Song Periods

Actual pictures of the practices and beliefs of mystical Daoism are mainly in the form of diagrams and are not directly related to child imagery as it developed in China. But illustrations of Buddhist paradise played an important role in defining the depiction of the auspicious child. Pure Land Buddhism was introduced to China in 252 with the first translation of the *Sukhāvatī-vyūha*, a description of the paradise of Amitabha Buddha. To end the cycle of human suffering, the faithful were admonished to exercise faith in Amitabha, who would arrange for a final rebirth in his Pure Land. From that realm of peace and beauty, free from the distractions of the mortal world, nirvana could more easily be obtained. The vivid and detailed account of the Pure Land given in the scriptures does not seem to have inspired many Indian depictions of paradise. But it was a catalyst for elaborate portrayals of heaven in China, including the bliss of Amitabha's land as well as the realms of other popular Buddhist deities such as Shakyamuni and Maitreya. Chinese pictures of paradise were modeled on the brilliance of the earthly imperial courts, with an emphasis on symmetry and the inclusion of palace architectural features. Perhaps it was the emphasis on "visualization" of the cosmos by the fourth-century Shangqing (Supreme Purity) Daoists, described by Craig Clunas in *Pictures and Visuality in Early Modern China* as a Chinese concept predating both the arrival of Buddhism in China and the formative period of religious Daoism,[11] that influenced these pictures. At any rate, it is within the context of Buddhism, especially in renditions of the Pure Land (also called by the Chinese the Western Paradise, a reference to the location of the peach garden of Xiwangmu [Queen Mother of the West] and the magical Kunlun mountains, abode of Daoist immortals), that the child as something other than a miniature adult is first seen with frequency.

An early example of this can be seen in a Northern Qi (550–577) marble stele in the Cleveland Museum of Art (fig. 1.3). At the top of the stele, two infant boys hover in the air, supporting the stupa of Prabhuteratna and Shakyamuni, Buddhas of the Past and the Present. Beneath them stands Maitreya, Buddha of the Future, with four attendants. The child as attendant to deity increased in popularity from this point. The small male escorts here are a variation on the flying attendants to Buddha called *apsaras*. Usually female (and not children), these angel-like beings were ubiquitous in Northern Dynasties (386–581) paradise scenes. Eight traditional *apsaras* decorate the front of the marble stele along with the two boys.

One cannot help but compare these infant attendants to the putti, the chubby naked boys seen in early Christian mosaics such as those at Santa Costanza in Rome,

Figure 1.3 Stele with Shakyamuni and Maitreya. Northern Qi, 550–577. Marble with polychromy; h. 119 cm. © The Cleveland Museum of Art, 2000, Leonard C. Hanna Jr. Fund, 1993.108.

the mausoleum built for Constantine's daughter, 320–330.[12] These putti, which eventually came to be associated with paradise in Christian art (and thus the tendency to think of them in reference to *apsaras*), had their origin in the decorative arts of the Roman empire, works that were easily transported to China and northwestern India via the overland trade routes through Central Asia known collectively as the Silk Road. Plump boys with grapes (a reference to Dionysius, the corpulent and carefree Roman god of wine) and other types of plants were a popular motif on cups and pitchers for several centuries (fig. 1.4). The months and seasons in Roman decorative arts were represented by female dancers and musicians interspersed with small boys among scrolling vines. Numerous works modeled on Roman prototypes, including fifth- and sixth-century works of Central Asian origin, have been found in excavations at Datong and other Chinese sites.[13] By the time the Northern Qi stele was made, plump-boys-with-vines was already a well-known motif in China.

Figure 1.4 Silver cup. Roman Empire, 31 B.C.–A.D. 50, probably from Syria. © Smithsonian Institution. Courtesy of the Arthur M. Sackler Gallery, Washington, D.C. Gift of Arthur M. Sackler, S1987.129.

In Chinese Buddhist art, the soul newly born into paradise also looks very much like the putto of Western art. The concept of the recently arrived soul as an infant is a purely Chinese invention. Nowhere in the *Sukhāvatī-vyūha* is the person saved in paradise described as a baby. On the contrary, the assumption is that those in Amitabha's world continue their adult consciousness in a seamless progression from Earth life, through the Pure Land, to nirvana. But the idea of a baby fits well with the Shangqing Daoist visualization of the self in embryo. This mystical form of Daoism was well-known in elite culture, the same circle of people who would have been responsible for the commissioning of Buddhist works of art and the most likely to dictate trends in art. The Chinese monk Zhi Dun (314–366) was the first to describe the reborn soul's entry into Suhkāvatī as occurring through the calyx of a lotus flower, a method of rebirth whereby the impurities of the womb would be avoided. An infant seated on a lotus pedestal thus became the standard way to depict the newborn soul. These new inhabitants of heaven, tiny infants on lotus flowers intertwined with scrolling vines, form the border of the halo around Maitreya on the Cleveland stele (fig. 1.3). In this case, they are in the paradise of Maitreya.

Some really spectacular scenes of paradise survive in the murals and scrolls found at the Mogao caves near Dunhuang. Many of these include depictions of children as attendants, gift bearers, and newborn souls (fig. 1.5 and plate 1). In this context,

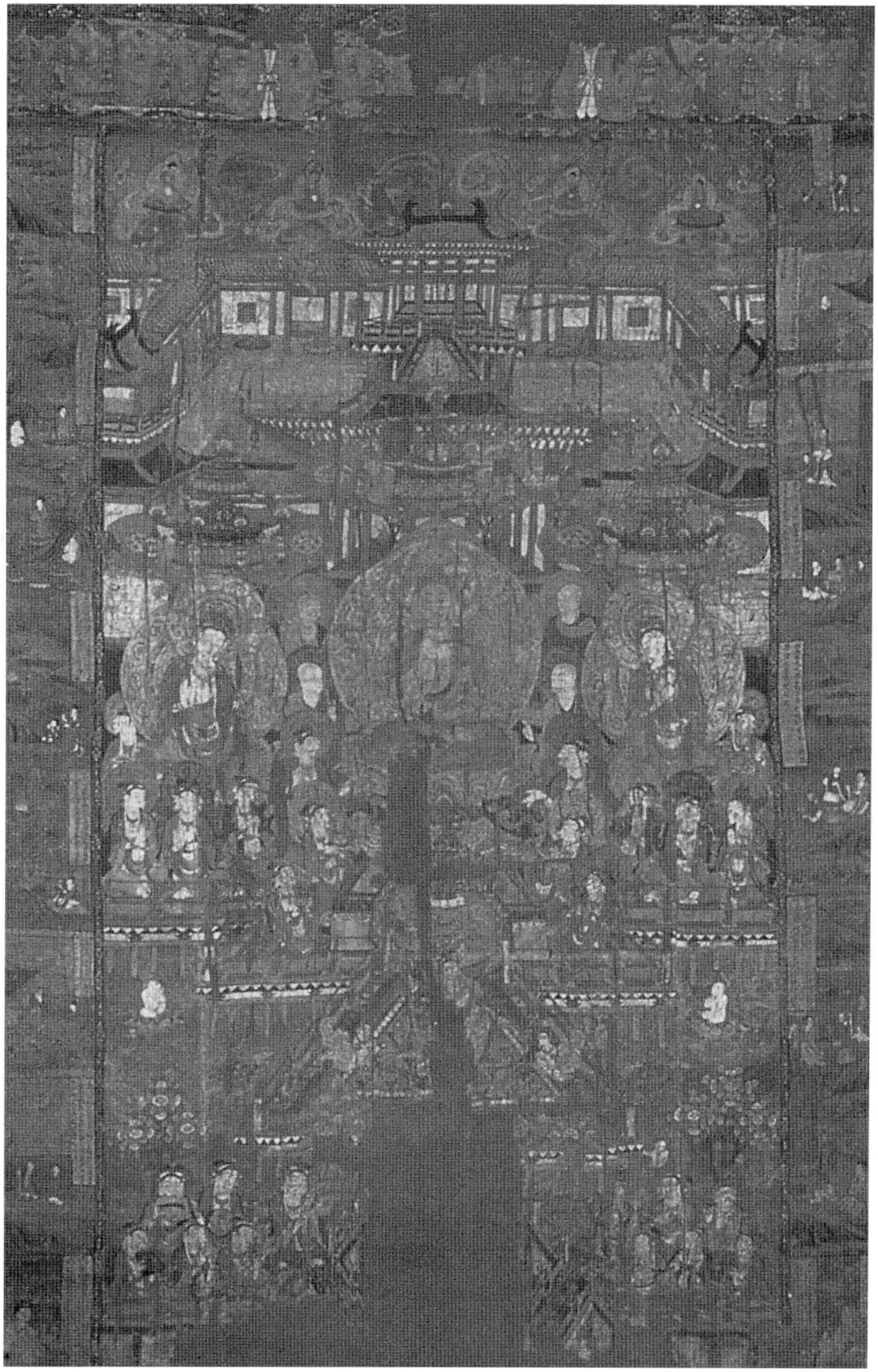

Figure 1.5 Paradise of Shakyamuni. Tang, eighth century. Wall painting from cave 17 at Mogao, near Dunhuang. © The British Museum, Sir Aurel Stein Collection.

the child took on the appealing characteristics that became the typology for the depiction of auspicious children. Referred to in painting as Tangzi (Tang boy), the child was outlined with a thin, even brush. His head was slightly enlarged to emphasize chubby cheeks, a manifestation of good health, and his hair was shaved except for a few tufts, which was the style for young boys. The typology of the child as a chubby, bare boy is consistent among the various paintings. Indian and Central Asian prototypes were available for all the major figures in Chinese paradise scenes. But there was no model in either Buddhist art or previous Chinese art for the depiction of children. Early Chinese pictures of children as diminutive adults did not adequately convey the spiritual changes represented by an infant. The model can be traced to Rome, and the spread of the Roman putti to Christian, Sassanian, and Central Asian art.

By the eighth century, the same cherubic image of boys began to appear outside the religious context in decorative arts made for elite consumption. At court and among the wealthy the child became an auspicious motif related to wishes for the birth of sons. A fragment of a greeting card preserved in the Shōsō-in shows that pictures of boys symbolized good wishes from one friend to another as early as the seventh century (fig. 1.6). A cherubic boy and a dog, cut from silk and attached to a plain silk ground, accompany the verse "On this propitious occasion, may happiness be renewed. May you find the peace of ten thousand years, and may life last a thousand springs."[14] The boy represents male progeny, the only certain way to prolong life, that is, in the sense of the patrilineal continuation. He plays next to silk cutouts of two auspicious plants, a *wutong* (paulownia) tree and an orchid growing from a rock. An intricate pattern of plum blossoms and scrolling vines, cut from paper and covered with gold leaf, is attached to the silk square and forms a border around the verse and figures. This type of colorful ornament was known as *rensheng*, and was given to friends on the seventh day of the new year in celebration of Renri (People's Day), a popular Tang festival.

Figure 1.6 Fragment of a greeting card. Tang, eighth century. From the Shōsō-in. Silk gauze, plain weave silk, and paper; 33.2 x 33 cm. Nara National Museum. After Ryoichi Hayashi, trans. by Robert Ricketts, *The Silk Road and the Shōsō-in* (New York and Tokyo: Weatherhill/Heibonsha, 1975), pl. 30.

Customs meant to encourage the birth of sons are tied in some way to all major festivals held in China, whether religious or secular. (In fact, most Chinese celebrations have long been a mixture of both religious and secular practices just as most celebrations in contemporary American culture are.) During the Tang dynasty it was customary to float small wax figurines in a basin of water, a reenactment of birth in the Pure Land, on the seventh night of the seventh month, the Festival of the Star-crossed Lovers. During the Song period, clay figures of infants holding lotus plants called *mohele* or *mohouluo* were produced for this festival, for sale to women hoping to become pregnant. Dramatizing this rebus for the birth of sons, real children ran through the streets carrying lotus as part of the Double Seven festivities. Ellen Laing identified a ninth-century Changsha-ware ewer with the design of a boy holding a lotus blossom as illustrating this custom (fig. 1.7).[15] The lively young boy is running vigorously, expressing robust physical health and the joy of movement. The combination of plants and boys, originally borrowed from the West, worked very well in China as fertility symbols, a subject that is explored in several of the essays in this volume. In this example, *lian* (lotus) is pronounced the same as *lian* (continuous). So a boy and lotus, a motif derived from both the Buddhist visualization of rebirth and the Roman celebration of the grape harvest, could symbolize "an endless succession of sons." Another example of this holiday motif is found on a small Song dynasty Qingbai-ware box, of a type used for cosmetics, that depicts a festively dressed little boy running and carrying lotus (fig. 1.8).

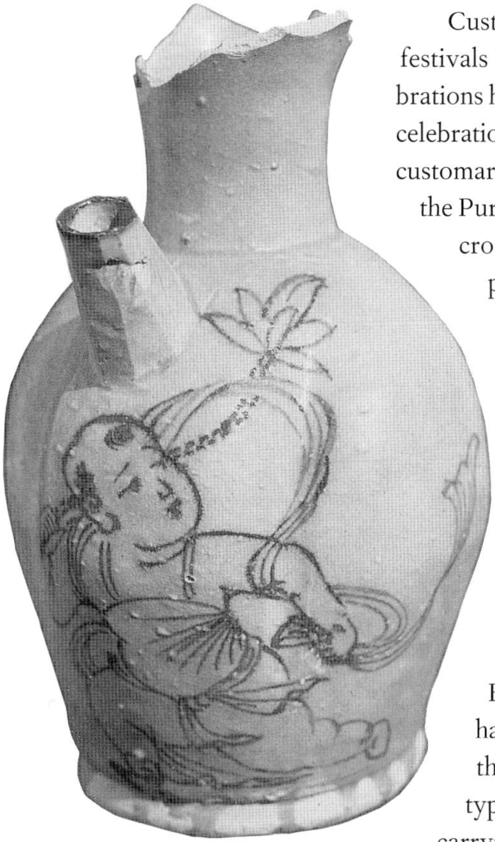

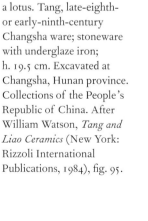

Figure 1.7 Ewer with design of a running boy holding a lotus. Tang, late-eighth- or early-ninth-century Changsha ware; stoneware with underglaze iron; h. 19.5 cm. Excavated at Changsha, Hunan province. Collections of the People's Republic of China. After William Watson, *Tang and Liao Ceramics* (New York: Rizzoli International Publications, 1984), fig. 95.

The appearance of children in Chinese Buddhist art only partially explains why auspicious images of children became increasingly prevalent after the Tang period. Chinese theories of child development also played a role. While genetics and fate were acknowledged, the thoughts and actions of mothers during both gestation and early childrearing

Figure 1.8 Covered box with design of a running child holding a lotus. Southern Song, twelfth- or thirteenth-century Qingbai ware; h. 5.7 cm; d. 10 cm. Private collection.

Figure 1.9 Pillow with design of an infant. Northern Song, eleventh-century Cizhou ware; glazed stoneware; h. 12.6 cm; length, 26.7 cm. © Royal Ontario Museum, George Crofts Collection, 918.21.392.

were also held accountable. Charlotte Furth's extensive work in the area of ancient Chinese obstetrical practices has yielded various examples of the belief that the fetus could be programmed by an attentive mother.[16] For example, she quotes Sun Simiao (581–682), who in his treatise *Beiji qianjin yaofang* (Prescriptions worth a thousand, for every emergency) described the third month of gestation as the time when gender was determined and the mother could influence the child's nature by "fetal education."[17] During this crucial stage, the development of the fetus could be governed by what a pregnant woman saw and ate, as well as by her thoughts and emotions.

The abundance in the Song period of ceramic pillows with designs of baby boys and other motifs symbolizing the birth of sons seems related to these ideas of controlling pregnancy, as if sleeping with such a pillow could perform some kind of sympathetic magic. The pillows served dual functions: first, to aid the onset of pregnancy, and second, to direct the dreams of pregnant women to positively influence fetal development. In the decoration of the Northern Song (960–1126) Cizhou-ware pillow illustrated here, the symbolism of fertility is reinforced by numerous tiny seeds that form a background for the boy and flowering plants (fig. 1.9). The child wears a scarf, a cloud-collar necklace, and a triangular apron that covers his navel. The apron, usually red, was a traditional piece of clothing worn by infants well into the twentieth century that served a symbolic protective function. The flower grasped in his hand is a lotus blossom. The scrolling peony and silver ingots that surround the infant, and the giant hibiscus *(furong)* that decorates the side of the pillow, are symbols of wealth and abundance.

During the Song dynasty, a time of reappraisal and renewed focus on classical Chinese culture, not just pillows but many of the ceramic articles used by upper-class women were decorated with boys and plants. An elegant example is a twelfth-century Ding-ware bowl in the British Museum, with a design of three infants, naked except for their scarves or necklaces and anklets, who cling to lotus and melon vines as if to prevent themselves from floating away (fig. 1.10). Lotus, beyond its Buddhist associations with rebirth and the "succession of sons" rebus, was also an

Figure 1.10 Bowl with design of infants among lotus and melons. Jin, twelfth- or thirteenth-century Ding ware; porcelain with molded decoration; h. 6 cm; d. 21.3 cm. © The British Museum, Oppenheim Bequest, OA 1947.7-12.62.

important symbol of marriage because one of its names, *he*, sounds like the word for "harmony." Melons, shown on the vines on this bowl, symbolize fertility because of their many seeds. The melons, blossoms, and vine together form the rebus *guadie mianmian*, meaning "May you have ceaseless generations of descendants." At the center of the bowl is a peony, used in literature to symbolize both feminine beauty and female genitalia. In combination with other flowers, the peony is also a symbol of wealth.

It was in the Song period that the subject of children became a recognized category of Chinese figure painting. As discussed in the essay by Dick and Catherine Barnhart, certain court painters were deemed specialists in the painting of children, the most famous of whom was Su Hanchen (twelfth century). The style of the Tangzi (Tang boy) described in the preceding text was the prototype for the develop-

Figure 1.11 Attributed to Li Song (1166–1243), *Skeleton Puppeteer*. Album leaf; ink and color on silk. Palace Museum, Beijing.

ment of a standard iconography for the child in the Song period. Su Hanchen's prolific output so successfully idealized the model child, that pictures of children by later artists were mostly variations on his style. In their essay, the Barnharts examine several works attributed to Su Hanchen. In addition, they discuss two prominent subcategories for Song pictures of children, the buffalo herder and the knickknack peddler. They boldly explore reasons for the artistic focus on children in the Song period, using literary sources to reinforce their argument that the unprecedented naturalism in the sympathetic rendering of children at this time reveals the Song to be a humanistic and enlightened age.

An album leaf attributed to the Southern Song (1127–1279) figure painter Li Song (1166–1243) in the Palace Museum, Beijing, is a startling aberration in the category of knickknack peddler paintings as discussed by the Barnharts (fig. 1.11). The pessimism revealed in the album leaf is out of place in the context of all other known Song paintings of children. The placement and expression of the women in the painting is particularly cynical. One woman sits nonchalantly nursing her son next to a skeleton posing as a puppeteer, while a girl gestures toward the skeleton's puppet as though to encourage a crawling boy to move closer to it, indicating that a woman gives birth and nurtures a man only to set him on the path toward death, and that other women along the way will hasten his progress to that end. This illustration of women as obstacles in an illusory life is given an ironic twist by placing it in the traditionally delightful context of a child at play.

Ming and Qing Variations

The bulk of essays in this book considers depictions of children in Ming and Qing art. During the Ming dynasty (1368–1644), the return to Chinese rule after a period of foreign domination encouraged a reinterpretation of traditional Confucian values and an endorsement of those ideals by the state. In order to preserve political dominance, the Manchu rulers of the Qing period (1644–1911) adopted many of the Chinese cultural norms that had been strengthened during the Ming. Portrayals of children in Ming and Qing art provided pictorial reinforcements of these values, which are discussed in detail by Terese Bartholomew, Ann Waltner, Julia Murray, and Ann Wicks.

Children at Play

Terese Tse Bartholomew documents the symbolism of specific games, toys, and seasons in Ming and Qing depictions of boys playing in a garden, elaborating on the topic of play, introduced in the essay by Dick and Catherine Barnhart. This traditional theme of the Song dynasty was given new life in the Ming period through large court-commissioned paintings and the prolific decoration of imperial ceramics, lacquerware, snuff bottles, furniture, and textiles. Bartholomew discusses the *baizi*, or hundred-boys theme, as a popular symbol for male progeny that was used to decorate any object bearing a wish for numerous offspring, but was especially the paraphernalia of the wedding chamber. Throughout Chinese history, the strong desire for sons was directly related to the need for male progeny to perform the ancestral sacrifices and to ensure the continuation of the family line. But by the Ming period, the birth of sons in itself was not enough. Families hoped for *guizi*, or noble sons, who would excel in their studies and take top honors in the civil service examinations, bringing wealth and the highest possible honors to their kin. Thus the boys depicted in Ming court paintings and the decorative arts are not just ordinary boys at play. Usually well dressed, they frolic in the gardens of the upper class. The garden plants indicate the season, and the toys and activities reflect the important festivals of China. As Bartholomew unravels the hidden meanings in pictures of boys at play, she illuminates the multitude of clever and playful methods used to reinforce one basic obsession among Chinese adults: the longing for talented sons.

Mothers and Sons

Ann Waltner's essay considers woodblock illustrations of late Ming editions of *Lienü zhuan* (Biographies of exemplary women), where children appear with their mothers in closed gardens or interior spaces. The interactions of the women and children, mostly in the absence of men, illustrate Ming views of the Confucian roles for different members of the family. Waltner interprets these pictures as paradigms of model behavior that dictate society's stern expectations for all adults, but especially women. The pictorial inclusion of children in illustrations to the text reinforces the importance placed on women's roles during the Ming period not only as child bearers but as significant educators during their sons' early formative years.

A Ming painting of palace women and children in the National Palace Museum supports the thesis of Waltner's paper (fig. 1.12). In late imperial China boys lived

Figure 1.12 *Royal Children*. Ming (attributed to Zhou Fang, eighth century). Handscroll; ink and color on silk; 36.7 x 328 cm. Collection of the National Palace Museum. Taiwan, Republic of China.

with their mothers in the women's quarters until the age of seven *sui*. At this point they were released from the inner quarters into the outside world of men. In this painting, the boys have been carefully arranged by age to show a gradual progression to the outside world. The tiniest infants are held by their mothers in the innermost part of the women's abode. They are visually the most confined, seen through a window in a separate room. Children at the crawling stage are slightly farther out, though still confined to a carpet surrounded by pillars, watched over protectively by their mother and two eunuchs. The next step outward is a boy learning to walk, holding on to the hand of an unmarried palace girl, most likely an older sister. Boys who can walk independently are shown farther out, and the interior space becomes even less confining. These boys are watched from a distance by the emperor's principal consort, but they still rely on their mothers, who bathe and comfort them. While not confined by walls, they are surrounded on all sides by palace women and servants. Two far more independent boys play on the edge of the veranda. One shakes an oversized lotus flower growing in a huge basin, causing petals to drop on a much younger child perched on the steps. This of course symbolizes a continuous succession of imperial sons. Finally, three older boys play in the garden, free of the palace building and having no association with the women. These are the sons who will soon leave the women's quarters. Since the handscroll would be viewed from right to left, it is fitting that the older boys are placed at the opening of the scroll, while the view progresses deeper into the inner quarters as the scroll is opened.

A notable aspect of child imagery in the Ming period is the frequency with which a child is depicted alone with his own mother, in addition to the more traditional pictures of young boys in the company of a large group of palace women or playing without adult supervision in a garden. As discussed in Ann Waltner's essay, the role of women as child bearers and early-childhood educators took on increasing significance in the Ming period. The Ming emphasis on the confinement of women is dramatized by works consistently showing the mother in an enclosed garden or indoors with no male company other than her little son. The isolation of the mother in these works may evoke sympathy among modern viewers, but we believe the intent

in the Ming social context was most often to focus on the importance of the mother's duty to her son. There are a few exceptional paintings, however, in which the artist does seem to identify with the woman's plight. A painting by Chen Hongshou (1598–1652) of an upper-class woman leisurely fumigating her clothing while her young son plays in the foreground is pleasant enough on the surface, but the dark undertones so often characteristic of Chen are also there (plate 2). The woman is framed by two beautiful but trapped creatures, a parrot tied to a perch and a butterfly caught under the boy's fan. These creatures elegantly symbolize her own entrapment. The boy's childish activity foreshadows the future subjugation of his own wife, who will also be kept in the inner quarters of his home while he is free to roam the outskirts. The bunch of loquats hanging from the parrot's perch could hint at the boy's future career as a literatus and visitor of high-class brothels, as the phrase "running under the loquat blossoms" was used to describe young examination candidates who visited famous courtesans. That this pattern of raising sons is the classic path to high social status and wealth is symbolized by the vase of mountain peonies *(fugui)* on a table next to the woman's raised wooden bed *(kang)*. The woman's dress is ironically decorated with cranes, a symbol of long life. It is not her personal longevity that matters, but the longevity of the patriarchal family that she is bound to preserve.

Noting that children are not usually portrayed in the context of a two-parent family, Ann Waltner asks the important question, "If the Chinese family is as central as we believe it is, why is it so seldom represented in art?" As she explores this seeming contradiction, she raises questions about the public-private dichotomy that has been a central issue in many recent interpretations of the dynamics of elite families. If women in the inner quarters are meant to be shielded from the public gaze, a reasonable explanation for the absence of men from pictures of their wives and children, how is it that we as viewers are given an undiscriminating view? Ann Wicks' essay on family pictures highlights the handful of depictions of nuclear families that do exist in Chinese painting. As in the Ming woodblock prints, these works most often serve as instructive guides to the correct ordering of family life.

Julia K. Murray focuses on depictions of child prodigies, celebrated individuals who are well-known in literary representations but whose pictorial biographies are only beginning to be known through Murray's pioneering work. Her essay points out conventions for the portrayals of three distinct types of prodigy: gods, sages, and scholar-officials. The dividing of prodigy pictures into recognizable types is another example of how art reinforced rigid expectations for all groups in traditional Chinese society, even among those who were exceptions to the norm.

Figure 1.13 Brush handle and cap with boys chasing butterflies among flowers. Ming, Wanli period, 1573–1620. Wucai porcelain; 19.2 x 2 cm. Percival David Foundation of Chinese Art, Pdf 753.

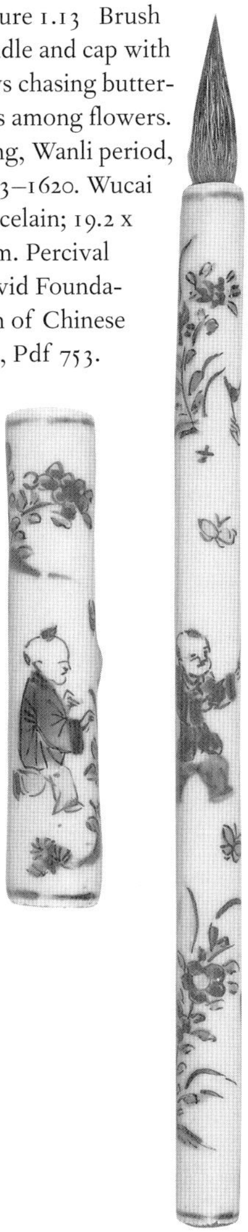

Children in the Material Culture of the Literati

As the link between a classical education and a prosperous family grew in the Ming period, luxury goods made for the literati increasingly portrayed boys and fertility symbols. Writing tools and desk ornaments—such as the ceramic brush handle, the ink cake, and the jade water dropper illustrated respectively in figures 1.13, 1.14, and 1.15—were decorated with stylized boys. As discussed in Terese Bartholomew's essay, many ceramics featured imagery specifically related to passing the civil service

Figure 1.14 Ink cake with design of one hundred children. Ming, 1368–1644. Design published by Fang Yulu (fl. 1570–1619). Disk shaped; d. 12.7 cm. © The Cleveland Museum of Art, 2000, Gift of Henry W. Kent, 1942.214.

Figure 1.15 Water dropper in the shape of three boys climbing on a jar. Yuan or early Ming, fourteenth or fifteenth century. Jade; 8.3 x 8.9 cm. Asian Art Museum of San Francisco, the Avery Brundage Collection, Chong-Moon Lee Center for Asian Art and Culture, B60J164. Photo Copyright © Asian Art Museum of San Francisco, 1997. All Rights Reserved.

exams, such as five boys fighting for a helmet, a boy riding a carp, and numerous variations on the theme of children imitating the activities of scholars. These pictures of children reinforced the image of the scholar-bureaucrat as powerful, and encouraged adults to view children as avenues of wealth.

Scholars' exchanges of poetry and paintings sometimes referred to the satisfaction of having numerous offspring, especially among retired government officials. For example, the well-known bureaucrat Wang Ao's (1384–1467) *Ode to the Pomegranate and Silk Gourd Vine*, inscribed on a painting by Shen Zhou (1427–1509) in the Detroit Institute of Art, was given as a birthday gift with a wish, written next to the poem, that the recipient's descendants be as numerous as the seeds of the pomegranate and as tall as the gourd.[18]

Beyond the wish for successful sons, the idea of childhood itself was taken up by the literati, who sometimes reflected on their own boyhood in poetry and painting. For example, in a painting by Cheng Sui (active ca. 1650–1680), a scholar seated in a garden pavilion instructs a young boy in the classics (fig. 1.16). The inscription on the painting reveals that the idyllic setting frames the artist's memory of his own childhood tutor, his great-uncle Cheng Yuanji:

> Mr. Yuanji was a member of my family—my father's uncle. Once he retired from the Hanlin Academy and returned home, he cherished righteousness and kept to himself. Brushing aside the confusions of the outer world, he would not set foot in the marketplace. His only intimates were the classics. He would, however, give instruction to the young boys in our family, and this is how I, too, came to study with him. His hope was that the hearts of those who would make an honorable career would remain true and generous. But, as I thought back, I realized that what Mr. Yuanji accomplished in opening our minds was very hard to come by, so I painted this to hang in my grass hut. When I wipe my eyes and sit in front of it for a long time, it is as though I were a boy again, and he were teaching me. . . .[19]

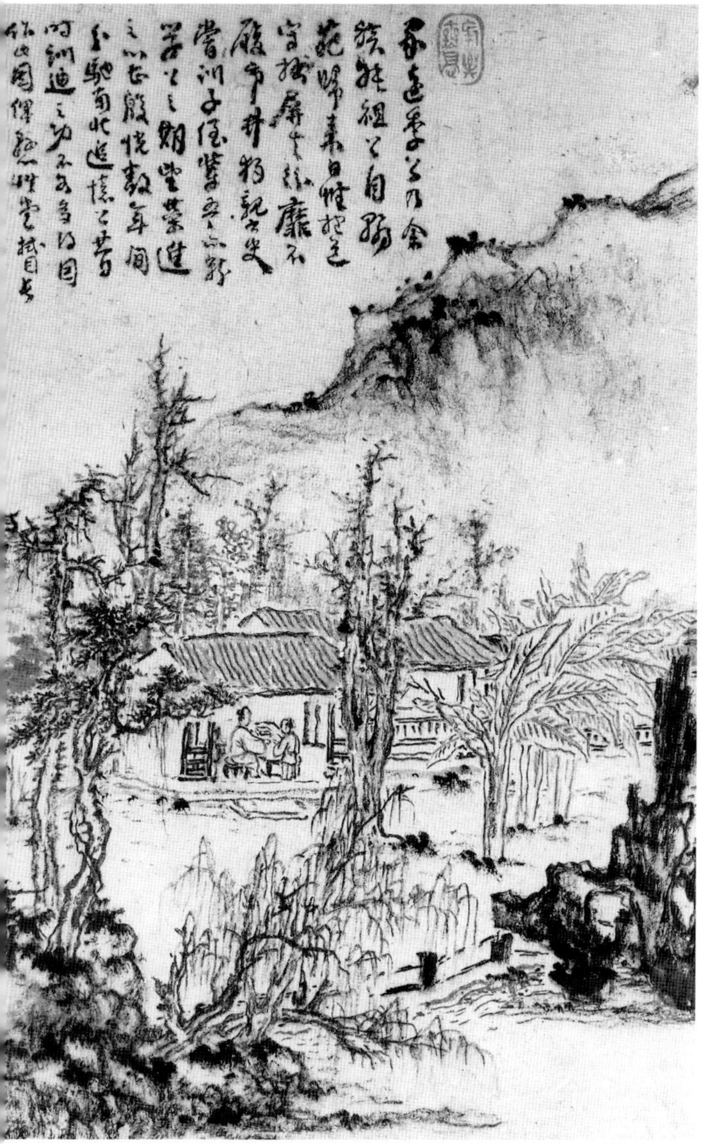

Figure 1.16 Cheng Sui (1605–1691), *My Teacher Cheng Yuanji*. Qing, seventeenth century. Calligraphy by Ji Yingzhong (not shown). Hanging scroll; ink on paper; 36.04 x 24.9 cm (image); 195.6 x 24.9 (calligraphy). Asian Art Museum of San Francisco, the Avery Brundage Collection, Chong-Moon Lee Center for Asian Art and Culture, B69D43. Gift from The Society for Asian Art. Photo Copyright © Asian Art Museum of San Francisco, 1997. All Rights Reserved.

Watching the Children Catch Willow Catkins, by Zhou Chen (ca. 1450–ca. 1535), a professional artist who painted literati themes, is a pictorial description of the reflections of a senior member of the literati class (plate 3). In a rustic garden set against an exquisite mountain landscape, a scholar watches three children play. Each child is in a different stage of male maturation, from an infant dressed only in a navel cover, to the preschool child with double-tufted shaved head and long gown, to the adolescent boy with trousers. The scholar himself, with beard and an official's cap and robes, represents the fourth stage, adulthood. By the Ming period, distinct stages of life were clearly recognized, and this is evident in Zhou's painting. Even the interaction with the catkins and the involvement in the game differ for each of the individuals. The posture of the infant is the most exaggerated, as he stumbles awkwardly in his attempt to catch the little seeds. The preschool child is standing, but with bent knees and both arms raised high; he too will surely miss catching a seed from the air. The oldest boy stands poised and upright, his hands in a position that will successfully capture the seed. The scholar stands aloof and dignified, his arms at his sides and his hands hidden by the long sleeves of his gown. His seeds were caught and planted years ago. Each of the children must journey through life to where the scholar now stands. Farthest from him is the infant, who has the longest way to go. The seedpods of the tree are a conventional reference to posterity. The subject itself was taken from a poem by Du Fu (712–770), but willow catkin imagery was used by other poets as well.[20] Su Shi (1037–1101) compared the catkins to human travelers searching for their lovers.[21] Zhou Chen's painting also incorporates the theme of travel, by illustrating the male journey of life. The contemplative mood of the scholar reinforces this interpretation. He stands removed from the children, wistfully acknowledging the long (and perhaps

Figure 1.17 Zhang Hong (1577–after 1660), *Village Schoolroom*. From the album *Figures in Settings*, dated 1649. Album leaf; ink on paper; 28.6 x 20.3 cm. © Allen Memorial Art Museum, Oberlin College, Ohio, AMAM 1997.29.14E. Gift of Carol S. Brooks in honor of her father, George J. Schlenker, and R. T. Miller, Jr. Fund, 1997. Photography by John Seyfried, January 2001.

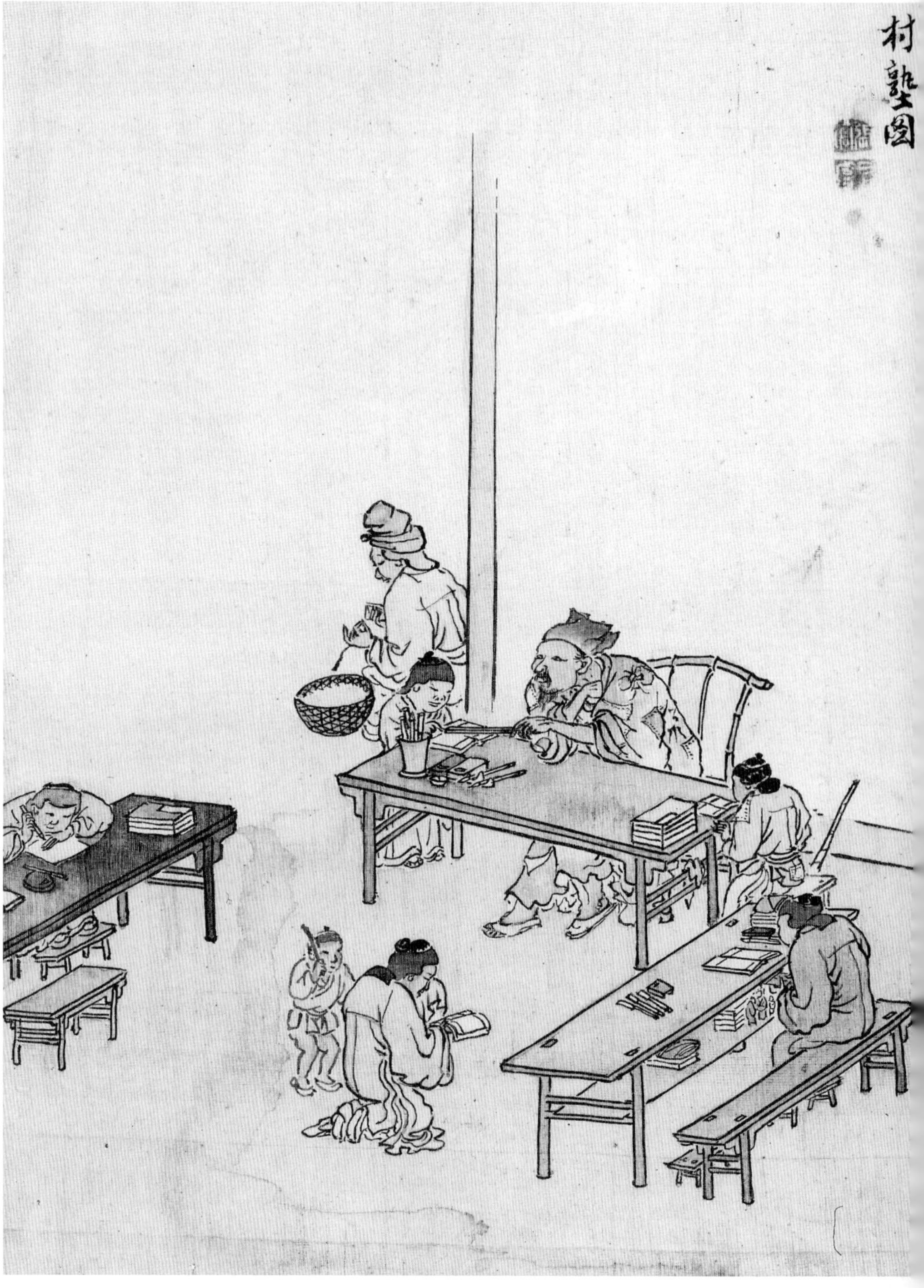

lonely, a common literary complaint of scholars that is illustrated with willow imagery) journey he has traveled.

Paintings, calligraphy, prints, and decorative arts owned by the literati reveal an intense ambition among the educated elite for their sons to achieve high intellectual status and preserve the literary prestige of the family. But at the same time, humorous paintings of schoolroom scenes, such as the one painted by Zhang Hong (1577–after 1660), poked fun at the intense competition among the families, who pushed their boys sometimes beyond the boys' limits (fig. 1.17). Intellectuals also broke free of the stylized court formula for painting boys at play. The spontaneous brushwork of Xu Wei's (1521–1593) *Boy Flying a Kite*, for example, expresses the concept of freedom that childhood represented to many of the literati (fig. 1.18). The relaxed brush of the "amateur" scholar-painter was eminently suitable for the depiction of childhood as an idyllic state that may well have been envied by the painter himself.

Admiration of childlikeness enjoyed a renaissance in the context of Neo-Confucianism in the late sixteenth century. Philosophers revived the ideas of the early-sixteenth-century thinker Wang Yangming (1472–1529), which reasserted the innocence of children in the centuries-old debate about the nature of man at birth. As pointed out by Pei-yi Wu, preserving the "child's heart" *(tongxin)* nearly reached cult status among the literati of the time.[22] Li Zhi (1527–1602), an outspoken literary critic and champion of spontaneity, wrote an essay called *Tongxin shuo* (On the infant's heart), in which he claimed, "The heart of the child is never false, but pure and true. . . . If you lose your child's heart, you will lose your true heart."[23]

A renewed interest in depicting herd boys in various media for elite consumption during that time represents the spontaneous and carefree life idealized by scholars and is perhaps related to the preoccupation with *tongxin* then in vogue. Boys herding water buffalo had been a popular theme in Song painting. The rustic depiction of commoners was consistent with the growing humanism and realism of Song figure painting as described in Dick and Catherine Barnhart's essay. "Returning home" on the back of a buffalo was also a metaphor used to explain the stages of Chan cultivation and enlightenment, which made the pictures meaningful to Song intellectuals.[24] But buffalo herders in Song art are not usually young boys. At best, they are adolescents. Ming idealism and playfulness, as well as the growing interest in depictions of boys and a recognition of childhood as a distinct stage in life, led to increasingly younger depictions of traditional herd boys. Guo Xu's (1456–after 1526) *Boy on Buffalo* (fig. 1.19) is a good example of this lighthearted treatment of the theme. As an urchin, the boy's figure is less chubby than imperial children playing in a garden. But his round head and small facial features retain the unmistakable stylized formula for depicting a child.

Figure 1.18 Xu Wei (1521–1593), *Boy Flying a Kite (Yuan yuan tu)*. Handscroll; ink on paper; 12⅞ x 55½ in. The Nelson-Atkins Museum of Art, 46–53. Purchase: Nelson Trust. © 1995, The Nelson Gallery Foundation. All Reproduction Rights Reserved.

The romanticized view of carefree childhood may have been a symbol of the enlightened mind of the Neo-Confucianist, but it contradicts the message of the decorative art owned by the literati that depicted academically successful sons as the ideal. It appears that for the men of the educated class, real childhood was sacrificed to the study of the classics, and they expected the same sacrifice from their sons. But childhood as an ideal was freely dwelt upon by grown men. Just as busy bureaucrats sometimes substituted landscape paintings or gardens for outings to mountains and lakes, imagining childlike spontaneity in playful ink paintings was perhaps vicariously enjoyed in place of an actual childhood experience.

The Impact of Social Consciousness and Western Ideas

During the Qing period, children were still seen as vital to the preservation of the patriline, but society's view of the child became increasingly sympathetic. As demonstrated in the writing of Angela Leung, by the latter part of the nineteenth century the child was considered a social being with rights of his own apart from his significance to the family. Evidence of the growing importance of the child is seen in the rising concern among the gentry for child welfare. Definite actions included the provision of vaccinations and health care specific to children, the establishment of children's cemeteries for all classes, and sustained efforts to integrate orphaned children into society.[25] This changing view of the child, initiated in the more affluent Jiangnan region, found expression in the paintings of Ren Bonian (1840–1895) and other members of his circle who lived as professional painters in Shanghai. The Rens specialized in figures, flower-bird paintings, and portraits in a whimsical, quasi-literati style inherited from the eighteenth-century Yangzhou professionals.[26] Ren Bonian's subjects are not completely free of the confines of symbolism, but for the most part, he painted ordinary children engaged in activities of no special significance other than snippets of the fabric of daily life. Most revealing of his progressive

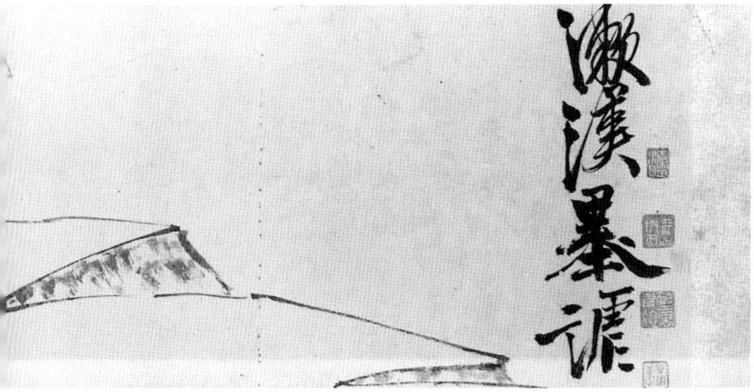

attitude toward children is the way he depicts their interaction with and importance in relation to the adults in the paintings. In *Figures,* two boys wrestle, with little notice given to the scholar walking next to them (fig. 1.20). A small child on the scholar's back glances scornfully down at the boys. The scholar, in a reverie of his own, pays no attention to any of the children. They are neither his servants nor his progeny, and he strides briskly by. But the scholar is in no way given a place of prominence in the composition. Each

Figure 1.19 Guo Xu (1456–after 1526), *Boy on Buffalo,* from the album *Miscellaneous Paintings.* Album leaf; ink on paper. Shanghai Museum.

Figure 1.20 Ren Bonian (1840–1895), *Figures*. Hanging scroll; ink and color on paper. After *Jen Po-nien hua chi* (Taipei: I shu t'u-shu kung-ssu, n.d.), 43.

figure assumes equal importance in the painting, each with his own right to existence.

The beautiful portrait of Jiang Shinong's granddaughter by Ren Bonian is another example of the recognition of the child as a social being (fig. 1.21). It also reveals the progressive attitude of the grandfather, who fostered the prodigious talent of his granddaughter and brought her out of the obscurity of the women's quarters to bravely meet the eye of the onlooker. This painting shows Ren's facility with Western-style realism in the depiction of facial features. In fact, many southern painters of the nineteenth century adopted this method as portraiture gained prominence as a category for painting.

James Cahill has suggested that the realistic facial features of figures by these Shanghai painters could only have been painted by artists exposed to the way human expressions were captured by photography.[27] I believe the visual impact of photography was important, and probably even necessary to effect the dramatic change in nineteenth-century figure painting in Shanghai. But photography alone was not enough to convince Chinese artists to change the centuries-old method for illustrating children. The view of childhood itself had to change along with the visual representation. Eighteenth-century court artists also had dramatic possibilities presented to them for the individualization of children's features by Western painters. But because of their less expansive view of children, it was much harder for them to act on those possibilities. Photography did provide visual ideas for change. But it was the social consciousness that developed in south China in the nineteenth century, and the awareness of adults of the special needs of children, that provided the motivation for artistic change. This climate is also partly responsible for the emergence of family portraits in the late Qing period, discussed in Ann Wicks' essay, "Family Pictures," chapter 7 in this text.

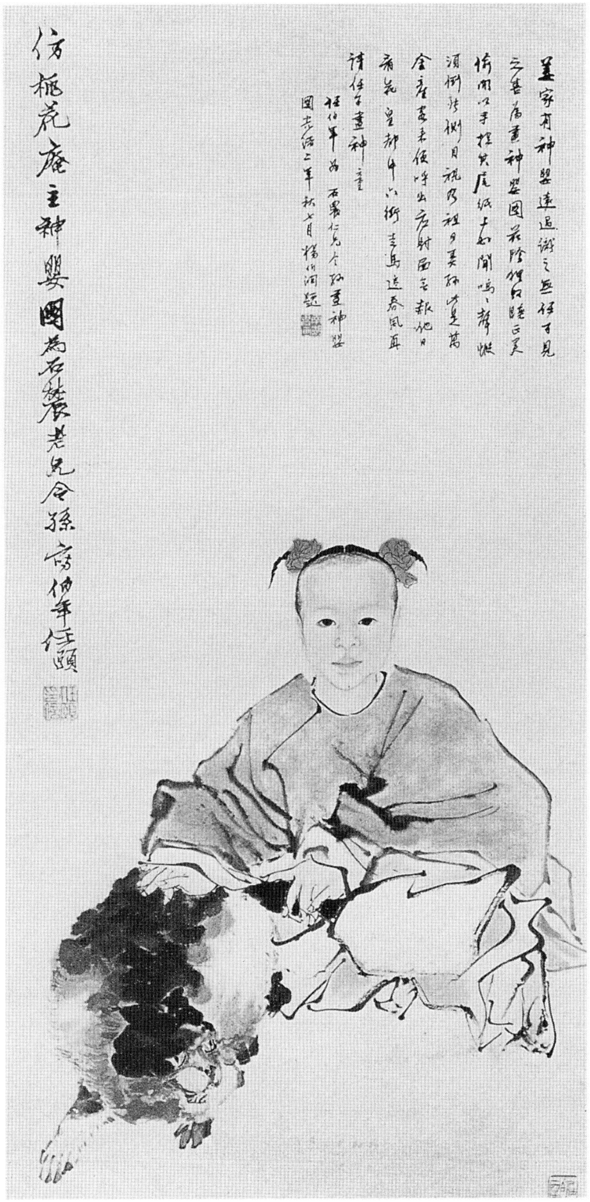

Figure 1.21 Ren Bonian (1840–1895), *Child Prodigy* (portrait of Jiang Shinong's granddaughter). Late Qing, 1876. Hanging scroll; ink and color on paper. Suzhou City Museum. After Richard Vinograd, *Boundaries of the Self: Chinese Portraits, 1600–1900* (Cambridge: Cambridge University Press, 1992), pl. 20.

Help from the Gods

Ann Wicks' essay on folk deities departs from a discussion of art depicting an ideal world with children as role models, to document art that illustrates the earthly concerns adults had about the safe birth and preservation of sons. The high mortality rate of infants and the vulnerability of young children to disease contributed to the supplication of specific gods on behalf of the young. Wicks discusses paintings and woodblock prints of some of the popular deities believed by the Chinese to deliver and protect children. While not comprehensive—the number of child protectors in folk religion is as numerous as the imaginings of parents in every time period and locale—it is a colorful documentation of the concern for healthy sons among prospective ancestors in every class of society.

Conclusion

In China, child imagery became a constant part of material culture, from the Song dynasty on. But until the nineteenth century, the focus was almost never on the child himself. It was the future role of the child as provider for aged parents and preserver of the patriline that mattered. Thus, once an acceptable image of the child was developed, there was no reason to change its elemental style. In fact, the use of child imagery was meant specifically to encourage obedience to tradition. A fluctuating style or an emphasis on individual characteristics would be counterproductive to that purpose. It was not until society recognized the child as a social being, that painters were able to individualize children in art.

So far, very little mention has been made of depictions of girls. Portrayals of girls in Chinese art do exist, but their numbers are few in comparison to those of boys. This should not be surprising to anyone familiar with traditional social norms in China, nor indeed even to one who has simply read the preceding introduction. There are, however, a few truly remarkable pictures of young girls to which we would like to draw attention. A smattering of girls is shown in the context of pictures of palace women. One of our favorites is a tiny child who playfully runs underneath a length of silk in *Ladies Preparing Newly Woven Silk*, a handscroll after Zhang Xuan (active 714–742) attributed to Emperor Huizong that is now in the Boston Museum of Fine Arts.[28] The painting shows women and girls of all ages—corpulent middle-aged women; slender women of childbearing age; unmarried girls with pigtails, who fan coals and hold the silk; and the small girl who is too young for a job. Imperial daughters are usually shown engaged in the same activities as the older women, performing at whatever level they are capable. Older girls share the women's work of embroidery, ironing silk, or the care of little boys. Unlike small boys, who must be entertained and watched over by the women, little girls in court paintings are left to their own resources, watching female activities until they have learned their role and can join in. There are no toys or symbolic plants pictured with the girls, and their number is always diminished in comparison to boys or even palace women. When boys and girls are shown together, the girl is almost invariably older than the boy and able to care for his needs.

There is at least one example of a pampered girl depicted in traditional Chinese painting. A section of *Gongzhong tu* (Women of the court) in the Sackler Museum at Harvard University shows a precious daughter cuddled in her mother's lap, playing with a dog (plate 4). This exquisite line drawing *(baimiao)* is a fragment of a Song copy after a scroll by Zhou Wenju (active 961–975). A similar handscroll in the Cleveland Museum of Art, once thought to be a section of the painting in Cambridge, has another small daughter, who holds a bird while riding in a carved chair carried by two adolescent girls.[29] This girl looks unusually solemn for her size. Her ride in the sedan chair may be an imitation of a wedding procession, playacting an adult role in anticipation of her future as a wife or concubine. Two more young girls romp playfully with a small dog at the far left of the Cleveland piece. Their demeanor is appropriately childish.[30] Like other paintings of court women made in the Tang manner, the *Gongzhong* scrolls still show only a few girls, growing up and learning their roles in the company of the many palace women. Little boys, typically smaller than even the youngest girl, are also included. The rare example of girls in favored positions, however, makes the *Gongzhong tu* especially noteworthy.

Tang ceramics show palace women and girls as we have seen them in the paintings, delightful creatures beautifully dressed and ready to serve the emperor. These eighth-century tomb figures help to authenticate the activities and style of women depicted in copies of Tang paintings. As in Emperor Huizong's painting after Zhang

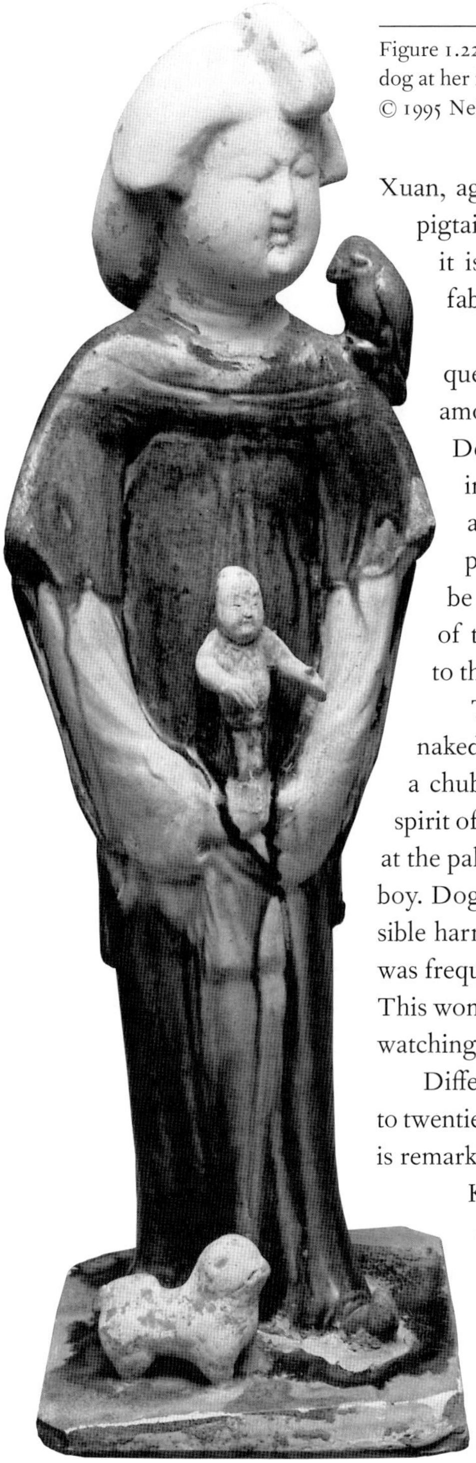

Figure 1.22 Tomb figure of a palace woman holding a child, with parrot on her shoulder and dog at her feet. Tang, eighth century. Earthenware with *sancai* (three-color) glaze; h. 40 cm. © 1995 Nelson-Atkins Museum of Art, Kansas City, Missouri, 39–27.

Xuan, age is defined by weight and hairstyle. The slenderness and the rounded pigtails of the figure with a duck on its shoulder illustrated in plate 5 tell us that it is a young girl. This girl is lively and playful; the richly embroidered fabric of her clothing is depicted in clay with relief flower patterns.

As in painting, girl figures appear among tomb ceramics far less frequently than grown women. But unlike painting, boys are not represented among tomb objects in the Tang period. One can only guess at the reason. Depictions of boys represent wishes for good things to come. Since the man in the tomb is already an ancestor, he is beyond the stage of producing heirs and is better served by living sons. Officials, court musicians, grooms, and palace women are enough to attend one in the afterlife. There might even be the lingering traces of distant human sacrifice represented by the choice of tomb figures. Certainly no powerful figure would take live sons with him to the afterlife. They were needed on Earth to perform the ancestral sacrifices.

There is one unusual tomb figurine that shows a palace woman holding a naked male infant upright by his feet (fig. 1.22).[31] The infant is not depicted as a chubby boy being raised among palace women. Perhaps he represents the spirit of a child already dead who accompanies his parent to the afterlife. The dog at the palace woman's feet could be interpreted as a playmate and guardian for the boy. Dogs are also associated with exorcism, and may be meant to repel the possible harmful effects of a dead child. On the woman's shoulder is a parrot, which was frequently used in Tang poetry as a symbol of the captivity of palace women. This woman appears doubly captive, accompanying the adult body in the tomb *and* watching over the spirit of a deceased infant.

Differences between boys and girls are not always clear in Chinese art, especially to twentieth-century viewers who are accustomed to clothing for young children that is remarkably gender specific in style, color, and decoration. But as pointed out by Karen Calvert in her study of American childhood, this is only recently the case. In the two centuries preceding our own, early American boys and girls under age seven dressed alike. Eighteenth-century portraits of boys in white dresses with long, curly hair look very much to us today like girls. Because the portraits are of specific, named individuals, their gender can be identified. But depictions of Chinese children are mostly anonymous. Our contemporary eyes, accustomed to gender-specific clothing, can deceive us as we try to distinguish gender. While Chinese adult costumes were specific to men or women, much of children's clothing in Chinese history is androgynous. Even when there was a difference, such as in the wearing of jewelry, boys sometimes dressed like girls to confuse malevolent spirits. Individually identified portraits would not necessarily help in this case, as boys were even given feminine names to hide their identity from ghosts who might covet them if they knew they were boys. Most children in Chinese art are in fact boys, whether they appear so to modern eyes or not.

One context within which girls are represented nearly as often as boys is that of acolyte, or attendant to deity, especially during the Ming and Qing periods. Child attendants, while certainly not unknown in earlier art, seem to become standard in Ming religious art. Guanyin, or Bodhisattva of Mercy and Compassion, is often attended by a little boy, most likely a reinterpretation of the youthful pilgrim Shancai. Nanhai (South Seas) Guanyin has a girl attendant as well, Longnü, the Dragon King's daughter. As was typical for portrayals of girls in court art or in the Confucian family scenes that are discussed in Ann Wicks' essay on family pictures, Guanyin's girl attendant is usually depicted as somewhat older than the boy. The same is true in depictions of the Golden Boy and Jade Maiden, who appear as attendants to Daoist deity. The cultural stereotype that boys are coddled and given the freedom to play while girls mature quickly and assume domestic duties is so pervasive that even an unrelated pair of children outside the human realm cannot escape it. The individualized portrait of Jiang Shinong's granddaughter by Ren Bonian finally broke the stereotype for depictions of girls (fig. 1.21). But this was not until the late nineteenth century.

Though the figural style used to depict children changed very little between the Song and the Qing dynasties, motifs and subject matter did vary in response to cultural aspects of the larger society. Thus it is possible to document trends specific to each time period by looking at the way children were depicted in art. The subtle differences are revealing. But even more telling is the remarkable consistency of one continuing concern, the production of male heirs. The overwhelming preference for little boys, reinforced by the decoration of clothing, utensils, wall hangings, New Year greetings, and even furniture, was solidly a part of Chinese public mores for centuries. The hundred sons of the legendary King Wen, prototype for the virtuous ruler discussed in Terese Bartholomew's essay, set the ideal precedent. No matter what the private feelings of individual Chinese might have been, art conveyed the accepted propaganda for a hundred generations: Multiple sons are the most precious treasure of all.

2

Images of Children in Song Painting and Poetry

Richard Barnhart and

Catherine Barnhart

The sudden appearance of sophisticated images of children in painting and poetry during the Tang (618–907) and Song (960–1279) periods comes after millennia during which children only occasionally and randomly appeared in the arts. But briefly, between the eighth and twelfth centuries, a great many memorable pictorial and literary representations of children appeared and several distinct genres of subject matter centered on children were invented. Gradually thereafter, children receded again into relative anonymity until the modern era, continuing to appear often in the auspicious imagery of family, clan, and society but only as stock players in institutionalized pageants and celebrations. Just briefly in Chinese art, therefore, do children appear to us as subjects of representation noteworthy in and of themselves, as individuals, as young human beings occupying their own personal and significant worlds.

Why this happened when it did, and why it did not continue, are questions considered but not directly addressed in this essay. Here, we examine the nature of works that define this distinctive era in the history of Chinese art and society and study some of the ways they may reflect other issues in Tang and Song history.

It may be well to observe at the beginning that the great humanist painters and poets in China always gave presence to children in their art. Here we are thinking of Gu Kaizhi (fourth century), whose *Admonitions of the Instructress to the Imperial Concubines* offers the earliest image of a complete family unit (plate 15); of Tao Qian (fourth and fifth centuries), whose poems often refer to his wife and children; and of Du Fu (eighth century), inspiration to the great Song poets later on.

Beyond this indigenous line of transmission, we should also consider the possibility that some pictorial influence from Central Asia and even further west may have played a role in encouraging the development in China of independent images of children. The genre of painting featuring chubby, lightly clothed babies and small children appears to have begun in China at the height of the Tang dynasty in Chang'an (modern Xi'an), the great Chinese city at the eastern terminus of the Silk Road. To this region had long come textiles, ceramics, jewelry, and gold and silver vessels of many kinds bearing decorative motifs from the Greco-Roman traditions that still flourished across much of the old Roman empire and in the various societies that succeeded Rome in Western and Central Asia. Plump cherubs in the form of putti and children of the gods arrived in China with trade, with Buddhism, and with Christianity, all of which traveled along the corridors connecting China to the Mediterranean. Some of these matters are discussed by Ann Wicks and Ellen Avril in their introductory essay in this text, and the role that images of children played in the imported religion of Buddhism is the subject of Julia Murray's essay.

By the eighth century, such images of children were commonly seen in a great variety of materials and forms, and it was then that the new artistic genre of children and mothers evolved in elite Chinese painting. The setting for this development was the imperial court at Chang'an, one of the most cosmopolitan political centers in the world, and one of the richest. The international culture that flourished at the Tang court drew upon the resources of the world to define a golden age of Chinese art and literature. The two painters credited with creating the new genre of "children and mothers" at that time, Zhang Xuan (active 714–742) and Zhou Fang (eighth century), were among the creators of classical Tang culture, along with the great master of Buddhist and Daoist subjects Wu Daozi, the landscape painters Li Zhaodao and Wang Wei, the genius of horse painting Han Gan, and the poets Du Fu, Li Bai, and painter-poet Wang Wei.

Both Zhang Xuan and Zhou Fang were aristocrats, and their subjects were mainly the aristocratic women and children of the imperial court. The models they created were closely followed later by Zhou Wenju of the Five Dynasties period and by many Song artists, and it is possible to trace the development of their tradition in some detail. Many later paintings of court women and children are still associated with the great patriarchs themselves. For example, in China's canonical national collection of painting now housed in the National Palace Museum in Taipei, most paintings of court women and children ascribed to the period from the tenth through the seventeenth centuries are catalogued under the names of Zhang Xuan, Zhou Fang, Zhou Wenju (tenth century), and Su Hanchen (twelfth century), even though it is not certain that an original work by any of these artists is still extant.

One of the earliest and most interesting illustrations of court women and children from the formative phase of this tradition is in a short scroll in the Metropolitan

Museum that depicts court women bathing their children (fig. 2.1). The Metropolitan scroll looks like a collection of basic motifs for the depiction of mothers bathing children brought together in a not quite coherent composition, perhaps to provide models for other paintings of these same subjects—and, probably, copied from other such works. We can see how the repetition of these basic motifs and compositional units functioned in principle, by examining a beautiful little round fan in the Freer Gallery of Art (fig. 2.2) that uses several of the same figures, sometimes reversing them, as was easily done with preparatory sketches *(fenben)* of the type that certainly lie behind these pictures. The brushwork and color of the Freer painting are far superior to those features of the Metropolitan Museum scroll, which might suggest that the former was done as a finished picture while the latter remains a collection of models from and for other paintings.[1]

Two later stages in this process of transmission and adaptation can be seen in a second round-fan painting, formerly in the collection of the great Ming collector Xiang Yuanbian, in which just two mothers and two children from the same set are introduced into a garden setting that suggests the Hangzhou palaces of the Southern

Figure 2.1 After Zhou Fang, *Court Women Bathing Children*. Southern Song, early twelfth century. Handscroll; ink and color on silk; 30.4 x 48.5 cm. The Metropolitan Museum of Art, Fletcher Fund, 40.148. All rights reserved, The Metropolitan Museum of Art.

周文矩

Figure 2.2 *Court Women Bathing Children*. Southern Song, twelfth to thirteenth centuries. Fan mounted as album leaf; ink and color on silk; 22.7 x 24.4 cm. Freer Gallery of Art, 1935.8. Courtesy of the Freer Gallery of Art, Smithsonian Institution, Washington, D.C.

Song emperors.[2] According to Ellen Laing, this painting is a result of the following sequence: a Tang-style model, followed by a Northern Song interpretation of the major theme (perhaps made at the court of Emperor Huizong as a part of his program of canonizing Tang models), which later became a Southern Song court production adapting the newly established classical theme to the then popular composition of imperial figures in a royal garden that is now extant in the form of a free copy by the Ming artist Qiu Ying.[3]

The most extended and elaborate form of this series of recensions can be seen in the National Palace Museum in Taipei, in a handscroll attributed to the patriarch Zhou Fang himself that uses all of the original Metropolitan Museum motifs and figures, and many more as well, in a composition of numerous palace women tending to their children (fig. 1.12). This appears to be a generic auspicious representation of the "one hundred" mothers and children, of the type that also exists of a hundred geese, a hundred horses, a hundred flowers, a hundred insects, and a hundred sons

Plate 1 Newborn soul in paradise. Detail of fig. 1.5. © The British Museum, Sir Aurel Stein Collection.

Plate 2 Chen Hongshou (1598–1652). *Lady Leaning on a Perfumer*. Late Ming, ca. 1639. Hanging scroll; ink and color on silk; 129.6 x 47.3 cm. Shanghai Museum.

Plate 3 Zhou Chen (active ca. 1486–1535), *Watching the Children Catch Willow Catkins*. Ming, early sixteenth century. Hanging scroll; ink and color on silk; 116.6 x 63.5 cm. Collection of the National Palace Museum. Taiwan, Republic of China.

Plate 4 After Zhou Wenju (active 961–975), *Women of the Court (Gongzhong tu)*. Song, ca. 1140. Handscroll detail; ink and traces of pigment on silk; 25.7 x 177 cm. Courtesy of the Arthur M. Sackler Museum, Harvard University Art Museums, Francis H. Burr Memorial Fund. Photo by Rick Stafford. © President and Fellows of Harvard College, Harvard University.

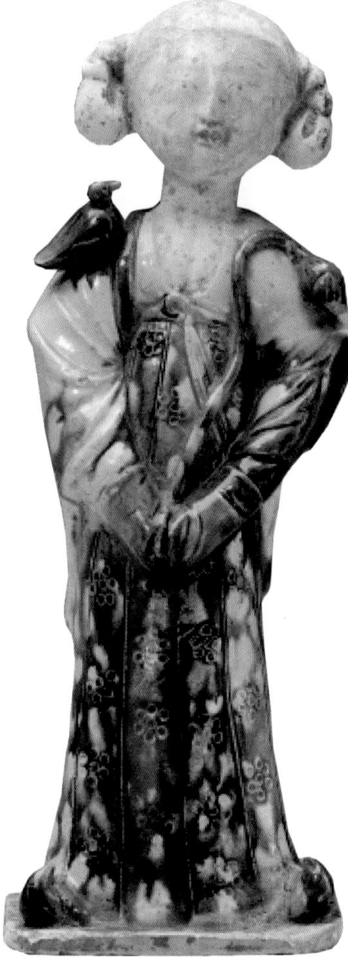

Plate 5 Tomb figure of a young girl. Tang, early eighth century. Earthenware; 30.2 cm. Private collection.

Plate 6 Su Hanchen (twelfth century), attrib., *Children Playing in an Autumn Garden*. Song, early twelfth century. Hanging scroll; ink and color on silk; 197.5 x 108.7 cm. Collection of the National Palace Museum. Taiwan, Republic of China.

Plate 7 *Winter Play*. Song, 960–1279. Hanging scroll; ink and colors on silk; 196.2 x 107.1 cm. Collection of the National Palace Museum. Taiwan, Republic of China.

Plate 8 Bowl decorated with boys at play; one of a pair. Qing, Yongzheng period, 1723–1735. Porcelain with enamel decoration; h. 6.8 cm; d. 14.8 cm. Asian Art Museum of San Francisco, the Avery Brundage Collection, B60 P1445.

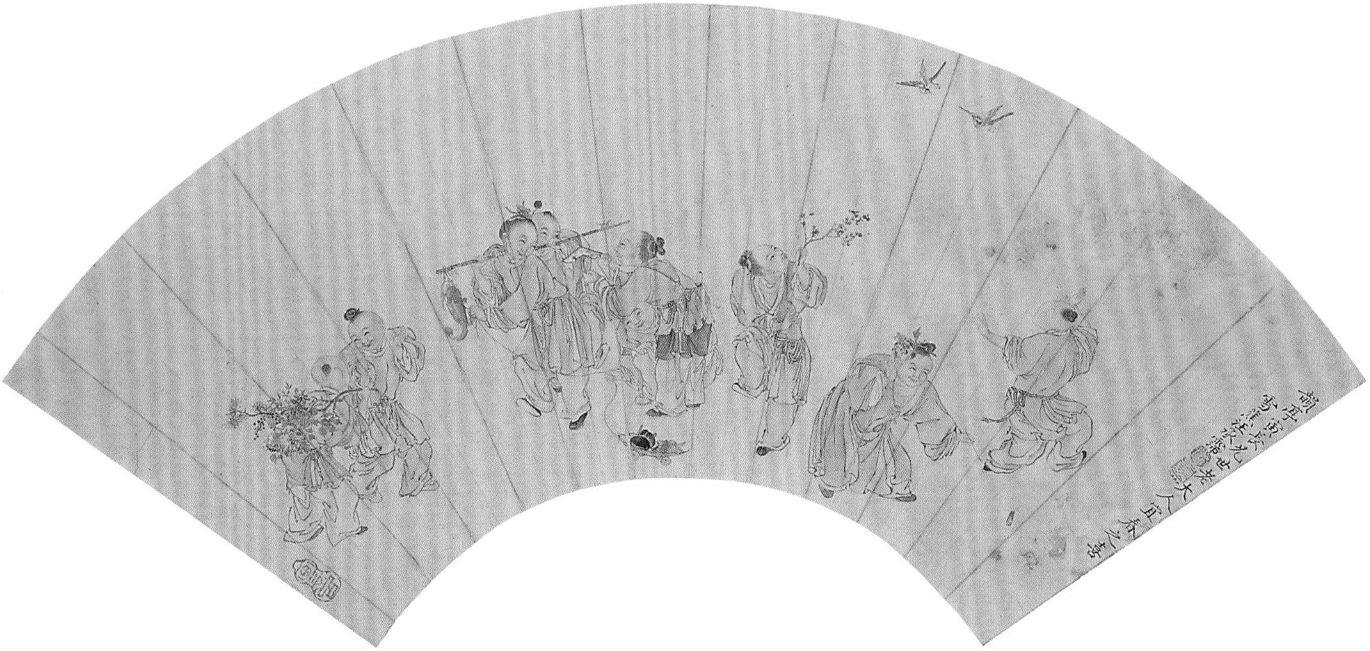

Plate 9 Wang Chengpei (d. 1805), *Boys at Play*. Qing, Qianlong period, 1736–1795. Fan painting; ink and color on paper. Asian Art Museum of San Francisco, 1998.32d. Gift of Joseph and Nancy Wang in memory of Dr. and Mrs. Hsin-chung Wang.

Plate 10 Purse with boys and oranges. Qing, nineteenth century. Embroidered silk; 11.5 x 10.7 cm. Asian Art Museum of San Francisco, 1988.32.7. Gift of Mrs. Ursula W. Bingham.

Plate 11 Dai Quheng (1755–1811), *An tu shen yin* ([Wang Wei] identifies the music by reading the notation), from the album *In Celebration of Child Prodigies*. Number six of eight album leaves; ink and color on paper. Phoenix Art Museum, Collection of F. Roy and Marilyn Papp. Courtesy of the Phoenix Art Museum.

Plate 12 *White-robed Child-giving Guanyin*. Early twentieth century. Woodblock print; ink and color on paper; 49 x 38 cm. Museum of the History of Religion, St. Petersburg. After Maria Rudova, *L'imagerie populaire chinoise* (Leningrad: Aurora Art Publishers, 1988), no. 10.

Plate 13 General Baotong bringing a child. Early twentieth century. Woodblock print; ink and color on paper; 37.7 x 22.5 cm. Nelson Atkins Gallery of Art. Photo: Robert Newcombe, 2000.

Plate 14 Hariti and her son. Ming, 1443. Wall painting; detail of fig. 6.14. After *Fahaisi bihua*, pl. 61.

Plate 15 After Gu Kaizhi (fourth century), *Family Group*. Detail of *Admonitions of the Court Instructress to the Imperial Concubines*. Late Tang or early Song, ca. tenth or eleventh century. Handscroll; ink and color on silk. © The British Museum.

Plate 16 Illustration to chapter 6 of the *Classic of Filial Piety*. Early Ming, fourteenth-century copy after Li Gonglin. Detail of handscroll; ink and color on paper; 20.5 x 702.1 cm. Collection of the National Palace Museum. Taiwan, Republic of China.

Plate 17 Lü Dongbin provides medicine for a filial son to cure his mother's blindness. Yuan, fourteenth century. Detail from mural painting of the life of Lü Dongbin, north wall of Chunyang Hall, Yongle Palace, Shanxi province. After *Yongle Palace Murals*, 84.

Plate 18 Giuseppe Castiglione (1688–1768), *New Year's Painting (Suichao tu)*. Qing, eighteenth century. Hanging scroll; ink and color on silk; 289.5 x 196.7 cm. Palace Museum, Beijing.

Plate 19 *Emperor Daoguang Enjoying the Autumn (Xiyi qiuting)*. Qing, mid-nineteenth century. Hanging scroll; ink and color on paper; 205.5 x 181 cm. Palace Museum, Beijing.

Plate 20 *Emperor Daoguang and Family in Spring*. Qing, mid-nineteenth century. Handscroll; ink and color on paper; 111 x 294.5 cm. National Palace Museum, Beijing.

Plate 21 Hua Guan (mid-eighteenth to early nineteenth centuries), *Mirror Grinding: Portrait of Xue Chengji*. Qing, 1799. Hanging scroll; ink and color on paper; 126.5 x 46.7 cm. Nanjing Museum.

Plate 22 Hua Guan (mid-eighteenth to early nineteenth centuries), *Sailing Back Smoothly: Portrait of Jiang Shiquan*. Qing, 1763. Handscroll; ink and colors on paper; 16 x 132.8 cm. Nanjing Museum.

in popular auspicious imagery.[4] It appears to be copied after a work of the kind associated with Qiu Ying, based in turn upon earlier models of the kinds we have observed as typifying the tradition of Zhou Fang, Zhang Xuan, Zhou Wenju, and Su Hanchen.

Throughout the evolution of this early and popular genre, children are inseparable from their mothers. The women of the imperial harem were regarded in much the same way as was the mother of the Buddha. The birth and early life of the Buddha were extremely popular subjects in painting at the same time, as Julia Murray illustrates in her essay, chapter 5, in this volume. These women gave birth to and raised young princes and princesses of the imperial family so that the structure of the Son of Heaven's rule over his earthly kingdom would continue.

Images of court women evolved in tandem with images of children, therefore, from the beginning. Indeed, the primary role women played in art was that of actual or potential mother of imperial children. There were few images of learned, talented women in Tang art, and there were few children unattended by their mothers and/or nurses. A rigorous patriarchal structure of social obligations and filial duties created the essential form and subject matter of art.

The emergence of images of women alone and of children separate from their mothers should probably be understood as a single development that reflects profound changes in Chinese society. We cannot explore the exact nature of those changes in this essay but refer to the general tendency toward a heightened appreciation of human life and of individual value that evolved as Chinese society slowly transformed itself from a hereditary aristocracy into a more broad-based meritocracy in the period of the ninth to eleventh centuries. This gradual humanization and individualization of the almost entirely aristocratic, hereditary imperial, institutional outlook of earlier society finds one of its most eloquent expressions in the painting and poetry of Song art.

In several recent studies of this phenomenon, Martin Powers focused on the discourse of human values he finds occurring between the ninth and twelfth centuries, and which he connects to the emergence of a new class of nonaristocratic, nonhereditary officeholders and scholars (see note 5). Men such as Han Yu (768–824), Mei Yaochen (1002–1060), and Su Shi (1037–1101) created new ideals of behavior and morality that emphasized human feeling *(renqing)* and promoted the welfare of common people *(min)*. Powers maintains that people of the twelfth century probably felt no more deeply about the welfare and happiness of their children than people of earlier periods, and that the discourse itself was a design for the redistribution of power. But surely, changes in feeling also occur, and heightened appreciation of human lives and their values does appear. People in different eras and cultures have placed varying values on children and others. The one-child policy of modern China, for example, appears to have intensified the devotion of parents to their only children and to have led to higher public value placed on daughters. Awareness of how such social, educational, and political policies can change feelings might suggest that the increased importance given to education and social advancement in China between the ninth and twelfth centuries, concerns so well described by Powers, acted to intensify feelings of love and affection toward the new population of slowly maturing, carefully educated children of the new scholar class while at the same time highlighting the importance of intelligent, cultivated mothers in nurturing knowledge and instilling proper values in these children.[5]

On the side of children, we see the first and perhaps still most satisfying pictorial result of those changes in a painting attributed to the Song artist Su Hanchen, *Children Playing in an Autumn Garden* (plate 6). This very large hanging scroll, formed of two panels of silk joined down the center of the scroll, shows us two children at play in a corner of a palatial garden. Blossoming hibiscus and chrysanthemums, as well as the jujubes with which the children are playing, identify the season as autumn. Their toys include a pair of cymbals dropped on the ground, a top on a round mottled tray, a beautiful pair of miniature archers on horses at either end of a spindle mounted above a board game, a small red-lacquer pagoda with a tiny Buddha inside, and a game known as "spinning jujubes." Behind the boy and girl stands one of the most beautiful garden rocks in all of Chinese painting, a small-scale mountain that recalls the great peaks of the classical landscape masters of the same period. The rock, a masterpiece in itself, together with the children's exquisite costumes and hair ornaments and the pair of elegant lacquer and mother-of-pearl tables on which they play leave no doubt of the luxurious upbringing of this pair of fortunate children.

What is most remarkable about these children is their separate existence. They occupy their own sheltered world, not the adult world, and are totally absorbed in their private activities. No mothers are visible nearby, there is no implication of social or familial obligation, there are no auspicious numbers or motifs signifying didactic purpose, and there is no apparent justification for their presence before us beyond their existence in the world and their identities as two distinctive children among millions. This is a new moment in the evolution of Chinese society, culture, and art, the moment when types of people previously seen in largely peripheral roles—children, women, the poor, foreigners—take center stage in the world of art and are presented to us as fully individualized human beings.[6]

In the face of such a compelling, focused, intimate, and deeply affecting human image as *Children Playing in an Autumn Garden*, we of course wish to know something about the artist responsible for it. But here we will fail, because without a

Figure 2.3 Su Hanchen (twelfth century), attrib. *Children Playing with a Balance Toy*. Song, 1120s–1160s. Round fan mounted as album leaf; ink and color on silk; 22.7 x 25 cm. John Ware Willard Fund, 56.98. Courtesy, Museum of Fine Arts, Boston. Reproduced with permission.

signature or even early documentation of any kind, we cannot retrieve the artist's name. Not surprisingly, it is attributed to Su Hanchen, to whom so many works (including a dozen large hanging scrolls in the National Palace Museum alone) are connected by later tradition. But the only extant plausibly signed painting by Su Hanchen, a beautiful round fan in the Boston Museum called *Children Playing with a Balance Toy* (fig. 2.3), does not immediately appear to have been painted by the artist who made *Children Playing in an Autumn Garden*. The latter might even date from somewhat earlier than the lifetime of Su Hanchen and could perhaps be associated with the now little-known figure painters who preceded Su Hanchen at court in the painting of such subjects. In iconographic significance and sheer physical presence, in our opinion, *Children Playing in an Autumn Garden* rests most easily with the paintings and painters associated with the reign of Emperor Shenzong (r. 1068–1085), such as the bird-and-flower master Cui Bai; the first master of gibbons and monkeys, Yi Yuanji; the greatest Song master of fish and aquatic creatures, Liu Cai; and the landscape painter Guo Xi, and could be a work of anywhere from the mid-eleventh century through the twelfth. The art historian Deng Chun in his *Huaji* (Record of paintings) of 1167 mentions two Northern Song painters of children, Liu Zongdao, famed for his painting of a child pointing to his reflection in the water and seeing the reflection point back at him, and Du Hai'er, a native of the capital whose works were popular at court in the Zhenghe era (1111–1117).[7] Liu and Du apparently were among the first to create the kinds of images of children that Su Hanchen produced slightly later. Purely stylistically, on the other hand, *Children Playing in an Autumn Garden* could have been painted as late as the lifetime of Liu Songnian, whose dated works fall into the period 1207–1210.

Perhaps representing the prevailing view of the matter, James Cahill regards both *Children Playing with a Balance Toy*, the Boston album leaf with Su Hanchen's signature, and *Children Playing in an Autumn Garden* as the work of Su Hanchen. He adds another anonymous painting in Taipei to this group, *Winter Play* (plate 7), pointing out that it is almost identical to *Children Playing in an Autumn Garden* in size and is similar enough in style and composition to suggest that the two were made as a pair, or possibly even for a set of four.[8]

Winter Play, like *Children Playing in an Autumn Garden*, is composed on the theme of two children at play in a garden, this one consisting of bamboo, blossoming plum, and camellias set around a cluster of garden rocks. As in the former picture, the children appear to be a slightly older girl and a younger boy, and similar attention is paid to the intricate and beautiful details of their hairstyles and ornaments. In the brief moment captured in this painting, they are gently teasing a kitten with a peacock feather attached to a banner. In Enlightenment-period France, Jean Baptiste Siméon Chardin (1699–1779) created a comparable child's world in painting, and in Periclean Athens the tomb memorials of children sometimes suggest a similarly private and fragile world. These observations might suggest that intimate, sensitive images of children can be associated with periods of enlightenment and humanistic thought throughout the world.

While there does not seem to be much doubt that *Winter Play* and *Children Playing in an Autumn Garden* were made as a set of some kind, as Cahill suggests, enough differences between the two, especially in the painting of the rocks and other elements of the setting, may indicate that even if the same painter was responsible for the figures of the children and the general design, others may have helped with the background. Nor does the relationship between the two paintings have any bearing on the question of who painted them, a question that remains in our minds unanswerable.

Conversely, a recent study of Su Hanchen by Liu Fang-ju concludes on stylistic grounds that the Boston fan, *Children Playing with a Balance Toy*, could not have been painted by Su Hanchen, despite the presence of his signature, but that both large

National Palace Museum paintings, *Children Playing in an Autumn Garden* and *Winter Play*—neither of which has a signature or seal of any artist—are by him.[9] At issue in such diverse opinions as those summarized here are traditional structural differences in the practice of connoisseurship that would take us far from any relevance to the subject of children in Song art. What we can observe with some certainty is that the painters of all of these pictures were professional masters active at the imperial court sometime between about 1075 and 1200. These painters were closer to the values of the *min*, or common people, than even the brilliant new scholars of the Song period, and we can appreciate in their art the forms they give to "human feelings," whether as part of a discourse of power or as a manifestation of the changing nature of human feelings at a time when human life was highly cherished. Professional painters offer a particularly promising entry into these matters, since they were of the *min*, yet also increasingly well educated and accustomed to the company of both learned scholars and wealthy aristocrats. They brought their unique skills as artists to these intersections of discourse, education, power, advancement, and the representation of "human feelings."

Another Boston fan signed by Su Hanchen (fig. 2.4) is also a work of affecting beauty, and is a subject not easily separable from *Children Playing*. In it is a single court woman, seated at her dressing table in what looks again like the corner of an imperial garden, looking at the enlarged reflection of her face in a mirror. A young maid waits in attendance behind her. Now the season is spring, the season of love and intensified emotion, and, sadly, the beautiful young woman contemplates the passage of time as she sits alone in her garden. As this is a court painting done by a court artist for a court patron, we assume that the image of the young woman is to be read as one of the hundreds of women of the imperial harem, a potential mother of more imperial offspring (we are also assuming that it would not have been appropriate for a court artist to depict an empress or wife of the emperor in such a way). The women of the harem were occasionally blessed by an imperial summons but were mostly alone with their beauty, growing a year older every spring.

It is as striking to see sympathetic attention paid by a leading court artist to such women as it is to see children playing alone in their garden. The very appearance of these new genres in the Song period helps to define an enlightened stage of human history. These images imply that even children and the women of the imperial harem are human beings with feelings and emotions, their lives worth representing. In Europe, similar attention to the domestic lives of women and children did not appear in art until the seventeenth and eighteenth centuries.

In Chinese poetry too, there is a new attention to the lives and feelings of children and women at this time, and a new consciousness of the integrity of the individual.

To the social consciousness and deeply humane sentiments of Du Fu, who is the inspiration for so much Song poetry, such Song poets as Mei Yaochen (1002–1060) and Su Shi (1037–1101) add a tone of affectionate directness and openness when writing of their families. As Martin Powers reminds us, they write of their wives as friends and confidants, and of their children as human beings instead of mere ideas or types.[10] Domestic emotions and mundane details of life and feeling become the substance of poetry between the ninth and twelfth centuries. That this phenomenon coincides with a discourse of human feelings can perhaps be connected to the late professor Kojiro Yoshikawa's observation "that the daily life of the [Song] period and the environment in which it was lived were in many respects radically different from the China of [pre-Song] times. They were, in fact, closer to those of modern times."[11]

Figure 2.4 Su Hanchen, *Lady at Her Dressing Table in a Garden*. Song, mid-twelfth century. Round fan mounted as album leaf; ink, color, and gold on silk; 25.2 cm x 16.7 cm. Denman Waldo Ross Collection, 29.960. Courtesy, Museum of Fine Arts, Boston. Reproduced with permission. © 2000 Museum of Fine Arts, Boston. All rights reserved.

Certainly among the most revealing and affecting poems of the kind to which we refer is Mei Yaochen's "Venturing Out and Home Again on the Night of the Fifteenth in the First Lunar Month," written in 1045 following the death of his beloved first wife:

> Staying home I'll only fret,
> Venturing out should ease my mind.
> Rich and poor, each with a mate
> My heart's pain intensifies.
> Creeping age dispirits me,
> Weariness overtakes my will.
> Returning, I see my boy and girl;
> My nose stings before words come.
> Last year with their mother they went out,
> Rouging their faces to copy her.
> Now she has gone to the springs below—
> Their faces are soiled, clothing worn.
> Knowing they are children still
> I hide my tears, lest they should see.
> Moving the lamp, I lie facing the wall,
> A hundred troubles coiled deep in me.[12]

This intimate view of Mei's family appears in a context common to many Tang and Song poems about mourning over the death of a family member, usually either a child or a wife and mother. Mei also refers to the pain and the material hardship suffered by children following the death of their mothers, another well-known theme in Tang and Song poetry. The sad condition of the children described by Mei implies that without the mother, there is no one capable of properly feeding, washing, clothing, or providing emotional support for the children. In this regard, poetry departs from painting in that visual images of children did not overtly express sadness or other negative emotions, most likely out of a sense that to embody such images in a tangible and clearly visible way would be inauspicious. In poetry, on the other hand, fewer such constraints existed, and some of the most detailed, individualized poetic portraits of children and families appear in poems of grief, loss, or separation from loved ones. A poem might be connected with a memorial portrait of a child, as Wu Hung shows in his discussion of an unusual Han-dynasty (206 B.C.–A.D. 220) funerary portrait of a five-year-old boy, Xu Aqu, who died in A.D. 170.[13] The stone relief carving shows the boy alive with other children running toward him, apparently entertaining him as he sits on a dais; below, lending a festive air, are two musicians, a dancer, and a juggler. There is nothing in these images to indicate death or sorrow. Yet the poetic eulogy accompanying the carving, written in the parents' voice directly addressing the deceased child, evokes the deep pain they felt upon losing their son:

> Your spirit wanders alone
> In eternal darkness underground.
> You have left your home forever;
> How can we still hope to glimpse your dear face?[14]

As Pei-yi Wu points out in his analysis of sources on Chinese childhood from the Tang to the Qing, this tradition of poetic expressions of grief over children continued later in China, flourishing in the Tang and beyond in two forms—lyric poetry lamenting the death of a child or a separation due to official posting far from home, war, or other circumstances; and ritual forms, such as the requiem, grave notice, or tombstone inscription similar to that described by Wu Hung. Pei-yi Wu notes, "From the Tang until at least the fifteenth century, children were more written about in China than in Europe."[15]

Especially in the Tang and Song, the death of a child inspired some of the most poignant, deeply personal images of childhood, as we can see in a poem Mei Yaochen wrote following the death of his younger son, Shishi, soon after his first wife's death, and even more movingly in a three-part poem written after the loss of his baby girl, Chengcheng, who was born to his second wife. The second part of the poem depicts the baby's fragility and the mother's intense sorrow:

> Flowers budding on the trees—
> Such was the freshness of my baby girl.
> They could not withstand the winds of spring,
> But were blown to the ground where they turned to dust.
> This too was the fate of the child I loved;
> Heaven knows nothing of sorrow!
> And the tears of blood in the tender mother's eyes
> Like the milk of her breasts
> have still not dried.[16]

The contrast between the fragile image of delicate blossoms he associates with the baby and the much earthier reference to flowing "tears of blood" and milk that represent the mother's sorrow heightens the sense of grief Mei feels for this tiny creature who so briefly belonged to her parents. The first two lines of the last verse express the gulf between his daughter's tiny being and his feeling for her even more graphically:

> In a coffin five inches high and five inches wide
> I have buried the sorrow of a thousand years.[17]

That these intimate details of children figure most often in poems of loss perhaps reflects the sudden intensity with which a parent would become aware of how important these small lives were once they had ended, or, in cases where the mother's death occasioned poems about the children left behind, how acutely the poet sensed his own inadequacy to preserve his children's well-being, to compensate for the loss of the mother as nurturing parent. Pei-yi Wu traces the rise of an "increasingly sentimental representation" of deceased children back to the ninth century, when poems, requiems *(jiwen)*, and grave notices *(kuangzhi)* for children appeared that went well beyond traditional Confucian prescriptions for mourning the death of young children.[18] Significant among these is a poem written by Han Yü (768–824) for his twelve-year-old daughter, Na, after her death in 819. He describes her suffering when his family left their home following his exile and expresses anguish over his own responsibility for her sad end:

> Strands of vine bound
> round the tree-bark coffin
> rudely interred in desolate hills,
> your white bones cold.
> Panic pierced your heart, your
> body already in pain
> palanquin-carried down the road
> whose hardships were known to all.
>
> No time was there to circle the mound
> thrice with lamentation,
> a single plate of rice, I heard,
> was your only oblation.
> Thus did my crimes bring you
> guiltless to this,
> and for me a hundred years
> of shame, remorse, and tears.[19]

A few years later, Han Yü included these same sentiments briefly in a tomb inscription, and more discursively in this passage from a prose requiem written for his daughter's reburial:

> You were helped into a sedan chair and traveled from early morning to night. Snow and ice injured your weakened flesh. Shaken and rocked, you did not have any rest. There was no time to eat and drink, so you suffered from frequent thirst and hunger. To die in the wild mountains was not the fate you deserved. It is usually the parents' guilt that brings calamities to their children. Was I not the cause of your coming to such a pass?[20]

The combination of these three memorial pieces underscores the deep remorse Han Yü felt over his role in her untimely demise, and the personal details emphasize that these pieces were written not merely to fulfill ritual custom but as an outlet for genuine parental grief.

Even more striking is a requiem Li Shangyin (ca. 813–858) wrote later in the ninth century for the reburial, several years after her death, of his five-year-old niece, Jiji. She also had been temporarily buried "amid pallid grass and withered roots next to an unused, weed-choked road," a lonely spot not very different from the first burial site of Han Na.[21] In this remembrance, however, Li includes a passage that, in its explicit attention to the small details of children's behavior, might almost be a caption for a Song painting of children playing:

> Since you died I have been blessed with several nephews and nieces. Clad in colorful swaddling clothes or short jackets, they often play with their hobbyhorses and jade hoops in the courtyard. Under the sun and in the breeze, they fondle flowers and crowd around me. Only you are missing and I wonder where your spirit has gone.[22]

Pei-yi Wu notes that Li "as a grieving uncle anticipates the expressiveness of a much later age," and goes on to note the shift that took place during the Song: "Simple words, direct observation, and plain narration give great immediacy to the representation of family life in an everyday setting."[23] Although Wu refers to the "deliberate obscurity and allusiveness" characterizing much of Li Shangyin's poetry in contrast to the straightforward, frankly affectionate prose requiem just cited, Li did write a delightfully observant poem, discussed later in this essay, about his son that also looks forward to the many simply phrased yet clearly personal and intimately detailed poems Mei Yaochen and other Song poets wrote about their own children and family life.

One question that arises with reference to these Tang and Song poems concerns the large number of poems written for daughters, whether deceased, bereft of mothers who have died in the prime of life, or left behind when the father has traveled far from home. Since daughters were generally less highly valued in conventional social terms than sons, it is interesting that so many poets wrote so emotionally about their daughters (or nieces), indicating that they actually felt very close to them, perhaps in a way that they could not feel toward boys, for whose moral development fathers were directly responsible. Pei-yi Wu suggests that "it was easier for little girls to be 'children,' while little boys were expected to behave in an exemplary manner, in a way that would prefigure the future men."[24] Mothers and other female relatives, of course, did take central responsibility for the moral and behavioral training of girls and often played a key role in boys' education as well, but fathers (the writers of these poems) did not bear the direct, day-to-day burden of girls' moral education and thus could express their affection more freely, especially in poetry written primarily for personal expression.

In paintings of children from the Song, it is seldom easy to determine whether all the young children depicted are boys or whether girls are also included, and scholars differ over the gender identity of children in the paintings discussed here. In both painting and poetry, children of both genders, despite the relatively subtle differences alluded to, emerge as natural subjects during the late Tang and Song, seemingly for the uncomplicated reason that parents were moved to write of children of either gender as people who were vitally important in their lives. Li Shangyin explains why he wrote as he did about his niece, who, although her youth and gender might have gained her far more perfunctory acknowledgment upon her passing, had obviously captured a part of his heart: "I know I am doing more than what proprieties would allow for a child, but how can I do less than my deep feelings demand?"[25] That such affection was real and openly expressed within the context of the household may be seen in Mei Yaochen's poem to Ouyang Xiu (1007–1072) following Ouyang's loss of his daughter. Ouyang's poem mourning his daughter, the third one he had lost, alludes principally to his own great grief,[26] but Mei's poem depicts the father-daughter bond he, as a family friend, had seen for himself:

> . . . Memories press me as I sit by a lonely bank
> How you loved this girl,
> So charming when she played below your knees!

She must have been clever as she grew,
Aping her mother, smearing on shadow and rouge . . .[27]

The lines about copying her mother's makeup routine are a convention, alluding to Du Fu's "Journey North" and to the poem Mei wrote about his orphaned children, cited above. Nevertheless, Mei's sketch of Ouyang Xiu and his young daughter is one that grows out of personal acquaintance and, like Li Shangyin's passage about his nephews and nieces playing around him, creates an image of a child that one might expect to see in a Song painting.

Complementing these poems of loss and mourning in the Tang and Song were poems that depicted children in a lighter tone. The dominant theme of these is observation of the children's—chiefly sons'—mischievous qualities that on the surface might seem to bode ill for a future official career but that inspire a certain fatherly satisfaction with their children's energy and irreverence. In this vein, the poem most often alluded to is the Six Dynasties poet Tao Qian's "Blaming Sons":

White hair shrouds both my temples,
my skin and flesh have lost their fullness.
Though I have five male children,
not a one of them loves brush and paper.
A-shu's already twice times eight—
in laziness he's never been rivaled.
A-hsüan's going on fifteen
but cares nothing for letters or learning.
Yung and Tuan are thirteen
and can't tell a 6 from a 7!
T'ung-tzu's approaching age nine—
all he does is hunt for chestnuts and pears.
If this is the luck Heaven sends me,
then pour me the "thing in the cup"![28]

Read with no knowledge of the father who wrote it, this poem might appear to be a sincere complaint, and to the extent that fathers in traditional China depended heavily on sons for support in old age, it probably was quite sincere in one sense. However, knowing Tao Qian's love of wine (the "thing in the cup") and looking at the sense of release he claimed following his own eventual removal from the "dusty net" of official life, we may read into this poem a hint of pleasure in his sons' preference for play over reading, writing, and arithmetic.

Following Tao Qian came a long chain of poems continuing this humorous expression of pleasure in sons who did not act like virtuous little scholar-officials in their youth. Li Shangyin's extended portrait of his young son stands out among these for its close and keen observation of a child at play and for the direct exhortation he gives his son to lead an active, useful life rather than become a moldering old scholar like his father. Li begins with a wry reference to "Blaming Sons," taking unabashed pride in the fact that his son is far more precocious than Tao Qian's lazy progeny:

> My little boy Kun-shih,
> no finer, no handsomer lad;
> in bellyband, less than one year old,
> already he knew six from seven;
> at three he could tell you his name,
> had eyes for more than chestnuts and pears . . .[29]

As the poem continues, however, we see not a junior scholar aping his father's ways but a very active boy, mimicking (and parodying) adult behavior in play, yet exuberant in the way children are when wrapped up in their own worlds:

> Elderly gentlemen come to the gate;
> at once he dashes out to greet them;
> in front of the guests, asked what he would like,
> he mumbles shyly and won't speak up.
> Guests gone, he mimics their faces,
> bursting through the door, snatching his father's staff,
> now aping Chang Fei's outlandish countenance,
> now making fun of Teng Ai's stutter.
> A brave hawk on high wings soaring,
> a noble horse with fierce snorting breath,
> he cuts stout green bamboo for a pony,
> gallops wildly, banging into things.
> Suddenly he is the General in a play,
> in stage voice summoning his groom;
> now beside the gauze-veiled lamp
> he bows his head in evening obeisance to Buddha . . .
> . . . Try to hold him—he wiggles and squirms;
> threaten and scold—he will not be ruled.

Li goes on to describe him playing with his older sister, evoking the paintings discussed above.

Though the boy is quite young, not yet at the age of reason when sons were expected to begin paying serious attention to the worthier pursuits of life, Li does not appear simply to be an indulgent parent who will crack down as the child grows older, but a wistful man who sees in his son the youthful vigor he himself has lost. He refers to himself as old and worn-out, and exhorts his son to become a true leader:

> My son, grow up to manhood quickly,
> seek out the cubs in the tiger's cave;
> make yourself lord of ten thousand households—
> don't huddle forever over some old book!

Several features of this poem anticipate the Song: the intense focus on domestic life, the thematic centrality of the child, and the pervasive sense that the important concerns of real life lie in a world apart from scholarly officialdom. Indeed, Li's poem is a much fuller and richer portrait of a child than we see in most other poems of the Tang or the Song. Echoes of Li's central sentiment persist in later examples, as in Su Shi's terse expression of hope in "Bathing the Infant" that his new son will avoid the pitfalls of the intellectual life:

> People raising sons hope for intelligence;
> Intelligence has misled me all my life.
> I just want my son to be foolish and dull,
> And to reach high rank with no suffering, no strife.[30]

The playfulness of this brief verse leads us back to Li Shangyin, whose son was anything but foolish and dull but who shares Su Shi's hope that his son will lead a truly fulfilling life. Even in one of Mei Yaochen's poems about the effects of his wife's death on their children's well-being, we find this playful air embedded in a scene of regret. Mei's eldest son, Xiushu (Zeng), has become so unkempt following the loss of his mother that he becomes a poignantly comical figure, crawling with lice, hair uncombed. Among the poem's many allusions is another ironic reference to Tao Qian's "Blaming Sons": "When does he have time to hanker for pears and nuts?" At the end, though, Mei's message is not very distant from Li Shangyin's or Su Shi's:

> Giving him a haircut would be easy enough,
> But I'd hate to harm that natural growth of his![31]

The idea of the child as natural and unspoiled, even in a disheveled state no Song artist would care to depict, lies at the heart of all these poetic images. Children live without pretense, without arrogance, and for that reason are vulnerable. Illness, poverty, parental neglect, the consequences of fathers' foibles, the sorrow of mothers' untimely passing, all may put children in harm's way. In their poetry, these fathers reveal a longing to preserve and protect the naturalness they ascribe to children, the innocence of children as we see them in Song paintings. Even from within poems of deep sorrow emerge the poetic complements to the paintings: Here are children as we wish they could stay forever, like the stone portrait of the deceased Eastern Han child Xu Aqu watching lively entertainment, belying the wrenching grief of the eulogy written in his parents' voice.

Poetry about children from the Tang and Song provided a persistent model not only for later poetry but for representations of childhood in fiction and personal essays as well, going beyond the stories of precocious youth that dominated much early storytelling to show children instead as ordinary, yet cherished, beings. For a final poetic example embodying all the qualities we see in the Song—intimate detail, personal references, domestic affection, playfulness, and regret over a young life too early curtailed—we turn to Gao Qi (1336–1374), whose life spanned the last years of the Yuan and the early years of the Ming. His "Seeing Flowers and Remembering My Deceased Daughter, Shu," written after Zhu Yuanzhang's siege of Suzhou at the end of the Yuan, combines in his portrait of her the mildly mischievous streak of Li Shangyin's son, the fragility of Han Yü's daughter Na, the desolation Ouyang Xiu felt upon his third daughter's death, and the open affection pervading all these poems and paintings.[32] There are echoes here of Du Fu's and Mei Yaochen's daughters imitating their mothers' makeup, and even, perhaps, of Tao Qian's son's fondness for fruit:

> My middle daughter I dearly loved,
> Until she was six I carried her in my arms.
> Holding her close, I'd feed her bits of fruit,
> Sat her on my knee and taught her to chant poems.
> Up at first light, she'd copy big sister's toilette,
> Straining for a glimpse in the dressing-table mirror.
> She'd begun to be fond of silk gauze and damask,
> Things we could not give her, being poor . . .

The end of the poem is very much like the end of Mei's "Venturing Out and Home Again" in its evocation of silent but intense grief:

> . . . A cup of wine brings no consolation,
> At dusk the curtains stir in the chill wind.[33]

The father can do no more for his child than to remember her vividly as she was, a small girl at play.

It seems to us that we glimpse in these Song paintings, and in the poems we have been reading, an age of enlightenment in the evolution of human kindness, decency, and consideration. Song painting and poetry speak to the modern world of values we can share and understand, even across the time and space that separate us from that distant age. And the fragility of the concept of human values Song art conveys is only intensified by our knowledge of the brutal and absolute end to Song society brought about by the Mongol conquest of China in the thirteenth century, and the increasingly rigid and limiting constraints imposed over Chinese society by later Neo-Confucianism.

If this appears to be a heavy weight to give a handful of paintings and poems about children and their mothers, one can of course simply admire these works for the skill of their representations and the beauty of their settings, and for the richness and subtlety of emotional content they embody. But the styles and techniques of these paintings are equally unusual in the long run of Chinese art history. We see in *Children Playing in an Autumn Garden* and *Winter Play* (plates 6 and 7) the essence of Song realism. Such realism differs profoundly from European realism and also precedes it by many centuries. But it deserves to be called realism for the ways it stands out from earlier and later Chinese forms of representation. Here, for example, we find the minute attention to details of structural forms, gesture, drapery, costume, decoration, and natural objects that allows any viewer to quickly grasp all of the physical nuances of the composition. Descriptive effort is given to precisely such details of identity as the surfaces of rock; the softness of cloth; the dense, massed complexity of flowers, leaves, and branches; the open hollowness of lacquer tables; and the full absorption of the two children in their activities. Later European oil paintings would not present these things more effectively, only more tactually.

Song realism of this kind presents us with the essence of scene and narration without many of the elements that European viewers later came to consider necessary for realism: clearly defined light and shade; perspective of the kind associated with "scientific" perspective in Europe; continuous, tactile grounding of space; and the construction of an interior box within which activity takes place. This realism is more like that of the Chinese poetic quatrain, in which what is of importance is described in a few carefully selected images, every word dedicated to the creation of a single basic mood. No elaborate preface is required, nor any continuity with what preceded the moment at which the poem begins, and there is no necessary connection to anything that may follow. This is a realism of artful choice, of suggestion, and of concentration on essentials. Here, two children play in a garden in a moment stolen from the larger responsibilities and cares of the world to come. While we realize that no two children in any garden anywhere looked exactly like this, we see enough of their physical reality to feel that we have glimpsed something true that also touches us with its intimacy. It is, in fact, only in a few paintings like this one that intimacy between two human beings is ever even suggested in Chinese art. The beauty and innocence of children may have been one concern of the painter, but the touching, sweet, physical interplay between two human beings was surely another. That Song painters unknown to us today were able for so brief a time to think of and depict human beings and human relationships in such tactile, intimate, and physical ways defies easy explanation, whether of discourse or essential feelings, yet remains necessary to our understanding of the nature of Song art and life.

Figure 2.5 Zhou Wenju (active 961–975), attrib. *Lady with a Flute*. Song, tenth century. Detail of hanging scroll; ink and color on silk; 86 x 30 cm. After James Cahill, *Chinese Paintings XI–XIV Centuries* (New York: Crown Publishers, Inc., 1962), plate 17.

For it is only in Song art that we can find such images. In the little album leaf in the Boston museum previously discussed, *Children Playing with a Balance Toy* (fig. 2.3), for example, we see two loosely clothed children playing together with the same kind of uninhibited and physical intimacy, as if there were no one else in the world but them. We wish to suggest that such paintings and the poems of the time that embody similarly intimate and tender attitudes cast a startling illumination on the nature of Song civilization.

A counterpart to Su Hanchen's poignant fan painting of two isolated children playing with a balance toy is a single figure of a court woman, dressed in male costume as was a popular practice in the women's palaces, presented in profile, standing before us full-figure, studying her fingernails (fig. 2.5). A flute is held at her side by a belt. This image corresponds to one described with deep appreciation by the Yuan critic Tang Hou (active ca. 1320–1330) as the work of the tenth-century master of the genre of women and children, Zhou Wenju, in a significant passage in which Tang discusses the whole tradition of the painting of court women and children:

> Skill in painting court women lies in attaining a true sense of life in the inner chambers. The Tang masters Zhou Fang and Zhang Xuan, Du Xiao and Zhou Wenju of the Five Dynasties, as well as Su Hanchen and the like all excelled at it. This is not achieved by decorative skills in applying cinnabar red and powdered white, or in depicting golden jewelry and fine jades. I once owned a painting of a court woman by Zhou Wenju. She had put her jade flute in the belt at her waist and was looking intently at her fingernails, giving the impression of a frozen moment. One felt that she was lost in thought.[34]

In a well-known passage the influential Song scholar and writer Ouyang Xiu noted, "Loneliness and tranquillity are qualities difficult to paint, and even if an artist manages to achieve them, viewers are not likely to understand them . . . it is difficult to give form to a sense of profound stillness or of deep feelings."[35] Yet in the paintings we have reviewed here, it is qualities such as loneliness, tranquility, tenderness, affection, and intimacy that the artists attained. And as Tang Hou's observations suggest, painters like Zhou Wenju and Su Hanchen were achieving precisely these effects in their paintings of court women and children, just as the antiquarian and textual scholar Ouyang Xiu was noting the near impossibility of their attainment.

While the paintings associated with Su Hanchen are the most significant body of early images of children in Chinese art, another popular Song subject of childhood play and bucolic freedom was that of the buffalo herd-boy. This separate genre also first appears in the eleventh century at the height of Song civilization. The poets Su Shi and Huang Tingjian (1045–1105) and their painter friend Li Gonglin (ca. 1041–1106) are among those who are first associated with the genre. For such scholar-officials as Su and Huang, herd boys held special meanings, among them memories of the countryside around their hometowns and the lost pleasures of their vigorous and spirited youth. In a reflective poem titled "Long Ago I Lived in the Country," written in response to a painting of herd boys done by his friend Chao Yuezhi, Su Shi wrote this reminiscence:

> Long ago I lived in the country,
> knew only sheep and cows.
> Down smooth riverbeds on the cow's back,
> steady as a hundred-weight barge,
> a boat that needs no steering—while banks slipped by,
> I stretched out and read a book—she didn't care.
> Before us we drove a hundred sheep,
> heeding my whip as soldiers heed a drum;
> I didn't lay it on too often—
> only stragglers I gave a lash to.
> In lowlands, grass grows tall,
> but tall grass is bad for cows and sheep;
> so we headed for the hills, leaping sags and gullies
> (climbing up and down made my muscles strong),
> through long woods where mist wet my straw coat and hat . . .
> But those days are gone—I see them only in a painting.

No one believes me when I say I regret
not staying a herdsman all my life.[36]

From the late eleventh century on, buffalo herd boys exemplify for many scholars and officials the simple life far away from ceremony, ritual, and social obligation, perhaps not unrelated to the life Li Shangyin and Su Shi wished for their sons in the poems discussed in the preceding pages. That most of those paintings still extant today were made for court consumption by artists employed by the court suggests how quickly the imperial court took over popular themes in art and made them into functions of imperial society and imperial values. The emperor of China, no less than a disaffected scholar-official, could thus seem to evince his deep admiration and wishful desire for a bucolic life of childlike simplicity. In fact, neither Su Shi nor the emperor is likely to have seriously wished for such a life, despite their pretenses. Such paintings easily fall into the realm of artifacts of the Song discourse on human feelings and values that Martin Powers describes.

Testifying to the popularity of the herd-boy theme is the huge number of paintings of the subject produced for the Southern Song court in the twelfth and thirteenth centuries.[37] Many of them are fan paintings. Such fans, held in the hand on a hot summer day, may also have been intended to evoke cool thoughts of shady streams and wind in the willows. Li Tang was only one of the many artists who painted this theme during the era of its greatest popularity in the twelfth and thirteenth centuries (fig. 2.6). And like so many popular Song painting subjects it was revived in the Ming period, especially at the Ming court where its celebration of rusticity was elevated to a monumental level.[38]

That the figures in ox-herding pictures need not be children—and as often as not they seem to be at least young adults—suggests, we believe, that childhood itself is not the central concern of ox-herding pictures. Poems about herd boys are often equally ambiguous regarding the age of the "boy." In rural regions, young boys often managed water buffalo, as we have seen, and such images may have evoked actual memories of rural childhood, but images of water buffalo alone, without herd boys, had the same symbolic function, as Scarlett Jang has shown in her detailed study of ox-herding pictures in the Song period.[39]

Ox-herding pictures and poetic images also had Chan associations. But above all they evoked the ideal of retirement and of a life far from the daily cares of public service. Quite possibly the innocence and carefree nature of childhood itself might have carried the same suggestions to many viewers, thus increasing the popularity of pictures of children in an age when the ideal of public service reached its peak.

Figure 2.6 Li Tang (ca. 1050–after 1130), *Herd Boy with Water Buffalo and Calf.* Song, eleventh or twelfth century. Hanging scroll; ink and light color on silk; 46.4 x 62.5 cm. Collection of the National Palace Museum. Taiwan, Republic of China.

Never again after the Song did that ideal motivate so many talented men. Landscape painting, another development of the tenth and eleventh centuries, can also be understood mainly as the creation of otherwise unattainable worlds of remote peace and tranquility, and as embodiment of the ideal of a life lived in the unclocked time of the natural world.

The final genre of paintings of children that developed during the Song period was that of the knickknack or toy peddler. In typical works of this genre we see numerous mischievous and excited children gathering around the portable stand of a peddler whose wares include a great array and variety of the popular children's toys and knickknacks of the time, including some of those we have seen in the paintings associated with Su Hanchen. The genre, often choosing to focus on peasant children, attained great popularity within Song court circles and further expanded the range of compositions focused on children. Many pictures of this genre were painted by a court artist named Li Song (active 1190–1230), whose art has been studied by Ellen Laing.[40] Sometimes, as in the example we have selected, there is also a nursing mother or amah, whose partially visible breasts are as unexpected in a court painting as the quarreling children in a society that esteems propriety and decorum (fig.2.7). Clearly such pictures served a special audience. As Ellen Laing points out, while the need for male offspring may have been a continuing preoccupation of all Chinese families, it was especially vital for the imperial family, whose rule of China depended specifically upon the regular production of large numbers of capable male offspring. Producing, nurturing, educating, and looking after the flourishing population of the children of the imperial palaces was a substantial enterprise, and a tightly regimented responsibility subject to strict requirements, programs, strictures, and schedules. It might be suspected, in any case, that these popular pictures of children, nursemaids, and toy peddlers found their main audience among the women

Figure 2.7 Li Song (active 1190–1230), *Toy Peddler*. Southern Song, dated 1210. Fan mounted as an album leaf; ink and light color on silk; 25.8 x 27.6 cm. Collection of the National Palace Museum. Taiwan, Republic of China.

of the imperial palaces who were most directly connected to the production and supervision of imperial children. Martin Powers has also shown how pictures of healthy, happy peasants were relevant to the discourse of human feelings *(renqing)* that he locates in the Song period. He observes:

> Unlike so many poems about the peasants' suffering, Li [Song]'s painting suggests that rural poverty is perhaps not so bad, after all, and that peasant women can raise fat, frisky children the same as anyone else. Perhaps this message would have appealed to the court. But there are further nuances, which color the ideological construction of poverty. In its touching narrative and its loving enumeration of childhood's charms, this painting asserts that even the poor possess feelings of [*renqing*] in common with people of all classes.[41]

If that is indeed the case, then we need to note further that all such pictures were painted by professional artists, artists whose values and experiences were shaped by the reality and the ideals of the common people, the *min*, of which they were a part. Similarly, many poems of the era—whether they depict rural family life in a positive light, the children poor but happy, or whether they stress the dark and desperate side of rural poverty—reflect the poets' direct observations of rural society and, more importantly, their need to maintain their connection with that world.

What we have today in which to glimpse the lives of children in Song China—from the spoiled young princes of the imperial family down to ragged peasants—are only some images of children with their mothers and wet nurses, of children playing in quiet gardens, of bucolic herd boys on willow banks, and of children excitedly gathering around toy peddlers displaying their wares. When joined especially to the rich imagery of childhood found in poetry and prose, and in the decorative arts, woodblock prints, and book illustrations, however, this is a substantially larger body of material focused on the lives of children in the tenth, eleventh, and twelfth centuries than can be found anywhere else in the world. This, we believe, suggests something significant about the character of Song society. The value placed on children in the Song, as expressed in painting and poetry, represented a significant stage in the development of decency, concern, mutual respect, and belief in the universality of "human feeling" not only within the context of Chinese traditions but in that of the larger world. Children would not receive such a high level of individual attention anywhere in the world again for several centuries.

3

One Hundred Children: From Boys at Play to Icons of Good Fortune

Terese Tse Bartholomew

The theme of boys playing in a garden was an established subject in the paintings of the Song dynasty (960–1279). It continued to be a favorite among artists and craftsmen of the Ming (1368–1644) and Qing (1644–1911) dynasties, but the iconography fluctuated according to the medium and the times. The focus of this essay is the changing emphasis of this theme in the decorative arts of the Ming and Qing periods. Exploring the subject of boys playing in a garden, the essay attempts to identify toys, games, and their hidden meanings, and to use the established themes as a means for assisting in dating art objects. Variously known as *yingxitu*, "pictures of boys at play," and *baizitu*, "pictures of a hundred boys," illustrations of boys playing in a garden appear frequently in the decoration of Ming and Qing porcelain, textiles, lacquerware, and other minor arts. *Yingxi* pictures feature a few boys playing, while *baizi* scenes usually depict a large group of boys, sometimes numbering one hundred as the name implies. The "hundred boys" is an allusion to King Wen (Zhou Wen Wang), legendary father of the founder of the Zhou dynasty, King Wu (r. 1122–1115 B.C.), who had twenty-four wives and ninety-nine sons. One day at Yanshan, he found an infant after a thunderstorm, and he adopted the baby so that he could have a total of one hundred sons.[1] King Wen thus established the ideal, and his one hundred sons became a popular motif in Chinese art. As a symbol for male progeny, the *baizi* theme was used to decorate any object bearing a wish for numerous offspring, especially items for the bridal chamber, including quilt covers, curtains, and valances for the wedding bed.

Song dynasty paintings depicted lively and varied scenes of children at play that eventually became standard themes for works of art in the Ming dynasty. These themes, such as groups of boys playing at school or pretending to be officials riding in procession, were repeated in various media, including porcelain, lacquer, and textiles. In this essay, a wide variety of toys and games were included to illustrate the activities of the hundred boys in a garden setting. Qing dynasty craftsmen continued to use Ming dynasty patterns, but new features also appeared. Among the more interesting developments are the pictorial puns, or rebuses, representing four-character auspicious phrases, usually having to do with passing the civil service exams with honors and achieving high rank.

The toys and games that became such important symbols in the Ming and Qing periods had their roots in the Song dynasty. Paintings by or attributed to artists such as Su Hanchen (ca. late eleventh through mid-twelfth centuries) and Li Song (active 1190–1230) include a wealth of information on games that have remained constant through the ages. According to the illustrations, Song dynasty boys played chess and other board games. They kicked balls, spun tops, rattled the *bolanggu* (a drumlike device on a stick with two beaters attached by strings), pumped swings, and played with toy carts. They liked percussion instruments such as the drum, cymbals, wooden clappers, and gong, and they accompanied puppet shows and lion dances with their music.[2] They flew kites and were entertained by paper windmills. Children enjoyed animals, and paintings show boys teasing cats, watching goldfish, chasing butterflies with fans, catching crickets and watching them fight, and playing with birds. During the Dragon Boat Festival, boys caught and teased each other with toads.[3] Elsewhere children played with masks and impersonated characters such as Kuixing, God of Literature. A child pretending to be the demonlike Kuixing wore a monster mask, held a brush aloft, and raised his leg to kick at the Dipper constellation. Plants were also utilized as toys and games. Children caught willow catkins in the spring, played with lotus blossoms, and carried large lotus leaves as umbrellas on hot summer days. When fruits ripened, the children would play at picking them. Harvesting red dates, or jujubes, was an especially popular subject, undoubtedly due to the fact that the Chinese name for the fruit, *zaozi*, is homophonous with the term for the early arrival of male progeny.[4] After children had their fill of the fruit, they used them to make toys such as the top made of bamboo sticks and jujubes used for the game *tui zaomo*, as shown in Su Hanchen's painting *Children Playing in an Autumn Garden* (plate 6).[5] Also prevalent in the Song period were highly detailed scenes of lively boys flocking around an itinerant peddler, who traditionally carried five hundred different kinds of goods, including a multitude of toys.

Ming Dynasty (1368–1644)

Very early in Chinese history, the strong desire for sons was directly related to the need for male progeny to perform the ancestral sacrifices and to ensure the continuation of the family line. But by the Ming period, the birth of sons in itself was not enough. Families hoped for *guizi*, or noble sons, who would excel in their studies and take top honors in the civil service examinations, bringing wealth and the highest possible honors to their kin. Thus the boys depicted in Ming decorative arts are not just ordinary boys at play. Usually well-dressed, these "noble sons" frolic in the gardens of the upper class. The garden plants indicate the season and often bear symbolic messages as well. The toys and activities included in the scenes are not merely representations of childhood fun but symbolize the four seasons and the agricultural-based festivals of China. Hidden in each object of play are symbolic references to wealth, fertility, and distinguished success in officialdom.

During the Ming, the boys motif is best exemplified by porcelain vessels with underglazed blue decoration, carved lacquer pieces, *kesi* (woven silk) tapestry, and robes excavated from the tomb of the Wanli emperor. The *baizi* motif is more commonly found on textiles and on lacquer pieces, while *yingxi* is a popular subject for porcelain vessels. Because of the space limitation on porcelain, the number of boys can range from a single boy at play to as many as sixteen, forty-six, and only occasionally one hundred.

The first examples of the *yingxi* motif in ceramic decoration come from the Tang dynasty (618–906). A pitcher from Changsha is painted with the motif of a boy carrying a lotus leaf (fig. 1.7.). Both the figure style of the infant and the scrolling vine motif painted on this pitcher are interpretations of designs originating in Rome and the Middle East that were exported to China by way of the trade and pilgrimage routes through Central Asia.[6] During the Song and Jin (1115–1234) periods, the ceramic centers of Dingzhou, Yaozhou, Cizhou, and Jingdezhen carved, painted, and pressed this borrowed motif of boys and plants into their wares. The chubby Western putto was thus adapted to express an ideal child in the Chinese idiom. Examples of the Tang figure style made in Cizhou kilns during the Song period begin to show the extension of the theme beyond boys and plants to include more active scenes of a boy fishing or riding a bamboo horse.[7]

The *yingxi* motif in ceramic decoration expanded into painterly renditions of numerous boys at play in a garden setting as early as the Chenghua era (1465–1487) of the Ming dynasty. But the height of the development of this motif for porcelain decor occurred during the Jiajing (1522–1566) and Wanli (1573–1620) periods when there was an explosion of the production of wares with this theme.

Figure 3.1 Covered jar with design of children at play. Ming, Jiajing period, 1522–1566. Porcelain with underglaze blue; h. 45 cm. Tianminlou Collection.

Porcelain and Lacquer of the Jiajing period (1522–1566)

An impressive illustration of the *yingxi* motif is a large jar with underglaze blue in the Tianminlou collection (fig. 3.1). It shows sixteen boys at play in a garden fenced by an elaborate railing and decorated with Taihu rocks, palms, banana plants, and pine trees. The boys appear in small groups. One group shows an older boy wearing a hat who sits in front of a tall screen, pretending to be a teacher. One of his students reads from a book. An erring student kneels before the teacher, while a third stands by with a bamboo staff to mete out punishment. In another group, an older boy sits on a stool by a square table on which is placed an opened cricket container watched by two younger children.[8] One small boy pulls a toy cart. Another boy is

Figure 3.2 Covered jar. Ming, Jiajing period, 1522–1566. Porcelain with underglaze blue. Collection of the National Palace Museum. Taiwan, Republic of China.

seated in a cart, pulled by his friend, while being fanned by a boy from behind. One boy appears to be holding a bow and arrows, and another carries a vase containing a branch of coral. The vase *(ping)*, a homonym of the word "peace," may convey the sentiment of "peace among sons and grandsons" *(zisun ping'an)*, or it could simply be a precious vase *(baoping)*. One boy, riding on a hobbyhorse, plays the role of an official. His companion shades him with a large lotus leaf. The motif "boy with lotus" is a reference to the Song dynasty custom of live children imitating fertility-cult figurines called *mohele* during the Qixi (Double Seven) festival.[9]

An underglaze blue-and-white covered jar in the National Palace Museum depicts a boy carrying a string puppet hanging from a long staff and waving it to the accompaniment of flute and gong music (fig. 3.2). The Song dynasty game of spinning a toy made of bamboo sticks and dates is seen on the same jar (fig. 3.3). Other activities depicted on porcelain from the Jiajing period include chess playing, kite flying, and riding on a caparisoned goat.[10] The theme of children riding goats goes back to the Yuan dynasty (1279–1368) and can be seen in examples of Yuan embroidered textiles in the Metropolitan Museum and the National Palace Museum.[11] Celebrating the arrival of spring, children ride goats in garden settings. Goats were an important part of the Mongol economy, able to subsist on the grasses of the steppes, providing both milk and meat. As an auspicious symbol, they also worked well in Chinese culture. Playing with goats *(xiyang)* is a rebus for propitiousness *(jixiang)*. And because the word for goat, *yang*, sounds the same as that for the male principle *(yang)*, a picture of boys and goats resonates with the wish for sons.

The same themes played out in garden settings of rocks and trees on porcelain are also featured in Jiajing lacquerware. The lid of a small covered box from the sixteenth century shows a boy beating a gong to announce the arrival of an official, played by a boy, riding a hobbyhorse, who is shaded by a lotus leaf canopy carried by his companion. The bottom of the piece is decorated with a scene of a boy shooting at a bird, while his companion stands by with a basket.[12]

Figure 3.3 Drawing of a boy playing the spinning-date game, detail of fig. 3.2.

Jiajing lacquerware also repeats the theme of the toy peddler, first introduced in Song dynasty paintings. Two similar but not identical examples of this

Figure 3.4 Front panel of one-hundred-boys jacket belonging to the Xiaojing Empress (d. 1612). Ming, Wanli period, 1573–1620. Embroidered silk. Excavated from Ding Ling. Palace Museum, Beijing. After the Institute of Archaeology, CASS; Museum of Ding Ling; and the Archaeological Team of the City of Beijing, *Ding Ling* (The imperial tomb of the Ming dynasty at Ding Ling), vol. 1 (Beijing: Wenwu Press, 1990), pl. 234a.

theme are found in circular dishes in private collections in Hong Kong and in the Palace Museum, Beijing.[13] The dishes are both made of carved polychrome lacquer bearing four dragons on the cavetto. The scene of the toy peddler takes place in the center, where he twirls a double *bolanggu*, or rattle drum, attracting the boys to his stand. The stand is constructed of a large round basket and a rectangular container stuffed full of merchandise, enclosed by four upright poles hung with lanterns and banners. The scene takes place in a garden with rocks, flowering bushes, and a peach tree bearing fruit. This is in contrast to the more realistic Song paintings, which depict urban and village street scenes of actual itinerant salesmen surrounded by ragtag commonplace boys. On each dish, eight boys are carefully arranged in groups of two. One older boy carries a toddler on his shoulders, allowing him a better view of the toys. The others play with a string puppet, watch crickets fight, spin a windmill, and point happily at the toys.

Figure 3.5 Back panel of one-hundred-boys jacket (Beijing: Wenwu Press, 1990), pl. 234b.

The Wanli Period (1573–1620): Hundred-Boys Jackets, Ink-Cake Designs, and Porcelain

Two imperial jackets bearing the hundred-boys motif were discovered between 1956 and 1958, when the tomb of the Wanli emperor at Ding Ling was excavated. These jackets were found in the coffin of the Xiaojing empress (d. 1612), one of the two empresses entombed with the emperor.[14] The jackets are of superior quality, making them aesthetically pleasing examples of this motif; they are also a substantial source of information about games and toys of the Ming dynasty. The hundred boys, wearing fancy garments, play in a garden setting with Taihu rocks, trees, and blossoms, on a floor scattered with auspicious objects and jewels. The boys' garments bear many symbols of longevity, such as a pine tree with its trunk twisted into a stylized *shou* (longevity) character. Both jackets, one of which is illustrated here (figs. 3.4, 3.5), are embroidered with large dragons and with two *wan* (ten thousand) char-

Figure 3.6 Drawing of a boy kicking a ball, detail of fig. 3.5.

acters in front and a large *shou* character in the back. The characters make up the phrase *wanshou*, or "longevity of ten thousand years," a traditional birthday greeting for an emperor or empress.

The activities of the hundred boys found on the jackets are similar to those found in other forms of decorative arts of the Jiajing and Wanli periods. Ming dynasty artists and craftsmen were extremely creative in depicting the motif of "a hundred boys." Whatever the medium, the boys are usually arranged in small groups, playing various games. Scenes embroidered on the two imperial jackets include boys dancing with lotus blossoms, waving flags, sleeping while being fanned by a friend, eating peaches and steamed buns, and fighting over a birdcage.

The coats are especially useful in illustrating specific games and toys that are discussed herein in some detail. Several of the games are related to the martial arts *(wushu)*. For example, on one of the jackets a boy exercises with a fencing pole, or *huagun*, illustrating one of the basic types of martial arts practiced in China. An early depiction of this exercise is found on a lacquer plate of the Sanguo period (A.D. 220–265), showing two young boys fighting with poles.[15] Two other boys depicted on the coats are wrestling: A boy stands behind his opponent and grips him around the waist. Wrestling has a long history in China and can be traced back to the Warring States period (ca. 475–221 B.C.).[16] In one scene, a group of boys watches while one boy kicks a ball (fig. 3.6). Football, known as *cuju*, was one of the earliest games of China. At first a form of martial art practiced in the Warring States period, it became a popular adult game in the Han dynasty (206 B.C.–A.D. 220). The ball was made of leather and stuffed with hair.[17] Often played in winter as a means of keeping warm and improving blood circulation, *cuju* is still a prevalent activity in China.

Another game depicted on the jackets is jump rope, with two boys swinging the rope while another leaps in. This game was called "to jump the white wheel" *(tiao baisuo)*, as the rope can resemble a white wheel when swung around rapidly.[18] In another scene, two boys, both blindfolded, play a version of blindman's bluff called "groping for the fish" *(moxiayu)*. One boy strikes the wooden fish *(muyu)*, a percussion instrument, so that the other boy can locate him by sound. Shen Bang (fl. 1550–1596) described this game in his *Wanshu zaji*, first published in 1593.[19] To play it, children hold on to a string to form a ring or "empty city" around the two blindfolded boys. One boy strikes the wooden fish and moves swiftly to another location while the other boy tries to snatch the wooden fish from him, then run out of the ring.

Hide-and-seek is a popular game the world over. The version embroidered on the jacket depicts one child covering the eyes of a boy seated in front of him, while the others hide among the openings inside a Taihu rock. A game that is peculiar to China is "flipping shoes" *(fanxie)*. First, the boys take off their shoes and line them

Figure 3.7 Drawing of boys flipping shoes, detail of fig. 3.4.

up in a row. A child hopping on one foot then tries to turn over as many shoes as he can (fig. 3.7). This game was still in vogue and played in the villages of northern China until the revolution of 1949.[20]

On one section of the jacket, two boys play a guessing game with their hands, called *caiquan*. Boys nearby kick a shuttlecock, a simple toy usually made of copper coins sewn into leather and stuck with feathers. The object of the game is to kick the shuttlecock with one's heel, trying to keep the game going as long as possible. Known as *jianzi* in Chinese, the shuttlecock was a pun for "to see a son," which is also *jianzi*. In Zhejiang province, it was a custom for the bride's family to give gifts when their daughter became pregnant. One or more shuttlecocks were included among the gifts, with the hope that the expecting couple would soon "see" a son.[21]

Imitating the activities of grownups is a game played by children in every society. The imperial jackets show boys in groups telling stories and giving each other baths. As shown in court paintings from the Song period, bathing infant sons was an important task of imperial mothers. In this playful version of the theme, one boy sits in a wooden tub, showered by a friend holding a long glass bottle, while two others try to upset the tub with a pole (fig. 3.8).

Children's imitation of the official on horseback is the imaginative play most frequently represented in early Ming art. Certainly the grandeur of officials as they appeared about town, on horseback, shaded by canopies, with attendants clearing their paths, would have been an impressive sight to any child who might have had the occasion to witness it. But it is difficult to know how often groups of imperial children actually played out this scenario. The coats have several boys depicted on single-wheeled hobbyhorses, accompanied by other boys who pretend to be attendants holding aloft large lotus leaves to shade the miniature "officials."

The children on the jackets also play school, a theme humorously portrayed in Song paintings. On one jacket, a boy dressed in formal attire pretends to be a teacher seated on a chair and giving a test. He holds a book and questions his "student." An erring student kneels on the ground, and two others in the back do last-minute cramming. On the second jacket, the boy playing teacher sits on a folding chair surrounded by studious pupils. One boy kneels in front of him, waiting to be reproved, while another boy holds a bamboo pole ready to mete out corporal punishment. The pole is held in exactly the same manner as officials held poles in courtroom scenes.

Figure 3.8 Drawing of a bathing scene, detail of fig. 3.4.

Toys are also prominently featured on the jackets. Illustrations of playthings seen

Figure 3.9 Drawing of a boy flying a kite, detail of fig. 3.4.

Figure 3.10 Drawing of boys spinning a top, detail of fig. 3.4.

in the Song period continued to be popular. These include the *bolanggu*, the rattle with two small beaters attached by strings (on the jacket illustrated, the particular rattle is a double one), paper windmills, stick puppets, string puppets, and spinning-date toys. Each of the toys is actively worked by the frolicking children. Some boys shoot marbles, others pull wheeled carts. The carts include a covered carriage on wheels and a banner-toting warrior seated on a lion with wheels. Boys fly kites with long streamers and play with two types of tops, spinning them with their fingers while seated, and twirling them with a whip while standing up (figs.3.9–3.11).

Musical instruments, especially percussion instruments such as drums, clappers, and gongs, are depicted as typical playthings of boys in garden settings. The jackets feature a new instrument as well, a glass trumpet called *liuli laba* (fig. 3.12). During winter, the Liulichang glass factory of Beijing produced glass trumpets for sale.[22] This practice began in the Ming period and became even more popular in the Qing. There were two types of glass toys—the *liuli laba*, a long glass trumpet with an open mouth shaped like a wine cup and a stem two or three feet long, and the shorter *bubudeng*, a gourd-shaped vessel with a stem. *Bubudeng* was the sound made by children when they breathed in and out of the gourd-shaped vessel. This type of vessel had a closed end and sometimes dealers sold goldfish in them. It seemed the shapes of the fish would change as they swam in the circular bottle, and children found them entertaining. These glass toys made a shrill sound and were popular among children during winter. Liu Tong (d. 1637) and Dun Lichen (1855–1911) both described the novel trumpets, respectively in *Dijing jingwu lue* (Scenes of the capital) and *Yanjing suishi ji* (Record of a year's time at Beijing).[23]

Animals and children have been a natural combination through the ages. The boys on the jackets watch goldfish, play with birds, tease dragonflies, and chase butterflies with their fans. Some boys stage cricket fights inside circular containers, while others catch the crickets and put them in cages. Elsewhere, after a cat has caught a butterfly, a boy sits on the cat and hits it with his fist (fig. 3.13).

Many of the toys and games are seasonal. One example on the Wanli jacket is the diabolo that two boys fight to hold (fig. 3.14). Called a *kongzhu* or *kongzhong*, the diabolo was a large humming top often used by street peddlers to attract customers. To play it, the diabolo was made to slide up and down on a string tied between two sticks and held in the hands of the player. It could make a shrill humming noise. It was also a seasonal toy for the spring.

Figure 3.11 Drawing of a boy whipping a top, detail of fig. 3.4.

Figure 3.12 Drawing of a boy blowing a glass trumpet, detail of fig. 3.5.

During the Ming period, children in Beijing used to chant a willow poem: "When the willow is green, let's play with the diabolo; when the willow is dead, kick the shuttlecock."[24] It was the custom to play the diabolo in the spring and kick shuttlecocks in winter. Summer activities depicted on the jackets include watching goldfish and playing with lotuses, the flower of summer. One boy takes a nap while being fanned by a friend, while others bathe and play with water. Autumn scenes show boys preoccupied with cricket fights or harvesting fruit and eating peaches straight from the tree.

Figure 3.13 Drawing of a boy beating a cat, detail of fig. 3.5.

Certain toys and activities represent annual festivals that were important in celebrating the orderly and cyclical movement of time in relation to the agricultural seasons. The New Year celebration is depicted with scenes of children lighting firecrackers, wearing masks, and carrying lanterns on the fifteenth day of the first month. Boys dressed in padded clothing and fur hats eat steamed buns and kick balls and shuttlecocks to keep warm.

Figure 3.14 Drawing of two boys fighting over a diabolo, detail of fig. 3.5.

To represent the Duanwu festival, held on the fifth day of the fifth lunar month, boys dress in light clothing and play with toads. The scene on the empress's robe shows the boys holding a contest for their toads, while one boy adds to the excitement by hitting a gong (fig. 3.15). Duanwu was believed to be the most poisonous day of the year, perhaps because the high humidity of the impending summer season encouraged plagues and pestilence. Catching toads was one of the activities designated for the fifth day of the fifth lunar month. Toads were used for medicine to combat disease and poisonous insects, and they were thought to be at the height of their curative power on this day.[25] Moreover, old ink sticks stored inside the carcasses of toads were believed to produce the blackest and shiniest ink. "The warty toads cannot escape the fifth day of the fifth month" became a popular saying. The Song painting *Children Playing with a Toad* by Su Zuo sets a precedent for pictorial descriptions of the festival (fig. 3.16). It shows a boy teasing his

Figure 3.15 Drawing of boys fighting with toads, detail of fig. 3.4.

companion with a toad. The impish boy carries a branch of pomegranate in his other hand, another indication that it is the fifth day of the fifth lunar month. Pomegranates, as well as artemisia, sweet flag, hibiscus, garlic, and loquats are associated with this festival as plants capable of dispelling evil spirits. Women wore pomegranate blossoms on this day in ancient China, for their fiery red color was believed to ward off evil.[26]

Figure 3.16 Su Zuo (twelfth century), *Children Playing with a Toad*. Song, 960–1279. Hanging scroll; ink and color on silk; 88.9 x 51.3 cm. Collection of the National Palace Museum. Taiwan, Republic of China.

The games played by the children also reveal local characteristics. Blowing long glass trumpets is peculiar to Beijing, while plantain trees and bathing scenes are more typical of the south. The imperial jackets, produced in palace workshops, reflect the combined work of needleworkers from all over China. Besides being garments of exquisite workmanship, these two jackets are securely dated to the Wanli period, which makes them important for dating purposes.

A covered dish ornamented in underglaze blue from the Asian Art Museum of San Francisco serves as an example of the treatment of the playing-boys theme in Wanli-period porcelain (fig. 3.17). Possibly a container for serving sweetmeats, the interior is divided into seven compartments, each decorated with two boys. Children featured on the rim of the cover and the sides of the container bring the total to forty-six boys at play. The center inside compartment shows a pair of boys flying a kite with three streamers. The six outer compartments feature pairs of boys with flags, fan, vases, *bolanggu* rattle, and string puppets (fig. 3.18). Two groups of eight boys each on the sides of the container fly kites and form a procession around a boy riding a hobbyhorse. A boy acting as attendant shades the horse rider with a large lotus leaf canopy. Along the rim of the cover, boys pull toy carts, carry vases, twirl the *bolanggu*, and lift wooden exercising poles *(huagun)*. Other boys look at lotus plants *(he)* growing from large porcelain containers, perhaps symbolizing the phrase *zisun hehe*, or "harmony among descendants."

Similar activities are featured on ink-cake designs by Cheng Dayue (1541–ca. 1616). In 1606, Cheng pub-

Figure 3.17 Sweetmeat box. Ming, Wanli period, 1573–1620. Porcelain with underglaze blue. Asian Art Museum of San Francisco, the Avery Brundage Collection.

lished his renowned catalogue of ink-cake designs, *Chengshi moyuan* (Mr. Cheng's ink compendium), the culmination of his life's work as a celebrated ink maker. The book consisted of some five hundred woodcut illustrations, designed by prominent artists such as Ding Yunpeng (1547–1621) and cut by the best woodblock carvers of his day.[27] His compendium was illustrated in colors, and included, remarkably, four western Biblical woodcuts, the first of their kind among Chinese publications.[28]

The circular design for a nine-sons ink cake *(jiuzi mo)*[29] in figure 3.19 shows nine boys in a garden setting framed by a Taihu rock and tall sweet olive tree on the left and palm trees on the right. The sweet olive, or *osmanthus fragrans,* is called *guihua* in Chinese. It is a rebus for *guizi,* "noble sons," and it also symbolizes literary success, for in ancient China, the phrase "to pluck a branch of *guihua* from the Moon Palace" *(changong zhegui)* meant to become a successful candidate in the imperial examination *(jinshi)*.[30] The presence of the sweet olive tree in the ink cake is no accident. It implies that the nine children are not just ordinary boys, but *guizi* destined to bring honors to their families. In the design, however, the boys are engaged in doing what was popular in the Ming period. The two boys in the background fly a kite, while in the foreground another pair play with a puppet on a stick. In the center of the design, a group of boys forms a procession with banner, gong, and drum to herald a boy on a wheeled hobbyhorse, pretending he is a scholar-official. As in the porcelain designs, the rider is attended by a boy holding a lotus leaf canopy.

Figure 3.18 Drawing of boys at play, detail of fig. 3.17.

Figure 3.19 Drawing of ink-cake design showing nine boys at play. Designed by Ding Yunpeng (1547–1621). Illustrated in Cheng Dayue, *Chengshi moyuan*, 1606. Redrawn from *Zhongguo banhua shi tulu*, vol.2: *Mingkan huapu mopu xuanji*, p. 16.

Figure 3.20 Drawing of two boys matching herbs *(doucao)*. After a dish, Ming, Wanli period (1573–1620). Porcelain with underglaze blue. Jingguantang Collection.

A game first appearing in the porcelain of the Wanli period is that of *doucao*, "matching herbs," or herb competition. It is also known as *doubaicao*, or "competition with a hundred herbs." A popular game for both children and adults in the Tang dynasty, it was originally associated with the Duanwu festival, where many herbs were gathered to combat the bad vapors. Children gathered various leaves and flowers and competed against one another for rarity, or strength, while grownups played a more sophisticated game of matching tiger's ear grass *(saxifraga)* to cock's comb, or lohan pine *(podocarpus)* to Guanyin's willow.[31] An example of this game is illustrated on a blue-and-white circular covered box decorated with sixteen boys at play.[32] A drawing from the box shows two seated boys holding herbs in their upraised hands, with a pile of grasses between them (fig. 3.20).

Decorative Arts of the Transitional Period (seventeenth century)

New elements appeared in the decorative arts at the end of the Ming and the beginning of the Qing dynasties. The changes are illustrated in two cut-silk tapestry *(kesi)* renderings of the hundred-boys theme, both attributed to the seventeenth century. One is published by Spink of London,[33] the other by Plum Blossom International of Hong Kong.[34] Both display a wide landscape with groups of boys playing among sizable blue and green boulders and a few large trees. The Plum Blossom example shows ninety-nine boys against a red background, interspersed with newly popular and highly symbolic trees: peach, associated with longevity; pomegranate, symbolizing numerous offspring; and peony, representing wealth and rank. The Spink tapestry features *wutong* trees, willows, palms, and plantains, plants traditionally used in Ming porcelains with underglaze blue decoration. Both tapestries display the red rising sun, suggesting the phrase "the sun rising in the eastern sky" *(xuri dongsheng)*, a symbol for vigor and youthful vitality.

The activities of the boys are almost identical in each of the two *kesi* examples. As in Jiajing and Wanli pieces, the boys fly kites, stage cricket fights, spin tops, and twirl *bolanggu*. They kick balls, play hide-and-seek, and sound musical instruments. A pond scene shows boys fishing and rowing. The ubiquitous processional scene is also included, but there are some noticeable changes. The hobbyhorse rider who pretends to be an official now wears the administrative robes of an official. The large lotus leaf carried by the attendant boy has been replaced with a silk canopy.

Some distinctly new themes are also introduced in illustrations of playing boys. Innovations include scenes of the four scholarly pursuits, with groups of boys poring over books, admiring a scroll, playing the musical instrument *qin*, and engaging in a game of chess. Another new theme is boys pretending to be immortals. One boy rides a toad in imitation of the immortal Liu Hai, the god of wealth. Two other boys carry a lotus blossom *(he)* and a box *(he)* to portray the Twin Genii of Harmony and Mirth (Hehe Erxian), the patron saints of happy marriages. In a hunting scene, boys brandish bows and arrows, and hold falcons.

One of the new activities is completely unrelated to traditional games played by actual children: Five boys fight for a helmet held aloft by one of the boys (fig. 3.21), illustrating the phrase *wuzi duokui* (five sons all take first place). During the Ming dynasty, the civil service examination was based upon the Five Classics, the *Book of Changes*, the *Book of Odes*, the *Book of History*, the *Book of Rites*, and the *Spring and Autumn Annals*. A candidate could select one of the five as his main subject. Those who finished first in each of the five sections were known as *"wujing kui."* The

Figure 3.21 Five boys fighting for a helmet. Qing, Kangxi period, 1662–1722. Jar lid; porcelain with underglaze blue, red, green, and yellow. Asian Art Museum of San Francisco, the Avery Brundage Collection, B60 P1232.

military helmet is also pronounced *"kui,"* so that grabbing the helmet is a visual pun on winning first place.

There is a second explanation for this motif. The five competing boys symbolize the five sons of Dou Yujun, each of whom achieved exceptional success. Dou lived at Yanshan during the Five Dynasties period (907–960) as a scholar, an educator, and an official. Epitomized as the ideal parent who raised five outstanding sons, he was included in the *Trimetrical Classic,* the primer for beginning readers from the Song dynasty until well into the twentieth century:

> Dou Yanshan had an unusual formula
> He taught five sons and they all became famous.

The five sons passed the civil service examinations with high honors, and became known as the Five Dragons of Yanshan (Yanshan wulong) and the Five Osmanthus Flowers (Wugui).[35]

Other new motifs of the transitional period include boys bearing meaningful gifts. One boy carries a vase *(ping)* containing a branch of coral, a precious object from the south seas, and another bears a vase holding a wish-granting scepter *(ruyi)*, a rebus for "may peace be with you and may your wishes come true" *(ping'an ruyi)*. Other boys present ancient bronze wine goblets, or *jue*, on a tray to represent the phrase *jinjue*, meaning "to be promoted to a higher rank." From the sky, the mythical *qilin* floats down on wish-granting clouds, carrying a boy holding the *sheng* (mouth organ) and a branch of *guihua*, a visual pun for *liansheng guizi*, or "continuous birth of noble sons." Together with the phoenix, dragon, and tortoise, the *qilin* is one of the Four Supernatural Creatures (Siling) and symbolizes good wishes. Traditionally, the *qilin* heralds the birth of a "noble" son. As Julia Murray illustrates in her essay, a *qilin* disgorging a book of jade appeared in Confucius' hometown the night he was born (fig. 5.13).[36] The motif of a *qilin* carrying a boy, *qilin songzi*, therefore conveys a wish for a clever and talented son.

These seventeenth-century innovations—such as the *qilin* carrying a boy; boys employed in the four scholarly pursuits, pretending to be immortals, and carrying symbolic objects—are important developments that suggest what was to come in the eighteenth century. The boys became more and more symbolic, rather than simply playing and having a good time.

QING DYNASTY (1644–1911)

Ming dynasty motifs persisted into the Qing. The following example from the Kangxi period (1662–1722) shows a conscious effort to recreate Ming dynasty boys at play. An elegant hundred-boys wooden box in the Palace Museum has black lacquered drawers inlaid with mother-of-pearl, gold, and silver.[37] The boys, richly garbed, appear in a beautifully terraced garden with trees and Taihu rocks. The cover shows children coming down a slide to the accompaniment of the *pipa* (four-string guitar) and gong. A small group, seated on the ground, watches the antics of a rabbit, which has been tied to a large weight. A side panel shows boys engaged in pulling a baby on a wooden cart, playing with a puppet, performing the lion dance and other dances, and spinning a top. The front panel shows a scene of hide-and-seek: A seated older boy covers the eyes of a younger boy, while companions hide among the large rocks. Other boys pull wheeled toys and stage cricket fights. On the side panels, boys watch a performance of string puppets, and others catch a butterfly, with a circular fan. On the drawers are scenes of boys with plants in their hands who are engaged in an herbal competition *(doucao);* a boy in ordinary clothes rides a hobbyhorse and is shaded by a boy with a lotus leaf while a companion in front with a large flag announces their arrival. Other boys spin tops with whips and play jump rope. Some of the scenes on this box were directly inspired by the ones shown on the garments of the Wanli empress. The craftsmen who made the box were familiar with the Wanli motifs of the "hundred boys" developed over a century earlier.

Porcelains of the Yongzheng period (1723–1735) are noted for their elegant decorations. The boys-at-play motif continues to be shown against a garden scene with terraces and trees. The Asian Art Museum has a pair of porcelain bowls decorated with this motif, in yellow and green glazes, from the Yongzheng period (plate 8). They show boys playing music on a garden terrace in front of pine trees. Two boys are dancing and two twirl paper windmills as four boys provide musical accompaniment. Besides the usual gong, drum, and cymbals, a new addition is the *yunluo*, or "cloud gong," consisting of four small brass gongs of different pitches arranged inside a bamboo frame. A simple tune is played by striking the gongs individually with a beater. The Yongzheng period was a short one, and the boys-at-play motif does not show a great deal of development.

The Qianlong period (1736–1795) was a time when the use of rebuses or pictorial puns became widespread. Many new ones were created during this time and came into common usage in the nineteenth and twentieth centuries. Chinese rebuses are made up of a group of seemingly unrelated objects, the pronunciation of which are used as homonyms to represent a four-character auspicious phrase. Some of these phrases have existed in China for at least two thousand years, and some rebuses had appeared as decorative motifs in the Ming dynasty.[38] The sudden flowering of rebuses during the Qianlong period may be attributed to the emperor himself, who delighted in the use of rebuses. One of his personal seals was a pun on his name and consisted of a circle enclosing the trigram *qian,* composed of three solid horizontal lines. He often used this seal as a substitute for the character *qian* in his reign name.

The playing-boys motif was especially popular during the Qianlong period. Often the boys were seen carrying auspicious objects such as halberds *(ji)* and L-shaped lithophones *(qing)* to represent the phrase *jiqing*, or "happy occasion." A sentiment such as the above had nothing to do with passing exams and achieving high rank. They were more representative of the times and reflected the auspicious motifs commonly used in palace decoration to wish for harmony and good harvest, therefore ensuring peace and prosperity for the kingdom.

There are many examples of the hundred-boys motif from the Qianlong period, one of which is a rectangular tray of carved lacquer found in the Palace Museum in

Beijing.[39] The lacquer was applied in layers of four colors: red, yellow, green, and purple. In the process of carving, the various colors were exposed. The tray shows a hundred boys at play. There are the usual scenes of hide-and-seek, jump rope, kite flying, matching herbs, and boys studying. Following the new trend, there is a boy on a hobbyhorse in the costume of an official, shaded by a proper cloth canopy. There are children playing with lanterns and making music. The musical instruments include the long glass trumpets popular in the Beijing area. Boys in two dragon boats race. New innovations include children performing a dragon dance with a long dragon, and a young acrobat executing a handstand on a bamboo pole. This piece is one of two that were commissioned from Suzhou in the seventh year of the reign of the Qianlong emperor (1742) and completed the following year. The bottom of the platter bears the inscription "Made in the reign of the Qianlong Emperor of the Great Qing dynasty" and the title *Baizi suipan*. *Sui* refers to a baby reaching the age of one year. *Suipan* was the name of the tray used for holding the various objects for a ceremony to take place when the baby completes its first year. Parents placed objects symbolizing the various professions on the tray, and the baby was allowed to choose. The objects chosen (or grabbed) by the baby were supposed to indicate its disposition and forecast its future. It is therefore appropriate that a Qianlong-period tray produced for such an occasion is decorated with the hundred-boys motif.

Many parents took this ceremony very seriously. A fictional example is Jia Zheng, the father of Baoyu, in the classic novel *Honglou meng* (Red chamber dream). On his son's first birthday, a tray of assorted objects was placed in front of the boy. When Baoyu ignored everything else and grabbed the powder box and rouge, Jia Zheng was "displeased and grumbled that the boy would grow up to be a dissolute and licentious sort, and from that day on did not care much for his son."[40]

An eighteenth-century Canton enamel dish in the Asian Art Museum depicts the one-year ceremony (fig. 3.22). While the father seated before a screen looks on proudly, an infant, supported by his mother, has just picked a wish-granting scepter *(ruyi)* from among the objects placed in front of him. The other objects include a sword for a military career, an abacus for a merchant, a brush and a book for a scholar, and an ingot for wealth. The choice of the *ruyi* symbolized that the boy would have a wonderful future, where all his wishes (or his parents' wishes) would come true.

There are many extant examples of lacquer boxes from the Qianlong period bearing the hundred-boys and boys-at-play motifs. There are single boxes showing the "hundred boys," as well as sets of two, four, and ten boxes that together make up the numbers of one hundred boys. The boys depicted on one lacquer box in the Asian Art Museum number fifty, which means it was originally one of a set of two boxes depicting the "hundred boys" (fig. 3.23). In an elaborate setting, with a pavilion and terrace enclosed by rocks and towering trees, boys on the cover of the box are fighting for a helmet, others are holding and lighting firecrackers, and four boys are playing drums, cymbals, and gongs. On the side of the cover, boys are exercising and doing handstands, watching cricket fights, and carrying auspicious objects such as the halberd and the lithophone. Decorating the bottom of the box are boys carrying lotuses, flying kites, and studying. Three boys, accompanied by a basket of flowers and grasses that they have picked, are having a *doucao,* or herb competition.

The lacquer boxes in the Palace Museum, Beijing, include other activities such as acting out the four scholarly pursuits by playing the *qin,* competing at chess, reading, and painting. There are also scenes of wrestling, dancing with masks, and quail and rooster fights.[41] Besides fighting with crickets, the Chinese delighted in gambling in conjunction with animal and insect fights.[42] Rooster fights can be traced

Figure 3.22 Dish depicting the ceremony to predict an infant's future occupation. Qing, late eighteenth century. Canton enamel; w. 20.6 cm. Asian Art Museum of San Francisco, the Avery Brundage Collection, B60 P2200.

Figure 3.23 Box with fifty boys at play. Qing, Qianlong period, 1736–1795. Carved lacquer; h. 7.4 cm; d. 9.8 cm. Asian Art Museum of San Francisco, the Avery Brundage Collection, B60 M406.

back to the Zhou dynasty. During the Han period, geese and ducks were trained for competition. Quails were kept as pets in the Tang period; during the Ming and Qing periods, quail fights were held north of the Yangzi River, especially after the first frost.[43]

The pervasive use of rebuses during the Qianlong period is exemplified by a fan painting by Wang Chengpei (d. 1805) in the Asian Art Museum (plate 9). Wang received his *juren* (provincial graduate) degree in 1747 and was noted for his paintings of landscape, figures, and flowers. On a fan intended as a New Year greeting to a friend, he painted a total of nine boys. One boy carries an arrangement of pine, nandina, peony, and chrysanthemum. These are auspicious plants that wish the recipient wealth and longevity. One boy brandishes a plum branch. The plum blossom is the first to bloom among the hundred flowers and symbolizes earning first place in the exams. Another boy holds a tall halberd *(ji)*, hung with the lithophone *(qing)* and a large fish *(yu)*, a symbol of abundance. These objects make up the phrase *jiqing youyu*, "happy occasion and may there be plenty." One boy strikes the *qing*, which produces a gentle and harmonious sound. The same boy who carries the halberd also pulls a boat *(chuan)* on wheels. The boat contains an official headdress *(guan)*, a jade belt *(dai)*, and a pomegranate *(liu)*. These form a rebus for the phrase *guandai chuanliu*, or "may the official rank pass on to the descendants" (fig. 3.24). The remaining boys, one wearing a peony blossom (a sign of rank) on his head, light a firecracker, while another boy looks up to the pair of magpies (birds of happiness) flying above.

The porcelain wares of the Qianlong reign often show groups of exquisitely painted boys in colorful enamels, carrying auspicious objects. An outstanding white porcelain vase with a Qianlong-seal mark in the National Palace Museum, Taipei, shows a group of boys celebrating the lantern festival, the fifteenth day of the first month (fig. 3.25).[44] The boys light firecrackers, blow a long trumpet, beat a drum, and pretend to be Kuixing, God of Literature, by holding a brush and kicking up a foot. Another carries a *ruyi*, dangling from one end a lantern made of two persimmons *(shi)*. This is a rebus for *shishi ruyi*, or "may everything be as you wish." One boy carries a long staff from which suspends a beautiful lantern *(fengdeng)* while a companion behind him holds up a stalk of grain. The grain stands for the five grains *(wugu)*. Together with the lantern, they make up the phrase *wugu fengdeng*, or "a bumper harvest of all crops." This rebus conveys the emperor's wish for a good harvest, therefore ensuring peace and prosperity for his kingdom.

Figure 3.24 Detail of pl. 9, fan painting *Boys at Play*, by Wang Chengpei (d. 1805). Qing, Qianlong period, 1736–1795. Ink and color on paper. Asian Art Museum of San Francisco, 1998. 32d. Gift of Joseph and Nancy Wang in memory of Dr. and Mrs. Hsin-chung Wang.

A Daoguang-period porcelain bowl painted in underglaze blue features boys engaged in a scholarly game (fig. 3.26).[45] A summer scene with boys standing around a winding waterway brings to mind the famous poetry contest first enjoyed at Lanting (Orchid pavilion) of the calligrapher Wang Xizhi (303–379). Floating wine cups down the meandering course of a stream, each participant was expected to compose a poem when the cup reached his spot, or forfeit by drinking the wine. The game was enacted by many groups of scholars, and at least one fictional group of children, Baoyu and his cousins in Prospect Garden in *Honglou meng*.

Another rebus is illustrated in the decoration of an embroidered wallet of the nineteenth century (plate 10, fig. 3.27). The auspicious phrase "taking three successive firsts" *(lianzhong sanyuan)* is acted out by children shooting at three citrus fruits. This phrase refers to the three civil service examinations of China. The top candidate of the *juren* degree is known as *jieyuan*, the person who places first for the *jinshi* degree is called *huiyuan*, while *zhuangyuan* is the top candidate in the palace examination. *Lianzhong sanyuan* therefore means one successively claims the titles of *jieyuan*, *huiyuan*, and *zhuangyuan* in one's lifetime. In the picture, three oranges *(san yuan)* impaled by arrows are on the ground. To successively hit on target is called *lian zhong*. Thus "hitting three oranges in a row" was the pictorial counterpart for "taking first place on the examinations three times in a row." Since this was the wish of the relatives of a candidate going for the exams, this motif was often embroidered onto his personal belongings, such as a wallet, to wish him success.

The same motif appears in a nineteenth-century *kesi* tapestry in the Asian Art Museum, illustrating ninety-nine boys (fig. 3.28). Three oranges are being shot in

Figure 3.25 Vase with boys at play. Qing, Qianlong period, 1736–1795. Porcelain with enamel decoration; h. 19.2 cm. Collection of the National Palace Museum. Taiwan, Republic of China.

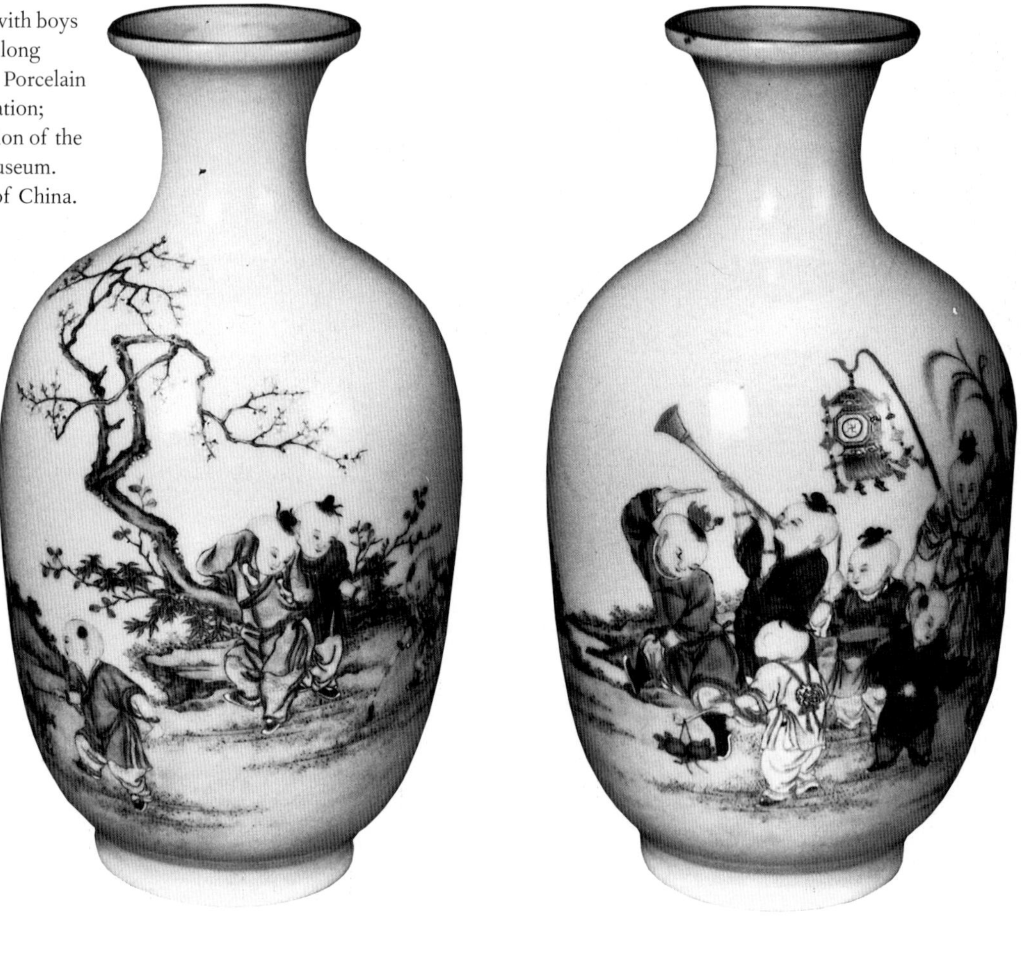

Figure 3.26 Bowl decorated with boys at play. Qing, Daoguang period, 1821–1851. Porcelain with underglaze blue; d. 15.5 cm. Kwan Collection.

one corner. Other boys are playing with lotuses, a rebus for *zisun hehe,* or "harmony among descendants." Others are performing a dragon dance and beating gongs and cymbals. Five boys grouped together try to snatch a helmet. Elsewhere boys are lighting firecrackers, staging cricket fights, playing with a rattle, holding a *ruyi* (a scepter symbolizing the fulfillment of one's wishes), playing chess, and carrying swords and books. There are children carrying lanterns and a child pretending to be the immortal Liu Hai by riding on a toad. Another boy pulls the boat, which carries an official headdress, belt, and pomegranate, representing the phrase *guandai quanliu,* or "may the official rank pass on to the descendants," the same rebus illustrated in Wang Chengpei's painting (plate 9). There are two processions woven into the tapestry. A young child dressed in official garments sits on the *qilin,* carrying an osmanthus blossom to signify that he is a "noble son" (fig. 3.29). Children marching before and after him wave banners and beat a gong. This image of a boy riding on a *qilin* continued to be a popular motif during the Qing dynasty, often depicted on silver locks given to infant boys at birth. Sometimes the boy depicted carries both the *osmanthus* blossom and the *sheng* (bamboo mouth organ) to represent *liansheng guizi,* or "continuous birth of noble sons." Another procession shows a top candidate *(zhuangyuan)* sitting on a horse, shaded by a canopy, with flag bearers in front proclaiming the fact that he has placed first in the imperial examination.

Figure 3.27 Drawing of a boy shooting at three oranges; detail of pl. 10.

The extensive use of symbols and rebuses in Qing dynasty depictions of playing boys is not confined to art made for the court; it is also prevalent in woodblock prints intended for common folks. Cutting across class lines, the same pictorial puns used by the upper class can be found among the prints of Yangliuqing, the printing

Figure 3.28 *A Hundred Boys.* Qing, nineteenth century. Table cover; *kesi* tapestry; 197 x 47 cm. Asian Art Museum of San Francisco, 1989.11. Gift of Katherine Ball.

center in Hebei province in operation since the Kangxi period.[46] Images of boys form an important category in these popular prints, which are still used for decorating the household during the New Year. They are too numerous to be described here, but it may be noted that besides being symbols representing the wish for numerous progeny, these boys are all "noble" sons doing what is expected of them. The *qilin* bringing a "noble" son is an important theme in the prints, as well as boys fighting for branches of plum blossoms or a military helmet that symbolize passing the civil

Figure 3.29 Boy riding on a *qilin.* Detail of fig. 3.28.

service examination with high honors. In single prints boys carry carp to represent abundance, play with lions to ensure high rank, or pull boats containing pomegranates, belts, and official headgear to guarantee that the rank will pass on to their descendants. Boys are shown with symbols for blessings, longevity, prosperity, and peace, all of which were luck-bringing rebuses popular during the Qing dynasty.

Conclusion

In conclusion, the hundred-boys motif in China developed from the basic wish for male progeny. This motif appeared in all types of decorative arts but especially on textiles such as bed curtains and women's robes, where the theme emphasized fertility and the prolific bearing of sons. When boys appeared on objects used by men, such as wallets or fans, the motifs chosen were more often those symbolizing passing the civil service examinations and less often directly related to fecundity. During the Ming dynasty, boys were depicted in gardens, playing with many of the same toys and games as were illustrated in Song paintings, but there was a new and stronger underlying theme focusing on education and high rank. This emphasis on proper education is seen in the pictures of boys playing school or pretending with their hobbyhorses to be scholar-officials on horseback. By the end of the Ming period, in the seventeenth century, pictures of boys immersed in the four scholarly pursuits, where they looked at paintings, studied, played chess, and performed on the *qin*, had become widespread. Boys were also shown in the guise of immortals, playing with the common attributes of popular deities such as the toad of Liu Hai or the box and lotus flower carried by the Twin Genii of Harmony and Mirth. The *qilin* carrying a "noble son" also became a standard motif. Passing the civil service examination with high honors is a recurring theme, with the boys holding branches of *osmanthus* and fighting for a helmet. By the eighteenth century, the activities of the boys are transformed into pictorial puns or rebuses for very specific four-character auspicious sayings. Not only are they involved in passing exams and retaining rank in the family, they also encompass universal wishes for a bumper harvest, peace, prosperity, and happy occasions. From the naturalistic and sympathetic depictions of actual children at play during the Song period, discussed in the Barnharts' essay, by the Qing period, images of children evolved into little more than stylized icons of good fortune.

4

Representations of Children in Three Stories from *Biographies of Exemplary Women*

Ann Waltner

Images of children are not uncommon in Chinese art. Sometimes children are portrayed with their mothers; more often they are portrayed in an idealized, timeless plane where all adults are absent. But pictures of children in family groupings with both parents are rare. This presents, at first glance, something of a mystery: If the Chinese family is as central to the construction of Chinese society as most scholars assert, why is it so seldom represented in works of art? There are a few instances of families portrayed in domestic settings, such as the Gu Jianlong (1606–after 1686) painting of Wang Shimin (1592–1680) at the Minneapolis Institute of Arts, and the portrayals of archetypal families discussed by Ann Wicks in the final essay of this volume. And, of course, since the use of photography became widespread during the course of the nineteenth century, there are ample examples of photographic family portraits. But prior to the photograph, we search nearly in vain for pictures of specific children depicted with both parents.

One cannot say that there are no Chinese family portraits because there are no portraits. As recent work, notably, though not exclusively, by Craig Clunas and Richard Vinograd has shown, there is a strong representational strain in Chinese art and illustration.[1] Perhaps artists and their audiences viewed family and family life as private and hence to be shielded from the public gaze. A good deal of theorizing would support this conclusion: Chinese cosmology and social theory both posit that in an orderly world there should be a distinction between the inner *(nei)* and outer *(wai)* realms.[2] Women and the family belonged to the inner realm and hence should be shielded from the gaze of the outer world. Men were cautioned about speaking of affairs of the world when they were in the inner realm, or of discussing their domestic lives when they were in the outer realm.

But if Chinese men had adhered to strictures about not speaking and writing of matters of the inner realm in public, we would know almost nothing of domestic life in traditional China. Men in fact wrote voluminously about the lives of women and the domestic realm in late imperial China. Much of the writing was to commemorate the lives of virtuous women. Writing about a woman's virtue involved complex negotiations: Despite the conjunction between privacy and virtue, one had to violate a woman's privacy in order to commemorate her virtue, and commemoration in its very essence is a public act. In spite of their discomfort at rendering their subjects' lives public, men wrote extensively and obsessively about female virtue. For example, the mammoth eighteenth-century encyclopedia the *Gujin tushu jicheng* (Imperial collection of books of all ages) lists more than thirty-six thousand biographies of Ming dynasty (1368–1644) virtuous women, culled from local gazetteers.[3]

Ming dynasty commemorations of virtuous women did not consist simply of words describing their lives: Lavishly illustrated texts commemorating lives of frugal female virtue were popular in the late sixteenth and early seventeenth centuries. Virtually all of the Ming texts in the biographies-of-exemplary-women genre are derived to some degree from *Gu lienü zhuan* (Biographies of exemplary women in history) by the Han historian Liu Xiang (80–9 B.C.), and many bear that name or some variation of it. Ming editors rearranged the stories, both adding more recent examples and eliminating some old stories. The Ming texts on illustrious women are ordered differently than their Han antecedent, and as Lisa Raphals has suggested in her recent book *Sharing the Light,* this is not an incidental difference. The biographies in Liu Xiang's Han dynasty text are categorized and ordered by the particular virtue illustrated by each life, an organization not all the Ming texts adopt. The sixteenth-century editor Lü Kun (1536–1618), for example, organized the stories around life cycles: One chapter is on girls, the next on wives, and the final on mothers. Other Ming texts organized the stories chronologically. Raphals has argued that these ordering principles diminish the importance of virtue as a category in the Ming texts.[4] Some editors added commentary to the biographies, though most left the text of the included biographies themselves more or less intact. Lü Kun was the most interventionist of the editors, and his emendations to the Han dynasty stories will be noted below.[5] These collected biographies are compendia of tales, many of them horrific and sad, of lives of exemplary and often heroic self-sacrifice. Most of the texts are quite short, and the illustrations often take up more space in the text than do the words. Thus it is no exaggeration to say that these texts are dominated by their illustrations.

These illustrations offer a window, though a very particular window, into the domestic realm, or rather into a representation of that realm. I began looking at these texts because I thought I might find family portraits in them. But I did not. Mothers and children are amply represented, but the patriarch is notable by his absence.[6]

Let us look at some of these images in detail. I selected the illustrations from three stories from a total of seven editions of biographies of virtuous women. All editions, except for the Qinyoutang edition, purport to date from the late Ming. (For details on editions, see the appendix at the end of this chapter.) The stories I have chosen do not cover the range of themes treated in *Lienü zhuan*. Indeed, I selected these particular examples because children figure prominently in the illustrations. The three stories I have selected are the story of Mencius' mother; the story of the Tushan woman (the consort of Yu the subduer of floods, and the mother of Qi); and the story of the public-spirited aunt of Lu. All three of these stories are contained in Liu Xiang's Han dynasty text and are reproduced with only minor emendations in the later texts. (The story of Mencius' mother is the only one that is reproduced in all of the later texts; presumably some editorial discretion was exercised when the other two stories were left out of one or more of the Ming editions.) The illustrations sometimes exist in tension with the text, and Ming versions of the text also sometimes exist in tension with the canonical text of Liu Xiang.

My discussion of these illustrations will attempt to show several things. The illustrations supplement, and in some cases resist, the text which they accompany. They are Ming commentary on Han dynasty texts. They are an indication of what the illustrator chose to be the central moment of the story, and a clarification of some details, which might have been left vague in the text. They have a strong dramatic and didactic value. Ming commentators realized the didactic value of images when they wrote that pictures can reach where words cannot.[7] Fang Ruhao, an early-seventeenth-century commentator, asserts that the word and the picture may have different kinds of functions:

> Illustrations might seem a childish thing, since the various weighty matters of history are all drawn with words. Yet what cannot be conveyed in words may yet be drawn in pictures.[8]

And indeed, the relationship between text and commentary need not be comfortable. As Hillis Miller noted in another context, an illustration might interfere with a text, "as two melodies playing simultaneously sometimes harmonize and sometimes do not seem to go together."[9] The texts are relatively immobile: They are arranged differently from their Han dynasty antecedents (and often from one another), but the texts themselves clearly stem from a common source. The illustrations do not; they vary greatly. Through close attention to the illustrations, we can suggest different ways in which these texts were read.

The Texts

Two of the illustration styles bear commenting on before we begin examining the stories. First is the style of the Qinyoutang text, which purports to be a copy of a text originally published in 1063. The style of the illustration is what Anne Farrer terms "cartouche illustration," a frame of illustration running across the top of the text.[10] The space in these illustrations is flat, and the figures and the objects in them tend to float, unrelated to one another. This mode of illustration looks very different from the late Ming texts. Doubtless there are reasons internal to the historical development of the woodblock print that would help to explain the shifting spatial representations. But I would suggest that in the treatment of space in the later texts, we see a domestication and containment of the subject matter. This conforms to what we know about an increasing concern during the course of the Ming with female chastity and the containment of female sexuality. This is visual evidence of the transformation in the concept of virtue, which Lisa Raphals has commented upon in the structure of the collections of biographies themselves.[11]

The Santaiguan edition (which is a reprint of a Fuchuntang edition) is distinctively framed in another manner. Both the Fuchuntang and the Santaiguan were important publishing houses, famous for their editions of illustrated dramas.[12] The text of the Santaiguan edition of *Lienü zhuan* captions each illustration with a four-character phrase. A couplet of poetry, one line on each side of the illustration, comments on the action in the illustration, which is in turn a commentary on the action in the longer text. The spatial composition of these illustrations is distinctive—the space is limited, and the spectator's space seems to be an extension of pictorial space. Shih Hsio-yen has suggested that in these illustrations the picture surface is like a stage: It is spatially shallow and the architectural features are dominated by the human figures.[13] The presence of the title at the top and a couplet commenting on the action at either side of the image reinforces the framing effect. As art historian Yao Dajuin has suggested in regard to his study of a splendid set of illustrations to the Hongzhi-era edition of the drama *Xixiangji* (Romance of the Western chamber), the framing of the page serves as a kind of proscenium.[14] The framing text also serves to limit and interpret the illustration—the illustration shows us how to imagine the story in the text, and the verbal frames tell us how to interpret the illustration.[15]

Mencius and His Mother

The story of Mencius' mother is the most famous and, in many ways, the most straightforward of the stories I will discuss. Mencius is an important early-Confucian thinker, whose dates are conventionally given as 371–287 B.C. Liu Xiang's *Lienü zhuan* contains two anecdotes about the ways in which Mencius' mother taught him when he was a child, and several more that show her guidance extended well into his adulthood. When Mencius and his mother lived near a cemetery, the child played at burial rituals, "happily building tombs and grave mounds." His mother said to herself, "This is no place to bring up my son." She then moved to a house near a marketplace, and her son began playing at being a merchant. Reflecting Confucian prejudice against merchants and commerce, she moved again, this time to a house near a school. Finally, at this dwelling, the child's imitative skills were put to good use: He played at being a scholar.

But Mencius' need for his mother's constant tutelage did not diminish. The next episode of the biography is the one consistently depicted in illustrations. Liu Xiang's text reads as follows:

> When Mencius was young, he came home from school one day as his mother was weaving. She said to him, "Is school out already?" He replied, "I left because I felt like it." His mother took the knife and cut the cloth she'd been weaving. Mencius was startled and asked why. She replied, "Your neglecting your studies is like my cutting the cloth. The superior person *(junzi)* studies to establish a reputation and investigates to gain wide knowledge. This being the case, when he is at rest, he is calm and poised, and when he is active, he keeps a distance from what is wrong. If you neglect your studies now, surely you will end up as a menial servant and will never be free from troubles. How is this different from a woman who weaves to support herself abandoning her weaving before she is finished? How can she clothe her husband and children? And before long, how could there be food for them to eat? If a woman neglects her work, or a man gives up the cultivation of his character, they may end up as common thieves, if not slaves." Shaken, Mencius studied hard from morning to night. He studied the philosophy of the master and eventually became a famous Confucian scholar. Superior men observed that Mencius' mother understood the way of motherhood.[16]

This text clearly allocates gender roles, and in a way that confounds simple stereo-

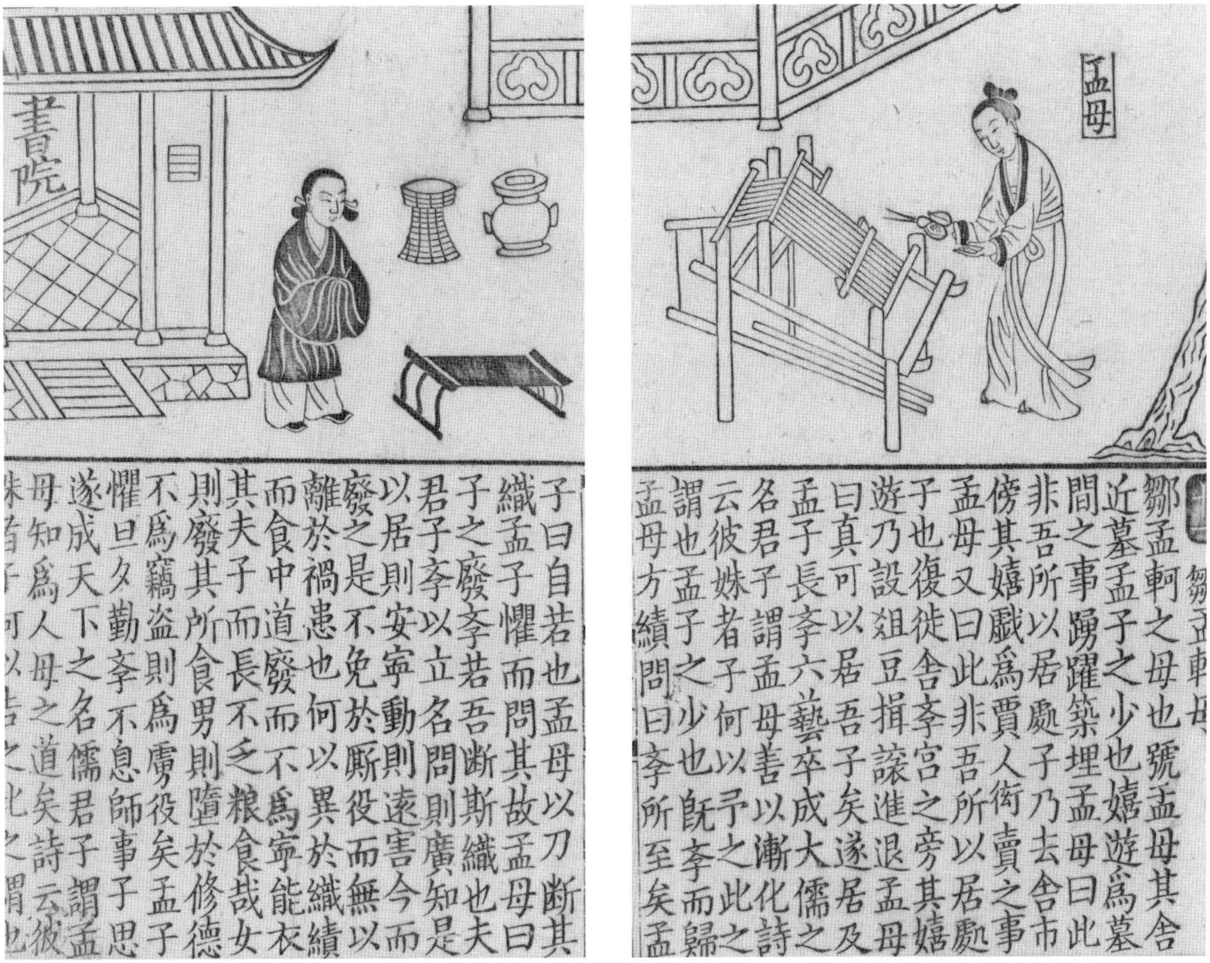

Figure 4.1 Illustration to the story of Mencius and his mother. Yuan. Woodblock print. From *Lienü zhuan*, Qinyoutang edition, late thirteenth to early fourteenth century. Reprinted in *Wenxuanlou cong-shu* (Yangzhou, 1842), *juan* 79–80. Photo courtesy of Harvard-Yenching Library.

types: Women provide for their families economically and men study to obtain fame and reputation. This is a conception of gendered duty that underlines the economic productivity of women. It gains its significance from the fact that Mencius' mother is a canonical mother, and this story is one of the most famous of all Chinese stories.

Liu Xiang's text does not suggest how old Mencius might have been when his mother took a knife to her weaving; it tells us that he was "young." A narrator may leave age indeterminate in a way an illustrator may not. And a quick glance at the various depictions of the story (figs. 4.1–4.7) shows that there is no agreement about how old Mencius was when his mother reprimanded him. The Santaiguan (fig. 4.2) and Huang Shangwen (fig. 4.4) editions both show an older child, wearing a cap. The Mencius in the Qinyoutang (fig. 4.1) version is also an adolescent, his hair worn in a manner suggestive of Mongol braids. In the Zhibuzuzhai version (fig. 4.7), Mencius seems rather younger than in the first three, and in the Huang Jiayu text, he is quite a small child (fig. 4.3). The prose in Lü Kun's texts varies from that of Liu Xiang's Han dynasty original, so that the qualifier "young" disappears. The illustrations to this passage in both Lü Kun editions (figs. 4.5–4.6) in fact show a grown man, wearing the cap that is the ritual marker of adulthood.[17]

Nor do the illustrations seem to agree on the degree of opulence in which the young Mencius was raised. One does not want to press a simple point too far, but late Ming followers of Wang Yangming stressed that Confucian sagehood was open to everyone: Social class should form no obstacle. Representing Mencius as a poor man would underscore the point that poverty need be no barrier to moral or intellectual excellence. Some of the illustrations portray the famous weaving scene indoors,

Figure 4.2 Illustration to the story of Mencius and his mother. Late Ming. Woodblock print. From *Lienü zhuan*, Santaiguan edition, 1591. Photo courtesy of Harvard-Yenching Library.

Figure 4.3 Illustration to the story of Mencius and his mother. Late Ming. Woodblock print. From Huang Jiayu, ed., *Liu Xiang gu Lienü zhuan*, 1606. Microfilm held at Harvard-Yenching Library.

some outdoors. In the Qinyoutang (fig. 4.1) and the Huang Jiayu (fig. 4.3) versions, the loom is outdoors (both in view of the schoolroom next door, which in the Yuan version is clearly marked as a schoolroom, with the Chinese characters *shu yuan*), suggesting that a small dwelling would not accommodate a large loom. Illustrations to the Huang Shangwen version (fig. 4.4) and both Lü Kun editions (figs. 4.5–4.6) portray Mencius and his mother indoors. The front of their modest dwelling is open to the air and to the viewer. Although the illustrations to the Lü Kun editions differ in their execution, the spatial organization is similar in both. The Huang Shangwen illustration (fig. 4.4) offers us an angled view into the room. The Santaiguan edition (fig. 4.2) has placed Mencius and his mother in an opulent setting, the ignored schoolbooks on a table to the side. What we learn from this multiplicity of representations is that there was no late Ming consensus on the social status of Mencius.

In the Santaiguan print (fig. 4.2), Mencius looks quite miserable, as if his mother's reproof pains him. The caption at the top of the illustration reads, "Slashing her weaving to teach her son," and the lines on either side read, "His teaching came from his mother, the *Poetry* and the *Rites*.[18] He received the benefits of her moving three times. His learning continued the past sages, their texts and their writings, and began a lineage of a hundred generations." Thus the ultimate source of Mencian wisdom is his mother—she began a lineage, which he transmitted. The picture can be seen as instructions on how to read the text. But further instructions on how to read both text *and* illustration are superimposed by the words that frame the picture.

Lü Kun recognizes the sagacity of Mencius' mother and uses it to reprove contemporary women. In his encomium to her biography, he explicitly compares her wisdom to the indulgence of contemporary mothers, who not only are lax in their discipline but protect their children from their fathers' correction. As a result, Lü Kun laments, children in his era grew up to be no good *(bucai)*.[19]

When the Yuan print (fig. 4.1) is compared to the Ming and Qing prints (figs. 4.2–4.7), we quite clearly see a transition toward enclosure of the domestic arena. Perhaps the most interesting enclosure is in the Huang Jiayu text, in which Mencius'

Figure 4.4 Illustration to the story of Mencius and his mother. Late Ming. Woodblock print. From Huang Shangwen, ed., *Guifan*, 1617. Photo courtesy of Harvard-Yenching Library.

Figure 4.5 Illustration to the story of Mencius and his mother. Late Ming. Woodblock print. From Lü Kun, ed., *Guifan*, She Yongning edition, late sixteenth to early seventeenth century. Reprinted as *Yinying Ming ge Guifan* (n.p.: Jiangning Weishi, 1927). Photo courtesy of Harvard-Yenching Library.

mother is weaving outdoors, behind a fence (fig. 4.3). The viewer is placed behind the fence too—Mencius' mother is shielded from the gaze of the world but not from us. We as readers and as viewers are privileged to gaze on a woman shielded from outside onlookers. The conventions of this illustration make it very clear that we are seeing what we ought not to be seeing; we are voyeurs.

The otherwise elegant lines of the Zhibuzuzhai text (fig. 4.7) are interrupted by an odd disjuncture between the two frames of the illustration. Mencius seems to be outdoors, and his mother seems to be indoors, yet they are looking directly at one another. The sense of disjuncture is reinforced by half a stool in the right-hand frame, which is not continued on the left. In most of the illustrations in the Zhibuzuzhai edition, there is clear continuity from the picture surface of one frame to the other. However, the disjuncture we see in this picture does appear in other illustrations in the text.[20] This suggests that the two halves of the frame were done separately, and

Figure 4.6 Illustration to the story of Mencius and his mother. Late Ming. Woodblock print. From Lü Kun, ed., *Guifan tushuo*, 1590. Photo courtesy of Harvard-Yenching Library.

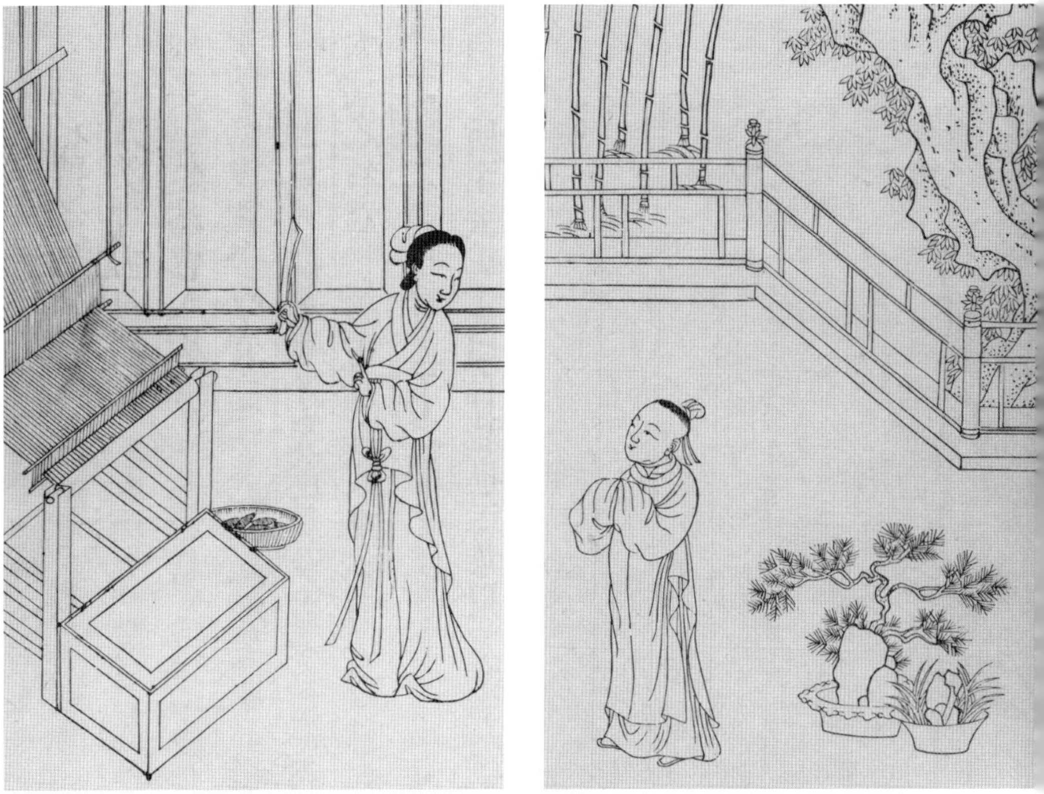

Figure 4.7 Illustration to the story of Mencius and his mother. Qing. Woodblock print. From *Huitu lienü zhuan*, Zhibuzuzhai edition, 1779. Reprint of a purported late Ming edition. Reprinted as *Retsujoden* (Tokyo: Zuhonsokankai, 1923–26). Photo courtesy of University of Minnesota Libraries.

were, at least in those instances, conceived of as separate elements illustrating a common narrative. This disjuncture has the effect of creating a distance not only between Mencius and his mother but between the reader and Mencius' mother. It is another solution to the problem of how we may look upon Mencius' mother without violating her privacy.

The Tushan Woman

The second story we will look at is also that of an exemplary mother and a heroic son. But there the similarities to the gentle remonstrance of Mencius' mother end.[21] The Tushan woman was the mother of Qi, the founder of the Xia dynasty, and the wife of the legendary sage-king Yu, the subduer of the floods. Some sources identify her as the deity Nüwa, who mended the sky.[22] The story of Yu is no less well-known than the story of Mencius and his mother, but the role his wife plays in most versions of the story is generally a minor one. There are a number of accounts of the relationship between Yu and the Tushan woman and the birth of their son, Qi, and the variations are quite stunning.

Let us begin with the text at hand. According to the *Lienü zhuan* account, the Tushan woman married Yu as a concubine, not as a principal wife. Soon after the Tushan woman bore Qi, Yu began the onerous labor of regulating the waters of China to bring floods under control. The *Lienü zhuan* text continues:

> Three times he passed his home but did not enter the door. Though she was alone, the Tushan woman understood how to teach and educated her son. As Qi grew up he was educated by her virtue and followed her teachings. He attained fame. When Yu became son of heaven, Qi was his heir. He maintained Yu's merit and did not fail. The man of noble sentiments *(junzi)* says Tushan was energetic in giving instruction. When the *Book of Songs* says, "You were given a woman that you might be succeeded by sons and grandsons,"[23] it could have been describing her. The encomium says: "Tushan, the mother of Qi, was taken as a mate by the emperor Yu but after [the four days] *xin ren gui jia,* Yu went to manage the floods and Qi wailed and cried. His mother alone taught him the right order and precedence *(lun xu)* in human relationships."[24] She instructed him to be good and in the end he succeeded his father.[25]

Yu was so occupied by his work that three times he passed by his house without stopping. He left home four days after the birth of his child. *Xin, ren, gui,* and *jia* are cyclical markers of days in the ten-day week—the eighth, ninth, tenth, and first days, respectively.[26] The education of the young Qi was entirely in his mother's hands, and she did a splendid job. The text tells us that she trained him well, so well that he grew up to succeed his father. Yao and Shun, the first two sage kings in Chinese mythical history, had sons who were unworthy, and so they chose unrelated men as their successors.[27] Qi is thus the first of the sage kings in Chinese mythology to inherit the throne. Indeed, one could regard him as the first legendary figure in patrilineal succession. The inclusion of the story of the Tushan woman in *Biographies of Exemplary Women* makes clear the centrality of the work of women in patrilineal succession.

The myth of Yu and the flood exists in many versions, some of them quite old and fragmentary. The fact that Yu ignored his family while taming the floods is acknowledged in virtually all versions of the story. One of the oldest versions of the story is in the *Shujing* (Book of documents) and is told in Yu's voice:

> When I was married in Tushan, I remained with my wife only the days *xin ren gui jia*. When my son Qi was wailing and weeping, I did not regard him, but kept planning with all my might my labour on the land.[28]

In *Lüshi chunqiu* (The spring and autumn annals of Mr. Lü), a text dating from the early third century B.C., the story is given thus:

> When Yu married the Tushan woman, he was not willing to harm the public *(gong)* for the sake of the private *(si)*. [He stayed home] from *gui* to *jia*, those four days, and then returned to taming the waters.[29]

Sima Qian records in the *Shiji* (first century A.D.) a report made by Yu to the emperor Shun:

> On the *xin* day and the *ren* day I married a woman of Tushan and stayed home through the *gui* and *jia* days. When Qi was born, I did not take care of him. For this reason I was able to accomplish the work of the waters and lands. . . .[30]

Lüshi chunqiu makes explicit the conflict between public and private, which is implicit in the *Shujing* and *Shiji* (Book of history) accounts. These accounts of the story of Yu's domestic life are not identical to the *Biographies of Exemplary Women* account, but neither are they at variance with it. Variant versions do, however, exist. Commentary to the official history of the Han dynasty written by Yan Shigu

(581–645) gives a version of the story that provides startling contrast with what we have seen so far:

> Yu went to appease the floods. He bore *(tong)* a passage through Huanyuan mountain and transformed himself into a bear.[31] He said to the Tushan woman, "If you want to bring me some food, come to me when the drum sounds." Yu leaped on a stone, drumming it by mistake.[32] Tushan came, and saw that Yu had changed into a bear. Mortified, she went to the foot of Songgao mountain, where she turned to stone. Yu said to her, "Return my son." The stone split on its north side, and gave birth to Qi.[33]

Yan Shigu writes that *Huainanzi* reports the story, but in fact, extant editions of the text merely report that Qi was born of a stone.[34] Another version of the story that would have been well known to educated Ming readers is that contained in the "Tianwen" ("Heavenly questions") chapter of *Chuci* (Songs of Chu).[35] The text in David Hawkes' translation reads:

> Yu labored with all his might. He came down and looked on the earth below. How did he get that maid of Tushan and lie with her in Taisang? The lady became his mate and her body had issue. How came they to have appetite for the same dish when they sated their hunger with the morning food of love?[36]

Later on, the text raises another question, even more startling than the earlier ones: "Why if he [Qi] was such a good son, did he kill his mother?"[37] Commentators agree that it was during the process of his birth that Qi killed his mother, because when the stone split, the Tushan woman died.

This version of the courtship of Yu and the Tushan woman is provided in *Wu Yue chunqiu* (History of Wu and Yue):

> Yu was thirty, and not yet married. He worried about the passage of time, and that he might violate the regulations.[38] So he prayed, saying: "Let there be a sign about my marriage." Then a nine-tailed white fox came to Yu. Yu said "White is the color of my clothing, and the nine tails are a sign of nobility." In Tushan, there is a song: "The white fox searches for a mate / Its nine tails, strong and glorious . . ." He takes this as an omen, and takes the Tushan woman as a mate.[39]

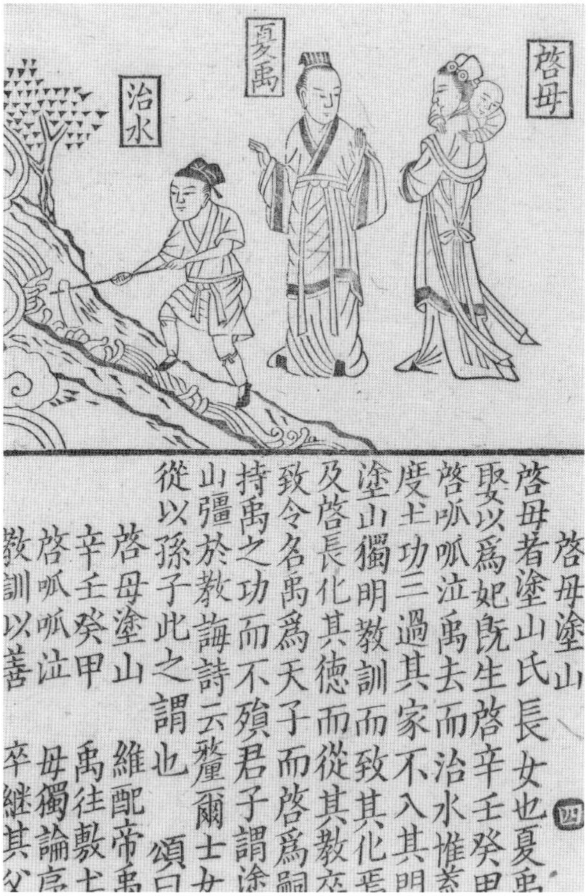

Figure 4.8 Illustration to the story of the Tushan woman. Yuan. Woodblock print. From *Lienü zhuan*, Qinyoutang edition, late thirteenth to early fourteenth century. Reprinted in *Wenxuanlou congshu* (Yangzhou, 1842), *juan* 79–80. Photo courtesy of Harvard-Yenching Library.

This is the clearest case of the three stories where textual accounts are in tension with one another. The *Lienü zhuan* version of the story is sanitized; it is domesticated and the illustrations reinforce the domestication of the prose. There is no whisper in the *Lienü zhuan* of Yan Shigu's bear, or of splitting stones and dying mothers.

In all of the *Lienü zhuan* illustrations of this story, Qi is still an infant in his mother's arms. But there are significant differences in the illustrations. The Yuan text (fig. 4.8) portrays the action all outdoors, in a largely undefined landscape. A raging storm and a highly schematic tree are all we see. The Tushan woman and Yu (identified by the cartouche as "Qi's mother" and "Xia Yu") converse while the workman tames the waters. (Indeed, the cartouche by the workman's head informs us that is what he is doing). Yu is engaged in conversation with his wife rather than in the actual labor performed by the workman. The infant Qi peers over his mother's shoulder. Nowhere in the text of her biography in *Lienü zhuan* is it recorded that the Tushan woman went out in search of Yu while he was engaged in his enterprise. What we see here on the part of the illustrator is sheer narrative extrapolation, combining narrative elements from sources other than the text it accompanies.

In the late Ming illustrations, the Tushan woman does not venture outside. The Zhibuzuzhai illustration (fig. 4.9) shows her bidding farewell to Yu at the door of the house. She is holding the infant, who is reaching out to his father. The father is smiling fondly at his family, all the while pointing to the workmen (and the work) in the next frame. (Just as traditional Chinese writing was read from right to left, so are illustrations to be read that way.) The domestic sphere and the work world are portrayed in separate frames: the Tushan woman is exposed to the gaze of the reader, but not to that of the workmen. Despite the fact that the open door leads our gaze into the house, we cannot quite see in. It is ironic that in one of the rare images we have of mother, father, and child, the father is on his way out the door.

Figure 4.9 Illustration to the story of the Tushan woman. Qing. Woodblock print. From *Huitu lienü zhuan*, Zhibuzuzhai edition, 1779. Reprint of a purported late Ming edition. Reprinted as *Retsujoden* (Tokyo: Zuhonsokankai, 1923–26). Photo courtesy of University of Minnesota Libraries.

In the Huang Jiayu text (fig. 4.10), the father has already bidden his family farewell. The Tushan woman and her child are within a room, which is in turn enclosed by a fence. The artist's use of perspective raises the house, so we can see within it. Yu and a workman stand outside the gate, on their way to subdue the floods. The viewer can see that the child is in good hands: The Tushan woman sits serene and elegant, in a patched thatch house. The genteel poverty underscores the irony of a man who saves a civilization but leaves his family to fend for themselves. The refined and graceful Tushan woman of *Lienü zhuan* patiently raises her son in his father's absence. She is rewarded when he grows up and succeeds his father. As the *Shiji* says, "The Xia came to power because of the Tushan woman."[40] Dynastic power for her progeny was her reward.

The Virtuous Aunt

The last story is also a perplexing one, and it caused consternation among Ming readers, who may well have perceived it as exemplifying values at odds with their own family system. The story in Liu Xiang's text recounts that when troops from the state of Qi entered Lu, they came upon a rural woman walking in the countryside, carrying her own son and leading her husband's elder brother's son by the hand.[41] Fearing that she did not have the strength to rescue both children from the invaders, she flung her own son down, picked up her nephew, and fled. Her son was captured by the Qi troops, and when they eventually reached her as well, the soldiers asked her why she had made the choice she did. She responded:

> My relationship to my son is private love *(si ai)*, and that to my nephew is public duty *(gong yi)*. If I had turned my back on a public duty and pursued private love, abandoning my brother's child to save my own child, even if by some good fortune I had escaped, still the lord of Lu would not succor *(xu)* me, officials would not nourish *(yang)* me, and ordinary countrymen would have nothing to do with me. If I were to do this, then my body would nowhere be at ease, and my tired feet would have nowhere to step. Although it is painful to lose my son, what is the meaning of righteousness *(yi)*? Although I can bear to abandon my son and practice righteousness, I cannot bear to live in the state of Lu without righteousness.[42]

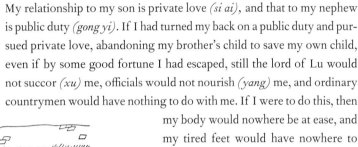

Figure 4.10 Illustration to the story of the Tushan woman. Late Ming. Woodblock print. From Huang Jiayu, ed., *Liu Xiang gu Lienü zhuan*, 1606. Microfilm held at Harvard-Yenching Library.

This particular story of sacrifice has a happy ending. The invading troops are so moved by her virtue, which exemplifies the ideals of the state of Lu, the home of Confucius, that they stop the siege. The text concludes:

> She was public spirited, upright, sincere and trustworthy *(gong zheng cheng xin)*. She truly put righteousness *(yi)* into practice. Oh, how great was her righteousness! Although she was just a com-

> mon woman, the country still depended on her. How much more should we use propriety and righteousness to rule the nation?[43]

Not only do both children survive, but the entire state of Lu is saved by the virtuous act of the public-spirited aunt.[44] Thus a rural woman educates the Han literati in propriety and righteousness. Propriety and righteousness remained important virtues in later periods, but the conflicting obligations of public duty and private love made the story a troublesome one for Ming readers.

Despite the fact that the story was troublesome, the Ming editor Lü Kun includes it in his *Guifan* (Female exemplars). His version is truncated: At 154 characters it is about half as long as the original Han text, and at 119 characters, his critical commentary is two-thirds as long as the text itself.[45] Lü Kun's strongest emendations are at the point when the public-spirited aunt is explaining her actions, and in some senses the emendations vitiate the point of the story. We saw in the preceding her elaborate invocations of community and community obligation. Lü Kun's version of the story reads as follows:

> The woman explained: "The one I am carrying is my nephew. The one I abandoned is my son. When the armies approached, I could not save both of them, and thought it best to abandon my son." The Qi general asked, "Who is closer to you, your nephew or your son?" The woman answered, "My son is private *(si)* and nephew is public *(gong)*. Although I suffer on account of my son, what does he have to do with duty *(yi)*?"

Lü Kun goes on to comment:

> Mr. Lü says: As for her public-spiritedness *(gong yi)*, yes, it was public spiritedness, yet she did not understand the true way *(dao)*. Her own son was also her husband's son; a woman's son cannot belong only to her. If her husband had many sons, or if he were still alive and could produce more sons, or if her [husband's] elder brother had died, or if his son was the heir to his father, then we could call her a public-spirited aunt. But if these conditions were not met, then what she has done is violate natural emotions *(qing)* on behalf of public-spiritedness. Throughout the ten thousand generations, this has never been a norm. What should she have done? I say, she should have asked the Qi general to allow them both to live. If he would not have permitted it, then he could have killed her. That the value of a child's life is set by the calculations of the Qi general—what

a tragedy! Among the officials of the state of Lu, how many are like the Public-Spirited Aunt?[46]

The concept of "natural emotion" was livelier in Ming discourse than it had been in the Han. Many late-Ming thinkers shared Lü Kun's conviction that properly understood emotions could be used as a reliable guide to human actions.[47] Not only were Ming families more strongly patrilineal than Han families had been, but as Lü Kun's comments suggest, conceptions of virtue had changed as well.

The illustration for the Yuan edition (fig. 4.11) is executed on either side of a folded page. The public-spirited aunt stands still, clutching her nephew, who looks

Figure 4.11 Illustration to the story of the public-spirited aunt. Yuan. Woodblock print. From *Lienü zhuan*, Qinyoutang edition, late thirteenth to early fourteenth century. Reprinted in *Wenxuanlou congshu* (Yangzhou, 1842), *juan* 79–80. Photo courtesy of Harvard-Yenching Library.

Figure 4.12 Illustration to the story of the public-spirited aunt. Late Ming. Woodblock print. From *Lienü zhuan*, Santaiguan edition, 1591. Photo courtesy of Harvard-Yenching Library.

over her shoulder directly at the viewer. Her own child, a miniaturized adult, seems to be beckoning the Qi general to come toward his mother. The general has a bow and arrow at the ready, but he is not aiming at the imperturbable aunt. All of the motion in the illustration comes from the general. When one turns the page, one sees the Qi troops, armed and armored, awaiting the results of the interview between general and aunt. The landscape is minimally represented: In both sides of the illustration, trees extend well beyond the frame of the picture, a style characteristic of the illustrations in this text. Both the soldiers and the aunt look very much like other figures in the text, suggesting (as others have noted) that the illustrations in this edition were put together from pre-drawn elements.[48]

The Santaiguan illustration (fig. 4.12) is much different. It is set in a wild and rocky landscape, just outside the city wall. The text tells us that the aunt was walking on the outskirts of the city when she was beset by Qi troops; presumably the city wall is to remind the viewer of that fact. The phrase at the top reads "Valuing righteousness, ignoring the private." The couplet on either side of the image reads:

> Abandoning her son, embracing her nephew in the desolate outskirts of the city: that is the heritage of the teaching of Lu.
> Valuing righteousness, ignoring the private, the whole country was gratified: that is the ——— of the troops of Qi.

The soldiers do not look particularly terrifying, but there is real dismay in the aunt's face. The nephew in her arms is a tiny infant (he cannot hold his head up, and she is too distraught to support it properly) and the son at her feet is no longer a toddler. Indeed, he looks very much like the Mencius in the Santaiguan illustration of that story. Looking at the two boys, it is scarcely plausible that previously their positions had been reversed—that she had been carrying her son and leading her nephew by the hand. I would suggest that the artist who designed this illustration is resisting the narrative: In his version, the son is old enough to fend for himself (or nearly so), while the nephew is a helpless infant. A similar, though somewhat less pronounced, difference in the ages of the children is present in the *Guifan tushuo* (Female exemplars, illustrated and explicated) illustration (fig. 4.13). These illustrations provide another explanation for the behavior of the aunt of Lu, an explanation more in line with Ming sensibilities, though one that runs directly counter to the texts they purport to illustrate.

Figure 4.13 Illustration to the story of the public-spirited aunt. Late Ming. Woodblock print. From Lü Kun, ed., *Guifan tushuo*, 1590. Photo courtesy of Harvard-Yenching Library.

The terror of the boy left behind is brought out in the *Guifan* illustration (fig. 4.14). The public-spirited aunt is in flight, her back to the viewer. The countryside is rocky and rugged, and the pursuing soldiers are armored and armed. Their attention is not on the aunt, but rather on her small son. He points to his fleeing mother with one hand, while with the other, wipes his face. His small form seems wracked with anxiety.

In the Huang Jiayu print (fig. 4.15), the terror has been muted. The aunt, the two children, and two soldiers (presumably one of them the Qi general) are in the foreground. From the background, connected by a path not visible to the viewer, two more soldiers approach. The organization of space in the mountains and streams crisscrossed by paths traversed by human figures evokes something of the spatial organization of a landscape painting. In the foreground, one of the soldiers is addressing the son, bending over slightly as he does so. The aunt has her back to the scene, as if she is fleeing, but her turned head indicates that she is attentive to the scene transpiring between her son and the general. In this representation of the scene, it seems as if the moment of danger has passed. These soldiers pose no threat to the family. This forms a distinct contrast with the dismay of the aunt (fig. 4.12) and the terror of the boy (fig. 4.14) evoked by the Santaiguan and She Yongning images.

Figure 4.14 Illustration to the story of the public-spirited aunt. Late Ming. Woodblock print. From Lü Kun, ed., *Guifan*, She Yongning edition, late sixteenth to early seventeenth century. Reprinted as *Yinying Ming ge Guifan* (n.p.: Jiangning Wei shi, 1927). Photo courtesy of Harvard-Yenching Library.

The various late-sixteenth- to early-seventeenth-century modifications described above may indicate a nod to Ming sensibilities. But the strongest editorial comment comes from the editors of the later Zhibuzuzhai edition, who have chosen to leave the story of the public-spirited aunt out entirely.

Some Conclusions

Let us return to the question with which we opened this essay, and talk specifically about the representation of the family in these illustrations. The focal point of the family dynamic that seems to be of interest in these three stories is the mother-son dyad. One recalls the work of the anthropologist Margery Wolf, who has suggested that within the patriline there lies nested another kind of family, which she calls the uterine family, consisting of a woman and her children. Husbands and fathers are not completely absent from these uterine families, but neither do they play the central role that patrilineal family theory would have us believe they do.[49] In the stories we have looked at, fathers and husbands are either entirely absent (and their absences unremarked) or on the way out the door, as is Yu. If this is propaganda for the patriline, it is odd and awkward propaganda. But, I suggest, it is indeed propaganda for the patriline: As the story of the Tushan woman makes very clear, the raising of sons is the central act that enables patrilineal succession. It is

Figure 4.15 Illustration to the story of the public-spirited aunt. Late Ming. Woodblock print. From Huang Jiayu, ed., *Liu Xiang gu Lienü zhuan*, 1606. Microfilm held at Harvard-Yenching Library.

second in importance only to bearing them, and as the myths of Yao and Shun illustrate, sons who are improperly raised are of no particular benefit either to their parents or to the imperium.[50] Mencius was great because he had a diligent mother, and Lü Kun used the story to reprove Ming mothers for what he saw as an epidemic of maternal negligence. Mencius' mother was the ultimate source for what became a male filiation of the *daotong*, the "transmission of the sagely way." It is harder to read the story of the public-spirited aunt as propaganda for the patriline. But it is a story that advocates the importance of communal, larger-kin values over those of the mother-child relationship.

The texts of these stories in Ming dynasty editions are fundamentally Han dynasty stories, retold and illustrated for a Ming dynasty audience, not as quaint relics of an antiquarian past but as living stories with the power to make things happen. (I should point out that the Ming editions of *Lienü zhuan* do contain new stories; these three, however, are old stories.) These stories reflect a society and social values that lay a millennium-and-a-half in the past. In the Han dynasty, widow remarriage had not become the touchstone of status and morality it would later become, nor was chastity the same sort of obsession it was in the Ming. Lineages did not function as powerful corporate entities in the same ways they did in later societies. The stories that date from one era are used as moral instruction for another, quite different era. One could, I think, argue that these are Han stories with Ming illustrations, embedded in texts whose structure and organization make them different from their Han antecedent. And part of what marks them as Ming texts is the fact that they are illustrated.

Conventional wisdom takes *Lienü zhuan* as a key text in the repression of women, in their socialization into good wives and wise mothers. But recent work, notably that of Katherine Carlitz, Sherry Mou, and Lisa Raphals, has suggested alternate readings, showing the complexity of representation of women in these texts.[51] Indeed, the question Raphals uses the Han dynasty text to answer is, "(How) can a woman become a sage?" The question, with its parenthetical "how," does not assume that a woman can become a sage; but neither does it preclude sagehood for women.[52]

Perhaps I was in error to expect to find family portraits in such a genre. The genre is perhaps not about families at all, but rather about enacting an abstract sense of virtue. The genre invokes moments of extreme moral crisis, which call forth acts of moral heroism. Ordinarily one does not slash one's weaving, or sit at home for years while one's husband fends off floodwaters, or be put in a position where one must choose which child will live and which will die. Texts that provide models of how to behave in such situations find their power in metaphor, not in practical advice. The *Lienü zhuan* is not, in either its Han original or in its Ming recensions, a genre that teaches people how to live in families. It is a text that instructs women to put public good ahead of everything else, including their families. For all its glimpses into domestic crises, it is not a genre about private life. As Katherine Carlitz has pointed out, these texts "knot the private to the public in a seamless web of idealized loyalties."[53]

Powerful virtue consists in behavior that transcends the ordinary, and part of what is assumed to be ordinary by both the Han compiler and the Ming commentators is attachment to family. Yu is implicitly praised for ignoring his family, and the public-spirited aunt is explicitly praised for risking the life of her son. Both of them valued the communal good more than their intimate family relations. In two of the stories, we see a strong language of public *(gong)* virtue being praised over private *(si)* attachments. *Gong* and *si* are a very different set of polarities from *nei* and *wai* (inner and outer). *Nei* and *wai* are spatial, relational, and shifting. They are metaphors that order families and societies. There are, to be sure, contexts where they might be translated by the English words *public* and *private* (though we are probably better served by the more literal *inner* and *outer*). But they are very different from *gong* and *si*, which refer to attitudes, not relationships. Indeed, one could say that the purpose of these texts is to inculcate the virtue of the public good *(gong)* in the inner realm *(nei)*. Children in this text are icons of the *nei*, who are sacrificed to the *gong*. We must look elsewhere, to other texts and genres, if we want to find representations of childhood that take actual children as their main subject.

Appendix

I. The Qinyoutang text (figs. 4.1, 4.8, 4.11)

Probably a copy of an edition dated 1063. The title page bears an inscription stating that the text was published by the Qinyoutang, the publishing house of the Yu family. Based on this inscription, T. K. Wu places the dating of the text as from the Dade reign period (1297–1307) of the Yuan dynasty. The edition I used was a Daoguang 5 reprint held at Harvard-Yenching University.

II. The Santaiguan text (figs. 4.2, 4.12)

This text is a reprint, done in 1591, of the 1588 *Fuchuntang Gujin Lienü zhuan*. The text is sometimes associated, perhaps spuriously, with the name of Mao Kun. The Santaiguan was the business place of the well-known publisher Yu Xiangdou. Both the Fuchuntang and the Santaiguan were important publishing establishments, famous for their illustrated drama texts.

III. The Huang Jiayu text (figs. 4.3, 4.10, 4.15)

Liu Xiang gu Lienü zhuan, in eight *juan*, edited by Huang Jiayu, dated 1606. This also exists in a twentieth-century reproduction.

IV. The She Yongning text (figs. 4.5, 4.14)

This is an edition of Lü Kun's *Guifan*, which takes more liberties with Liu Xiang's text than do other editions. This text exists in two modern reprints—one dated 1927, the other 1994.

V. Guifan tushuo (figs. 4.6, 4.13)

This is another edition of the text edited by Lü Kun, dated 1590. A copy of this exists at the Harvard-Yenching Library, and another exists at the University of Michigan. The illustrations differ substantially from those of the She Yongning text. A Kangxi era reprint, entitled *Lü Xinwu xiansheng Guifan tushuo*, exists at Princeton University.

VI. The Huang Shangwen text (fig. 4.4)

Guifan by Huang Shangwen. Published by Huang Yingtai in 1617.

VII. The Zhibuzuzhai text (figs. 4.7, 4.9)

Huitu lienü zhuan in sixteen *juan*. The earliest extant edition of this text is 1779, but it purports to be a reprint of a late Ming edition, with illustrations done by the famous figure painter Qiu Ying (early sixteenth century). Although the elegant ladies in the text do bear some relationship to the style of Qiu Ying, the likely dating of the text is several decades after his death. There are several modern reproductions.

5

The Childhood of Gods and Sages

Julia K. Murray

Stories about deities who once lived on Earth are found in the literature of many cultures. Such accounts invariably claim that these divine beings were conceived and born in an unusual manner. It is also typical of hagiographical narratives to describe supernatural abilities or behavior that these individuals demonstrated as children.[1] For example, prodigious events are prominent in Christian accounts of the conception, birth, and youth of Jesus Christ.[2] First, the angel Gabriel appeared to the Virgin Mary to announce that the Holy Spirit had become incarnate in her through an immaculate conception. Immediately before Jesus was born, a supernova appeared in the sky and guided the Three Wise Men on their long journey to give homage to the newborn baby. While Jesus was still a young boy, he amazed his elders by preaching authoritatively in the temple. Over the centuries, innumerable paintings and other kinds of religious pictures have depicted these important Christian themes.

Geographically closer and culturally more relevant to China are Indian stories about the conception, birth, and childhood of Prince Siddhartha, who became the Buddha Shakyamuni.[3] Although the many accounts of his life vary in detail, some basic features appear in most versions, whether they originated in India, Central Asia, or China. Shakyamuni was conceived when his mother, Queen Maya, dreamed that a bodhisattva descended to her in the form of a six-tusked white elephant and entered into her right side. When she reported her dream to her husband, King Sudhodhana, he summoned Brahmin prognosticators, who interpreted it to mean that her son would be a great man. Ten months later, when the Queen was strolling in the Lumbini Garden, a tree bent down for her to grasp, and the baby was born from her right side without causing her pain. At the same time, thirty-two miraculous events occurred:

Dead trees flowered, heavenly lights appeared, simultaneous births took place in the animal kingdom, and so forth. The newborn infant immediately took seven steps, pointed upward, and announced his identity, and heavenly beings provided water for his first bath. The elderly sage Asita examined Siddhartha and identified thirty-two auspicious features *(laksana)* on his body, such as a fleshy protuberance from the top of his head (the *usnisa*) and white hairs between his eyebrows that emitted light (the *urna*), and predicted that he would become a world leader. Seven days later, Queen Maya died. The young Siddhartha exhibited superhuman intelligence and physical abilities, which he demonstrated by tossing an elephant in the air and shooting an arrow through iron targets. Some of these events are depicted in early Indian religious art, such as in the reliefs carved on the stone railings of the stupa at Bharhut.[4]

With the spread of Buddhism to China, pictorial representations of the Buddha's life became a staple of Chinese Buddhist religious art. As discussed below, certain motifs in his conception, birth, and childhood were modified to conform to Chinese tastes or conventions. For example, while Indian images portrayed the bodhisattva in the form of an elephant, the Chinese depicted the bodhisattva in human form, riding on an elephant. Chinese elements also appear in architectural forms, clothing styles, and ethnic features. In addition to receiving Buddhist hagiographies from India and Central Asia, however, China had its own legends concerning divine beings who had been born on Earth. Some of these indigenous accounts were composed many centuries before the introduction of Buddhism, such as the story of Houji, presented in the following text. Because Buddhist accounts conformed to Chinese expectations concerning the conception, birth, and childhood of a god, visual representations of these events in the life of Shakyamuni provided a model for pictorializing the hagiographies of Chinese deities. It seems likely that the interaction of native and foreign elements gave rise to a common stock of imagery in Chinese depictions of the early lives of divine beings. These conventions also served as a template for shaping the hagiographical narratives concerning Chinese gods of much later origin.

Deities who had lived human lives were not the only individuals for whom Chinese accounts claimed heavenly manifestations and prodigious qualities in childhood. These features also appear in the biographies of certain men who achieved recognition as sages or who succeeded in founding a new dynasty. Although such men were not exactly gods, they are often described as "semi-divine" because of their superhuman ability to mediate between heaven and Earth.[5] Moreover, some of the same motifs emerge in accounts of men who achieved distinction within the purely human realm, typically as exemplary scholar-officials or erudite recluses. Often described as preternaturally learned at a young age, these child prodigies went on to pass the civil service examinations or to realize their exceptional potential in some other respectable pursuit. Although Chinese biographies and hagiographies typically paid little attention to the subject's childhood, in contrast to his or her later life, an extraordinary birth and/or childhood might be mentioned as a means of foreshadowing or justifying the individual's later career.[6]

A close examination of literary and visual representations suggests that there are consistent patterns in the kinds of unusual occurrences and/or childhood behaviors that are associated with gods, sages, founding emperors, and various kinds of exemplary individuals. In the following text I present examples from each group and explore depictions of their early lives.

The Childhood of Gods

For convenience and simplicity, the term "god" *(shen)* is used here to refer to a being who was thought capable of bestowing blessings and other benefits in response to prayers and sacrifices offered by people from different families, regardless of whether or not the religion or cult was officially recognized by the state.[7] By this definition I mean to exclude ancestors who were worshiped just by their own descendants, and officials who were posthumously canonized by the emperor and received sacrifices in the state cult. The Chinese religious landscape was populated by an immense number of gods, only some of whom were identified with the institutionalized churches of Buddhism, Daoism, and state Confucianism.[8] A number of establishment deities were simultaneously the focus of popular cults, which might emphasize characteristics that were downplayed or even absent from the conceptions promoted by the established religions.[9] Other gods were worshiped only by popular cults in a limited geographic area.

The earliest Chinese account of the birth and childhood of a god is recorded in the *Shijing* (Book of odes), the ancient anthology whose compilation is conventionally ascribed to Confucius (ca. 551–479 B.C.). The poem "Birth of the People" ("Shengmin"), which is believed to date from the ninth century B.C., describes the miraculous life and prodigious achievements of Houji, the god of agriculture.[10] Houji was conceived when his mother Jiang Yuan stepped in the giant footprint of Shang Di (Lord on High), to whom she had offered prayers and sacrifices in hopes of obtaining a child.[11] As a further sign of his divine origins, his birth entailed none of the usual trauma of labor and delivery—"no bursting, no rending." Abandoned three times as an infant, he was protected first by animals, who avoided stepping on him (fig. 5.1); next by woodcutters, who found him in the forest; and finally by birds, who warmed him with their wings as he lay on the ice. In childhood, Houji's divine powers enabled him to gather food for himself and to cultivate crops. His great con-

Figure 5.1 *(facing page)* Houji as a baby among animals. Ming, dateable to 1507. Detail of wall painting at the Jiyimiao, Xinjiang county, Shanxi. After *Jiyimiao bihua*.

tribution to Chinese culture was to teach the people the principles of crop cultivation, thus introducing a more reliable livelihood. As Anne Behnke Kinney has written, Houji's conception and early life as described in "Birth of the People" became the model for the biographies of other gods and extraordinary beings, which were written in some numbers in the Han period and shortly thereafter.[12] The key motifs in such accounts are miraculous conception, unusual birth, a period of adversity, and extraordinary childhood behavior.

The Zhou dynastic house (ca. 1050–221 B.C.) claimed Houji as its progenitor and regularly offered sacrifices to him, and the lengthy poem may have been sung as part of a sacrificial ritual. Later dynasties included sacrifices to Houji as part of a much larger state cult maintained by the emperor and government officials, in recognition of his contributions to Chinese culture. During the late imperial period, Houji was also worshiped in popular-cult temples in parts of Shanxi and Shaanxi, where he was believed to have lived. Pictorial representations of his life survive in some of these temples.[13] However, there is no evidence that events in the early life of Houji were illustrated in antiquity. Although paintings of poems in the *Book of Odes* can be traced to the Period of Disunion (220–589), no illustration for the poem "Birth of the People" is known today.[14] Moreover, the pictures for other *Odes* poems suggest that a depiction for "Birth of the People" is more likely to have been a portrait of the adult Houji than a narrative illustration of several events in his early life.[15]

Extant representations of Houji's biography date only to the Ming dynasty (1368–1644), and his early life is depicted in murals on the walls of temples that were built in the region of his purported activity. For example, several events are illustrated in the upper section of the east wall of the Jiyimiao, a temple in Xinjiang county, southwestern Shanxi. These murals were completed in 1507.[16] The sacrifice by Jiang Yuan is portrayed, although not her stepping in the giant footprint. Next is an intimate scene in the birthing chamber, where Jiang Yuan rests on a bed and three maids bathe the infant Houji, observed by two others who point in amazement at him (fig. 5.2). Subsequent scenes show each of the three contexts in which Jiang Yuan abandoned Houji to the elements (cf. fig. 5.1). Her change of heart and acceptance of Houji are conveyed by showing mother and child riding together in a carriage. More abbreviated illustrations of Houji's infancy appear in some late Ming woodblock-printed editions of Liu Xiang's *Biographies of Exemplary Women (Lienü zhuan)*, accompanying Jiang Yuan's biography in the chapter on good mothers (!).[17]

There is no question that the mythical elements of Houji's life came from the ancient Chinese textual tradition, and the iconographical details of its Ming depiction are based on the *Shijing* poem, "Birth of the People." Nonetheless, the visual representation of Houji's life owes certain of its conventions to pictorial narratives

Figure 5.2 *(facing page)* Houji's first bath. Ming, dateable to 1507. Detail of wall painting at the Jiyimiao, Xinjiang county, Shanxi. After *Jiyimiao bihua*.

of the life of the Buddha, which were based on various teachings and scriptures brought from India and Central Asia in the Han (206 B.C.–A.D. 220) through Tang (618–906) periods. As noted above, the recitation of events in the Buddha's life included supernatural elements that made his biography comparable to Chinese accounts of extraordinary individuals who became gods. In contrast to the lives of Chinese gods, which seem not to have been pictorialized in antiquity, visual representations of the Buddha's life played a role in spreading the foreign religion in China. I have argued elsewhere that pictorial narratives presenting linked episodes were not made in China before the introduction of Buddhism,[18] and the multiple-scene form of pictorial biography may itself be of foreign origin. In any event, depictions of the Buddha's life provided a model for the pictorial biographies of a range of extraordinary beings and, indeed, may have inspired the devotees of other gods to produce such accounts. Accordingly, it is useful to examine the evolution of Chinese conceptions of the life of the Buddha, before returning to Houji and other Chinese gods and sages.

Pictorial Biographies of the Buddha

The earliest surviving Chinese depictions of the life of the Buddha Shakyamuni are incised on the backs of votive stone stelae dating to the Period of Disunion. Probably based on or similar to drawings and paintings in more perishable media, these stone pictures shared techniques and styles with other subjects of metropolitan pictorial art. A well-known portrayal of the life of the Buddha, discussed by Nagahiro Toshio, appears on an Eastern Wei (534–550) stele from Henan, dated 543, which is now preserved only in a rubbing (fig. 5.3).[19] The decorated back of the now lost stone is divided into several horizontal registers, each of which is subdivided into several scenes by columns of inscriptions. The pictures illustrate excerpts from the life of the Buddha as well as two *jatakas*, tales about earlier lives of the being who became the Buddha in his last incarnation. The scenes associated with Prince Siddhartha's birth and infancy occupy three-quarters of the second row and proceed in a simple linear sequence. At far right, Queen Maya is dressed in Chinese-style voluminous robes and stands under a tree, grasping a branch over her head. The already haloed baby emerges from under her right arm, seemingly out of her pendant sleeve, into the waiting hands of the kneeling attendant. In the next scene, at left, the infant stands and makes his proclamation, pointing upward. A few dragon heads can be seen in the sky, a reference to his first bath, and the entire scene is observed by the same kneeling attendant. Further still to the left is the visit of Asita, the Brahmin seer, who holds the baby on his lap to examine the child's thirty-two bodily signs. The

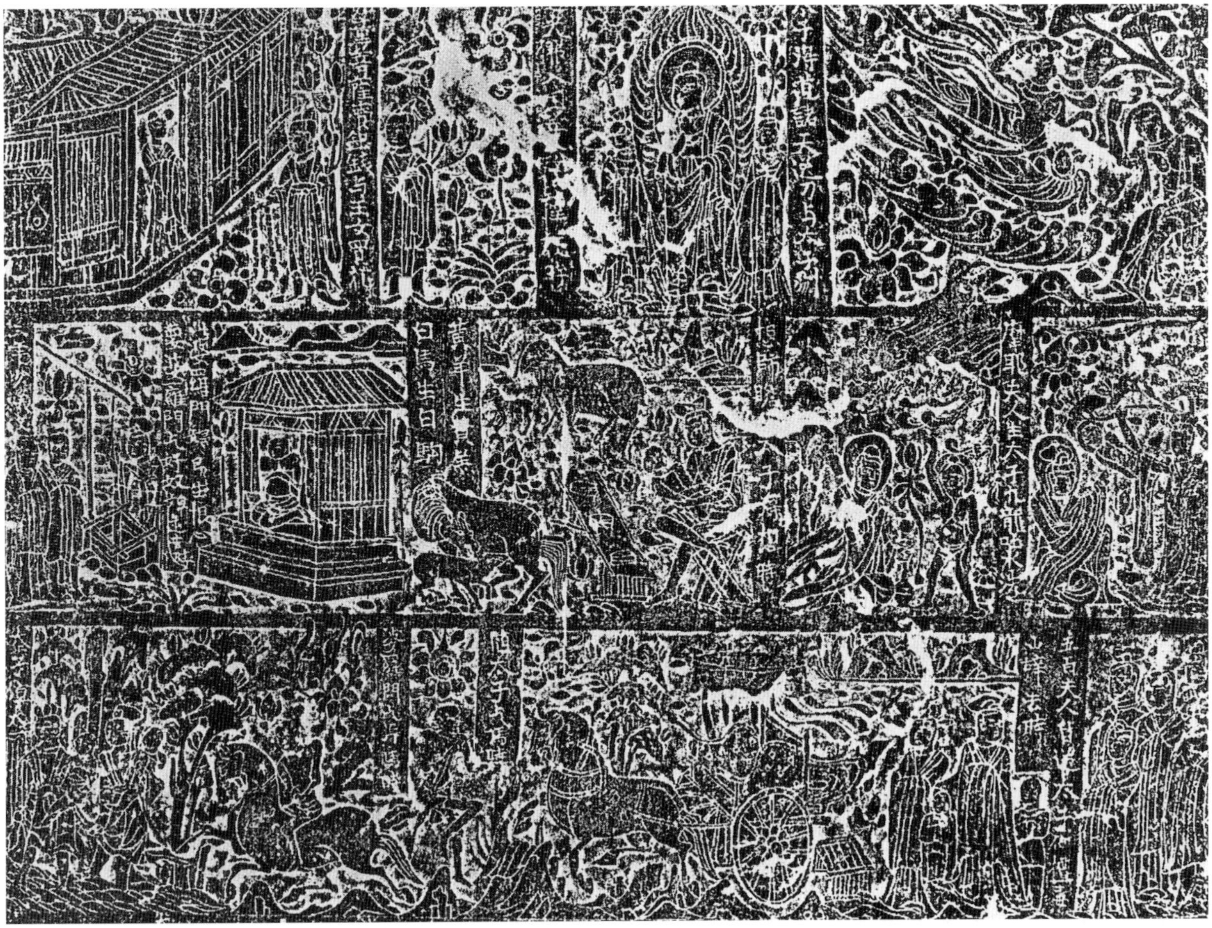

Figure 5.3 The life of the Buddha. Dated 543. Stone stele. After Nagahiro, *Rikuchō jidai bijutsu no kenkyū*.

sequence ends with the representation of two of the auspicious events that occurred when the Buddha was born, the simultaneous births of a yellow lamb and a white colt. The registers are read from top to bottom, and the order of scenes is consistently from right to left.

Other early Chinese stelae arrange the birth and childhood episodes somewhat differently. On the back of a 471-dated Maitreya, Buddha of the Future, found in Xingpingxian near Xi'an, the narrative scenes follow a zigzag path from bottom to top through six registers, which are subdivided by vertical bands into compartments of varied widths (fig. 5.4).[20] The sequence begins at lower right, above a row of seated Buddhas, with depictions of several events from a previous life; and the scenes relating to the conception, birth, and young childhood of Prince Siddhartha occupy the top two rows. Queen Maya's dream appears at the right end of the

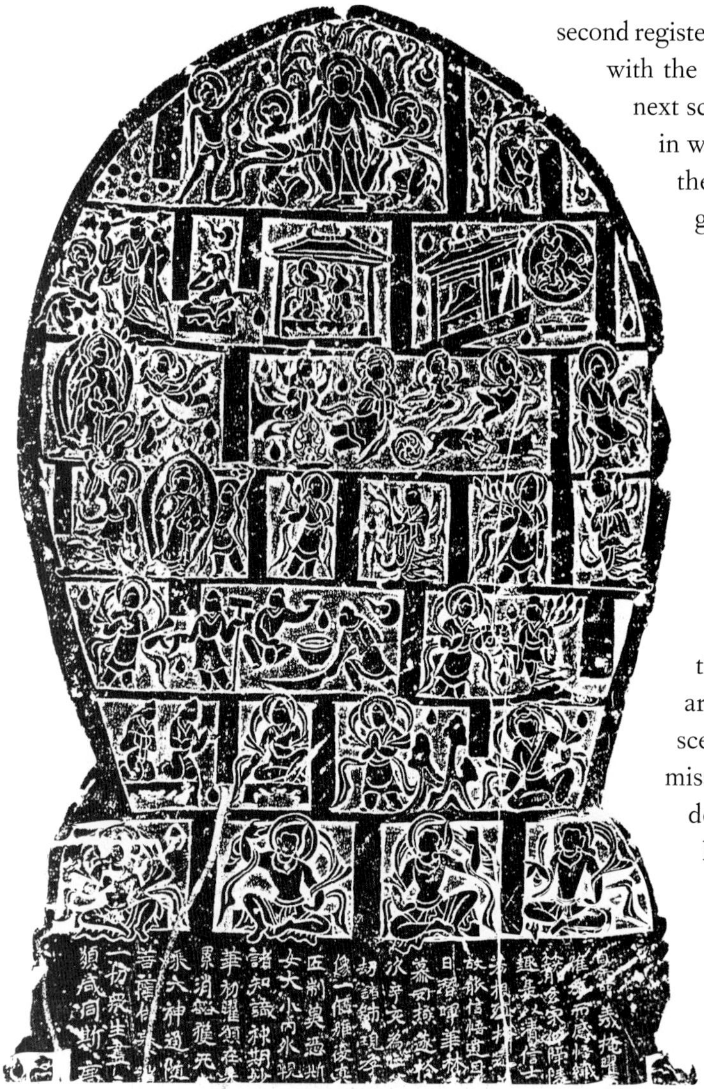

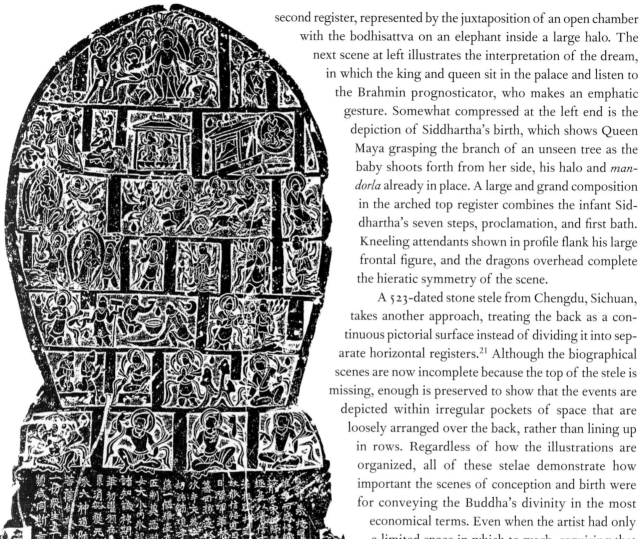

Figure 5.4 The life of the Buddha. Dated 471. Stone stele. After *Zhongguo meishu quanji, huihuabian*, vol. 19.

second register, represented by the juxtaposition of an open chamber with the bodhisattva on an elephant inside a large halo. The next scene at left illustrates the interpretation of the dream, in which the king and queen sit in the palace and listen to the Brahmin prognosticator, who makes an emphatic gesture. Somewhat compressed at the left end is the depiction of Siddhartha's birth, which shows Queen Maya grasping the branch of an unseen tree as the baby shoots forth from her side, his halo and *mandorla* already in place. A large and grand composition in the arched top register combines the infant Siddhartha's seven steps, proclamation, and first bath. Kneeling attendants shown in profile flank his large frontal figure, and the dragons overhead complete the hieratic symmetry of the scene.

A 523-dated stone stele from Chengdu, Sichuan, takes another approach, treating the back as a continuous pictorial surface instead of dividing it into separate horizontal registers.[21] Although the biographical scenes are now incomplete because the top of the stele is missing, enough is preserved to show that the events are depicted within irregular pockets of space that are loosely arranged over the back, rather than lining up in rows. Regardless of how the illustrations are organized, all of these stelae demonstrate how important the scenes of conception and birth were for conveying the Buddha's divinity in the most economical terms. Even when the artist had only a limited space in which to work, requiring that he portray just a few events from the Buddha's life, he consistently chose to illustrate the birth scenes because they signified the Buddha's transcendent nature.

A far more detailed pictorial biography of the Buddha is painted on the ceiling of the antechamber in Dunhuang cave 290, which is attributed to the mid-sixth century (fig. 5.5).[22] The two slopes of the pitched ceiling are divided into three registers each, and the illustrations are arranged in a linear sequence, which begins in the top register and changes direction in each subsequent row. In contrast to the terse pictorial accounts on the early stelae, where the restricted space accommodated only a few excerpts from the Buddha's hagiography, the eighty-odd scenes in the Dunhuang mural permit a much more discursive approach and place heavy emphasis on the events of his early life. For example, an entire register is devoted to various miraculous events that coincided with Siddhartha's birth, and the visit of the seer Asita to examine the infant does not appear until the middle of the third register. It seems likely that concise and discursive approaches coexisted as alternative ways to depict the Buddha's life, and the choice depended on both the purpose and the format of the representation. Nonetheless, no matter how many scenes are depicted, the early Chinese illustrations of the Buddha's life do little to articulate or characterize the surroundings in which the events take place. Even in the detailed presentation on the ceiling of Dunhuang cave 290, the actions occur in the foreground of a very shallow pictorial space, and only vague settings are suggested by the schematically portrayed buildings and trees, which often serve primarily to separate the scenes.

As Chinese illustrations of the Buddha's life evolved over the centuries, his birth and childhood took on an ever more "Chinese" appearance, not only in terms of the figural types and clothing styles, but also in more detailed depictions of the material environments. As portrayed in a mid-twelfth-century (Jin dynasty, 1115–1234) mural at the Yanshansi, Siddhartha's home came to be modeled on the Chinese imperial palace, even down to the inclusion of civil service officials wearing long

Figure 5.5 The life of the Buddha. Mid-sixth century. Section of painting on the east side of antechamber ceiling in Mogao cave 290, Dunhuang. After *Zhongguo meishu quanji, huihuabian*, vol. 13.

Figure 5.6 *(facing page)* Officials awaiting audience at King Sudhodhana's palace. Completed in 1167, by Wang Gui and assistants. From *Life of the Buddha*, detail of a wall painting at the Yanshansi, Fanzhi County, Shanxi. After *Yanshansi Jindai bihua*.

gowns and stiff-eared caps, waiting for an audience with his father, King Sudhodhana (fig. 5.6).[23] The scene of miraculous conception is somewhat revised, perhaps to accommodate Chinese expectations concerning the appropriate "look" of a paranormal event. Instead of juxtaposing Queen Maya's bedchamber with the bodhisattva riding on a white elephant, the two are widely separated. Far away in the sky, the bodhisattva sends down a beam of light that touches the palace roof, and colored arcs of light radiate from the closed building, creating a dramatic spectacle at a focal point of the mural just right of center. The Yanshansi wall painting also conflates the birth with the baby's bath and first steps, which are depicted in the upper left. Surrounded by a glowing cloud, he sits in a magnificent golden basin being showered by nine Chinese dragons, whose sinuous bodies are fully drawn. His first seven steps are portrayed with a scattering of flowers that lead to a halo, inside which the infant stands and makes his declaration. Further to the right, in the upper center of the mural, Siddhartha's youthful feats of strength are given great prominence. Looking for all the world like a Chinese heir apparent surrounded by his princely companions, he hurls an elephant (fig. 5.7) and shoots iron targets from horseback.

Figure 5.7 Siddhartha throws an elephant. Completed in 1167, by Wang Gui and assistants. From *Life of the Buddha*, detail of a wall painting at the Yanshansi, Fanzhi County, Shanxi. After *Fanzhi Yanshansi*.

Figure 5.8 Bringing the infant Siddhartha from the Lumbini Garden back to the palace. From *Shishi yuanliu*, episode 8. Woodblock-printed book, early-Ming edition. National Central Library, Taiwan, Rare Book no. 8967.

The more detailed formulations in late imperial China of the life of the Buddha gave additional scope to portrayals of the prodigious events surrounding his conception, birth, and childhood. A particularly influential example is *Shishi yuanliu* (Origins and evolution of the Shakya clan), also called *Shijiarulai chengdao yinghua shiji ji* (Record of Shakyamuni Buddha's attainment of the way, and transformation of his life's traces), a woodblock-printed illustrated book compiled by the early-Ming monk Baocheng.[24] The compendium includes over two hundred pictures, each accompanied by a four-character title and a lengthy quotation from one of several sutras in the lower half of the page. Each folio displays an illustration in the upper half and the associated text in the lower half, giving them equal weight. Chronologically arranged and encyclopedic in its detail, the compilation covers not only the Buddha's life, but also a number of events preceding and following it, including milestones in the evolution of the early Buddhist church. Siddhartha's early life is treated in great detail. For example, an episode entitled "Returning from the garden to the palace" *(cong yuan huan cheng)* shows King Sudhodhana after he had received news of the miraculous birth and had gone to the Lumbini Garden to fetch the baby (fig. 5.8). According to the accompanying sutra text, he asked where he might find an appropriate vehicle for conveying the child. In response, the god Visvakarman[25] transformed his body into a seven-jeweled carriage, the four *deva* kings turned into strong young men to pull it, and *apsaras* and jade maidens burned incense along the way in celebration.

Shishi yuanliu was widely circulated as a woodblock-printed illustrated book and was reprinted several times over the centuries. Besides being a religious work in its own right, the compendium also appears to have served as a sourcebook for large-scale colored paintings of the life of the Buddha. Close counterparts can be found in Ming temple murals, such as the wall paintings at the Jueyuansi in northern Sichuan, which were completed in 1489.[26] Covering all four walls of the main hall, the paintings illustrate the same episodes as the woodblock-printed series. Moreover, most of the titles given to individual scenes are identical, and the compositions very similar, to those in the book. The mural scenes are divided among fourteen separate panel-like surfaces, which are defined by equally spaced columns that are set partially into the walls. Each panel illustrates between four and twenty sequential episodes. The panels are arranged counterclockwise around the hall, beginning and ending at the main entrance on the south wall. The conception, birth, and early life of the Buddha are treated in seventeen scenes on the second panel, which is placed at the south (right) end of the east wall. One scene in this group, showing King Sudhodhana declaring a great amnesty in celebration of the birth of his heir, is without counterpart in *Shishi yuanliu*.[27] In contrast to the monochrome woodblock-printed illustrations, the wall paintings contain bright colors and gold, particularly on the figures, which create a regal ambiance.

The iconography of the early life of the Buddha receives a very expansive treatment in early-Ming wall paintings at the Chongshansi in Taiyuan, Shanxi. Although the original murals were destroyed by fire in 1864, their contents survive in a meticulously painted album of copies, which bears the date of 1483.[28] The copies suggest that the murals enlarged upon *Shishi yuanliu*'s treatment of the Buddha's early

Figure 5.9 The birth, seven steps, and first bath of Siddhartha. From *Shishi yuanliu*, episode 7. Woodblock-printed book, early-Ming edition. National Central Library, Taiwan, Rare Book no. 8967.

Figure 5.10 *(facing page)* The first bath of Siddhartha. Ming, dated 1483. Leaf four in an album of paintings after early-Ming wall paintings in the Chongshansi, Taiyuan, Shanxi. Ink and colors on silk. After *Taiyuan Chongshansi wenwu tulu*.

life in two ways. First, they gave separate compositions to events that appear within a single illustration in *Shishi yuanliu*. For example, where the woodblock book combines Siddhartha's birth, bath, and first steps into one picture (fig. 5.9), the Chongshansi album of copies gives a separate leaf to each event (fig. 5.10). Second, the Chongshansi series contains several scenes of heavenly beings giving gifts to the child and of the youth's supernatural feats. In all, some twenty-one compositions in the Chongshansi series cover the same period of the Buddha's early life as do fourteen pictures in *Shishi yuanliu* and seventeen in the Jueyuansi mural. In addition, most of the Chongshansi scenes include a larger number of subsidiary figures and much more lavish settings, all painted in sumptuous detail with brilliant mineral pigments. In these respects they closely resemble Ming palace painting, perhaps an indication that palace artists were involved in creating the murals. This possibility is consistent with the research of Zhang Jizhong and An Ji, who have proven that the Chongshansi was built under the patronage of Zhu Kang (1358–1398), the prince of Jin and third son of the Ming founding emperor.[29] In any event, the splendid setting given to events in the early life of the Buddha reflects Ming ideals of aristocratic material culture and social life.

Pictorial Biographies of Other Gods

Figure 5.11 *(facing page)* The first bath of Lü Dongbin, by the workshop of Zhu Haogu. Ming, dated 1358. Detail of mural in the Chunyangdian of the Yonglegong, Shanxi. After *Yonglegong bihua quanji.*

Chinese pictorial narratives of the Buddha's life, particularly the later renditions, provided a template for illustrating the hagiographies of other gods. It seems likely that Daoist temples were first to adopt the form, perhaps as a way of competing with Buddhism for support from the state and the populace. From Daoist deities, pictorial hagiographies spread to gods on the state register of sacrifices and to those of popular cults. Because many gods were worshiped by more than one group, accounts of their lives were broadly disseminated, if somewhat differently conceptualized by each. In addition, hagiographical legends were further developed and transmitted in oral and written literature, and ritual theater performed them before mass audiences.[30] Although the specific details might vary, people expected a god's life to include a miraculous conception, unusual birth, remarkable behavior in childhood, and the exercise of supernatural powers. The ubiquity of these elements was visually reinforced by theatrical spectacles, illustrations to printed books, and temple murals. As Paul Katz has pointed out in his studies of the pictorial hagiography of Lü Dongbin at the great Daoist temple Yonglegong, even a representation sponsored by the clergy to portray orthodox interpretations of church doctrines was likely to be infiltrated by popular ideas, because it was executed by painters who participated in popular culture.[31] Moreover, Daoist temple decorators also accepted Buddhist commissions, as did the workshop responsible for painting the Lü Dongbin hagiography at the Yonglegong. The life of the Buddha was undoubtedly within the repertoire of such painters, and its conventions stood ready for application to the lives of other gods.

Even a cursory search turns up many examples of Daoist and popular gods whose conception and birth present only minor variations on the same miraculous themes. For example, Lü Dongbin was conceived when a white crane flew down into the family courtyard and awakened his mother. When she gave birth, an unusual fragrance filled the room. As portrayed in the first scene of the Yonglegong hagiography, the focus of attention is on the baby (fig. 5.11).[32] Rays of colored light stream upward from his body, turning into a rosy cloud under the hovering figure of a large crane. Other members of the household and passersby in the street outside look up in delighted amazement. Lü's mother, sitting upright in a formal chair, watches calmly as her maids bathe the infant, an event that is not described in written accounts but probably was inspired by the life of the Buddha.[33] As a child, Lü showed his prodigious ability by mastering the classics, but he chose not to take the civil service examinations, after encountering the immortal Zhongli Quan, who converted him to Daoism.

The visual conventions for presenting the conception, birth, and childhood of a god became so well established that they might even distort or contradict the

details of a particular deity's story. For example, in the Jiyimiao mural mentioned previously, the illustration of Houji's birth gives no indication that Jiang Yuan miraculously delivered the baby without experiencing any pain or disturbance (cf. fig. 5.2). Instead, the event is represented simply with a generic scene of upper-class childbirth: The mother rests in bed while maids wash the infant. Although Houji was one of the most ancient Chinese gods in terms of textual origins, his hagiography was pictorialized long after this compositional scheme had become the standard way to portray a birth scene.

Miraculous conception is a constant theme in these hagiographical accounts, but there is interesting variety in the ways that the mothers of the gods became impregnated. Of the women discussed above, the Buddha's mother dreamed that a bodhisattva in the form of a remarkable elephant entered her side, Lü Dongbin's mother was visited by a crane, and Houji's mother stepped in a god's giant footprint. Other stories describe additional methods of miraculous conception: The mother of Zhenwu (originally called Xuanwu, the guardian of the North) was touched by a ray of sunlight,[34] the mother of Jigong (Sire Ji, or Crazy Ji) dreamed that she swallowed rays of sunlight,[35] the mother of Wenchang (the lord of Zitong) dreamed that she swallowed a pearl,[36] the mother of Mazu (Tianhou the empress of heaven and protector of sailors) had a dream in which the bodhisattva Guanyin gave her a special pill,[37] and so forth. As presented in these accounts, the mothers range from completely passive recipients of divine attention (e.g., they were touched by something) to more active participants who played a part in the process (e.g., they chose to swallow something). A related set of distinctions could be drawn between mothers who had prayed beforehand for a child and those who had not. Usually the women who had sought to conceive were the ones who cooperated actively in the process of divine conception. It is the rare hagiography that includes the human father alongside the mother in sacrificing to the gods for a child, as occurs in Mazu's case. Divine conception explicitly effaces the human father, and even if he helped to raise the child, he received no credit for the glorious accomplishments of his offspring.

The Childhood of Sages and Emperors

Many of the elements common to the early lives of gods also appear in those of figures who are characterized as sages rather than as full-fledged deities. A sage *(sheng)* may be considered a person whose extraordinary moral attainment and insight permit him to perceive and act in accordance with the patterns of heaven, usually to the benefit of humankind.[38] The sages of distant antiquity were often described as culture heroes who contributed to the formation of Chinese livelihood and civilization. Although identified with historical human beings, they demonstrated a superhuman level of wisdom and were sometimes thought of as gods. Accounts starting in the Han period also imputed supernatural characteristics and powers to more recent sages, and a distinction between god and sage was not sharply drawn.[39]

The archetypal sage of historical times was Confucius (Kongzi), venerated over the centuries as the great teacher and transmitter of core cultural values. In the earliest written biography of Confucius, Sima Qian (145–86 B.C.) mentioned certain details that suggested Confucius' special nature, but the account contains nothing that seems blatantly supernatural.[40] Sima's narrative began with a recitation of Confucius' patrilineal ancestors, who came from the state of Song and may have been related to the Shang royal house. Confucius' father, Shuliang He, formed a "union in the wild" *(yehe)* with a woman of the Yan family in the state of Lu, and a child was conceived after he/she/they sacrificed on the top of Mount Ni (near modern Qufu in eastern Shandong).[41] At birth, Confucius had an unusual head that was said to resemble Mount Ni, for which he was named "Hillock" (Qiu) and styled Zhong Ni. His father died immediately after he was born, and his mother passed away a few years later. As a child, Confucius liked to play at performing sacrifices by setting up a sacrificial table and arranging ceremonial vessels on it (fig. 5.12). By mentioning

Figure 5.12 Confucius as a boy plays at performing rituals. Rubbing of stone tablet. Early-Qing reconstruction of Zhang Kai's 1444 original series. From *Shengji tu* (Pictures of the traces of the sage, or Life of Confucius). After Baba Harukichi, *Kō Mō Seiseki zukan*.

Figure 5.13 The *qilin* brings the jade tablet to the mother of Confucius. Woodblock print. From *Shengji tu*. Late-Ming edition purporting to be 1444 original. Beijing Library, Rare Book no. 16645. After Zheng Zhenduo, comp., *Zhongguo gudai banhua congkan*.

this unusual way of playing, Sima Qian established Confucius' exemplary character from the start and foreshadowed the preoccupations of his adulthood.

The comparative restraint of Sima Qian's account is missing in the so-called apocryphal texts of the Han and post-Han periods from which stories were incorporated into Kong family genealogies of later centuries.[42] The apocryphal accounts injected mystical elements into Confucius' life story and claimed superhuman powers of prognostication and wisdom for him. To establish that Confucius was extraordinary from the outset, these writings described his conception and birth as miraculous. In response to the sacrifice on Mount Ni, his mother received a visit from a *qilin*, a large, scaly beast with a single horn, whose appearance was considered extremely auspicious as the portent of a future ruler (fig. 5.13). The fabled creature carried in its mouth a jade tablet inscribed with *"Shui jing zi ji shuai Zhou er wei su wang"* ("The child of the essence of water will succeed the declining Zhou and become an uncrowned king"). Upon accepting this mysterious proclamation from the gods, she was pregnant.[43] During the period of gestation, further signs heralded the imminent arrival of an extraordinary being. On the morning of Confucius' birth, two dragons appeared above the house, and five gods descended into the courtyard. When the baby was born, the sounds of heavenly music and celebration filled the air. The newborn's body bore forty-nine auspicious signs, among them an inscription on his chest announcing that he was "created to stabilize the world" *(zhi zuo ding shi fu)* (fig. 5.14).

As Han followers of Confucius succeeded in establishing in Chinese political philosophy a central place for his teachings, and his books became the core curriculum of the governing elite, a state cult of Confucius began to take shape. By the early Tang period, semiannual sacrifices were offered to Confucius in official temples throughout the empire.[44] Even though his cult became established during the first few centuries of our era, a pictorial narrative of his life was created only in the Ming period.[45] The earliest example, produced in 1444 under the auspices of the censor Zhang Kai (1398–1460), was a modest series of pictures annotated with edited excerpts from Sima Qian's humanistic biography of Confucius. However, by the end of the fifteenth century, it was superceded by pictorial hagiographies that drew upon the supernatural lore, and these adopted the standard conventions for portraying the life of a transcendent being (cf. figs. 5.13–5.14).

The prophecy that Confucius would be an "uncrowned king" implied that heaven had endowed him with the essential nature of a ruler, which Han cosmology

Figure 5.14 The birth of Confucius. Woodblock print. From *Shengji tu*. Late-Ming edition purporting to be 1444 original. Beijing Library, Rare Book no. 16645. After *Zhongguo gudai banhua congkan*, comp., Zheng Zhenduo.

conceived in somewhat mystical terms. As Julia Ching has described, the ruler came to be seen as the mediator between the heavenly and earthly realms, interpreting heaven's signs and keeping the seasons in harmony—functions already associated with sagehood.[46] Although no ruler since the ancient golden age was truly a sage, sageliness itself was a qualification for ruling.[47] Not surprisingly, as the superhuman competence of a sage came to be attributed to earthly rulers, auspicious omens, bodily signs, and unusual behavior in childhood also figured in stories about emperors. Nonetheless, in contrast to deity hagiographies, the biography of an emperor rarely claimed that he was actually fathered by a god.[48]

The belief that superhuman powers appropriate to a sage ruler had to be inborn and could not be attained by ordinary mortals was particularly useful to men who established a new dynasty. Because founding emperors often achieved power by violent means, rather than through normal succession, extraordinary features in their early lives served to demonstrate that heaven had ordained their ascent, thus conferring legitimacy on actions that might otherwise be considered reprehensible. Moreover, the assumption that only a supernaturally endowed individual was destined to succeed in setting up a new order would discourage ordinary men from daring to rebel against the current regime. Auspicious anomalies associated with birth and childhood could also be important in legitimizing the actions of a member of a dynastic house emperor who achieved the throne outside the normal line of succession, prefiguring his unexpected elevation and justifying his potentially questionable deeds.

One such ruler was Song Gaozong (1107–1187; r. 1127–1162), the first emperor of the Southern Song. As the ninth son of Song Huizong (r. 1100–1125) and younger brother of Song Qinzong (r. 1125–1126), he was not expected to rule. However, he took the throne after two emperors and most of the royal family were captured in the Jin invasion of 1126, leaving him the only prince still at large. Twelve omens that foretold Gaozong's destiny to rule were recorded and illustrated during his reign.[49] The first three concerned his birth and childhood. When he was born, a golden light filled the room and four sages attended him. While he was still a small child in his mother's care, she dreamed that a god came and sternly admonished her to stop feeding him leftovers. Later, he became so strong that he could carry two large sacks of rice for several hundred paces. Although the illustrations for these three portents no longer survive, early Qing catalogues describe them in enough detail to indicate that the scenes were exactly what we would expect.[50] The first showed palace maids washing a baby while his mother rested, the second portrayed her both lying asleep in a pavilion and also in conversation with a deity, and the third depicted the future Gaozong standing in a courtyard holding a heavy sack in each hand.

The Childhood of the Exemplary Literatus

In addition to the special cases of emperors and of men who posthumously became powerful cult deities, biographies of other historical individuals sometimes describe auspicious phenomena associated with the subject's birth, an unusual physical appearance, remarkable ability or behavior in childhood, and so forth. As in hagiographies, such elements served as signs that the individual's exceptional nature was inborn.[51] Despite such shared features, historical figures who distinguished themselves in purely earthly pursuits must be considered a different category from gods and sages or even emperors, because their achievements as adults remained within the realm of human ability rather than involving the supernatural. Moreover, even though outstanding literati or military men might be posthumously canonized and awarded sacrifices in the state cult, most of them did not become deified in a popular sense. In contrast to cult figures, for whom it apparently was desirable to create pictorial hagiographies, ordinary men seldom became the subjects of illustrated narratives.

Even single-scene representations of famous people as children were rare, and they usually occurred in a morally instructive context. Mothers were sometimes depicted with children who achieved renown as adults in the illustrations of the *Biographies of Exemplary Women*, discussed by Ann Waltner in chapter 4 in this volume. In pictures for the *Biographies* chapter on "Good Mothers," the presence of a son who became famous served to affirm the mother's superior qualities: The proof of her exemplary mothering was that she raised an outstanding son. The didactic message of these stories was directed primarily to women and girls.[52] Other depictions of famous individuals as children seem intended as role models for boys. Certainly the written biographies of men who attained public position provided exemplars for scrutiny and emulation by later generations. Anecdotes about the precocious learning and moral attainment that such men demonstrated as children might have spurred young boys to study hard and cultivate their moral awareness, so that they too could eventually obtain official positions.[53] For this kind of exhortation, however, visual images seem much less effective than written biographies, perhaps because the intangible qualities of erudition and morality are difficult to pictorialize.

The limitations of pictures are vividly demonstrated by an album called *In Celebration of Child Prodigies*, which contains illustrations of anecdotes about eight men of the Han through Tang periods (plate 11). The Tang poet and official Wang Wei (699–759), shown in plate 11, is by far the most renowned of the group.[54] The Qing court artist and official Dai Quheng (1755–1811) created the album at the behest of the Jiaqing emperor (r. 1796–1820), who ordered his son, Prince Miankai (1795–1839), to study it and to write a eulogy for each exemplar. Each illustration shows a generic child engaged in some interaction, usually with several other individuals, within a panoramic landscape. Without the aid of Dai's identifying inscriptions, viewers probably would not recognize most of the children and would miss the point of their stories.

Concluding Remarks

From the preceding discussion, it should be evident that Chinese depictions of the early lives of transcendent figures exhibited a pattern of common elements concerning the manner of conception, birth, and early childhood. The origins of this pattern can be traced to two major sources: textually, the life of Houji in the *Shijing;* pictorially, the life of the Buddha in narrative illustrations associated with the spread of the Indian religion. Illustrated hagiographies of individuals who were regarded as deities or near-deities typically included a miraculous conception, auspicious omens associated with birth, an unusual delivery, and unchildish childhood attainments. Although the textual biographies of exemplary individuals who were merely human sometimes described similar phenomena in the early lives of their subjects, the events were not pictorialized; indeed, the lives of such men generally were not illustrated at all. The practice of illustrating life events in narrative pictures seems to have been reserved for deified individuals who were worshiped by a cult.

6

The Art of Deliverance and Protection: Folk Deities in Paintings and Woodblock Prints

Ann Barrott Wicks

Art objects that celebrate and promote children as an essential family asset are widespread both geographically and chronologically in China. But individual members of the groups that produced these artworks had no effective control over the birth of healthy boys or the protection of young children from disease. Problems with infertility, infant mortality, and desired gender were thus frequently linked with supernatural forces. Stories of malignant spirits harmful to children illustrate the creative methods used to explain what is inexplicable to the human heart, the death or debilitating illness of a child. For example, an early tale recorded in the third century by Gan Bao recounts the origin of a devil whose specialty was to frighten children, then describes steps taken to bring the demon and other evil spirits under human control.

> Of old, Emperor Chuan-hsü had three offspring who, when they died, became baneful ghosts. One haunts the waters of the River and became the pestilence demon, one dwells in Juo River and is known as the "Wang-liang" water spirit, and one inhabits the houses of men, where it specializes in frightening human children—it is known as Little Demon.
>
> After these evils appeared, the hereditary office of the Fang-hsiang family was established, which, on the first day of the new year, was charged with conducting exorcism ceremonies to drive out demons.[1]

It is important to note that the exorcism was performed by an official family on a ritually significant day. While demons may vary from region to region in name or description, the importance of institutional rank and respect for the lunar/agricultural calendar in controlling unknown forces is common to every period and place in Chinese history.

As early as 1500 B.C., heaven was ritually consulted through oracle bones to try to ascertain gender and the likelihood of a safe birthing. Oracle bone graphs existed for pregnancy, parturition, and safe delivery. The most frequently asked questions were about the gender of the expected child, the date of birth, and whether or not the child would be safely delivered. The question "Boy or girl?" was answered with "Good" or "Not good." "Good" indicated that the child would be male.[2] Bronze vessels of the Zhou period, used in ritual sacrifices to imperial ancestors, were also inscribed with phrases related to male progeny. "May sons and grandsons forever treasure and use [this vessel]" was a standard phrase placed at the end of most every inscription, whether that inscription was a lengthy description of the reason the vessel was made, such as to commemorate a military success, or was simply a date. There was a direct connection between the power to rule and the ownership of bronze sacrificial vessels. And the birth of sons and grandsons was essential in order to ensure the continuance of power in successive generations. The inscribed wish embodied both the desire for male descendants and the hope that those descendants would use the vessels properly to revere the ancestors who initially commissioned or otherwise acquired the bronzes.

In later centuries, specific deities became known as child deliverers and child protectors. Visualization of these supernatural beings in paintings and woodblock prints helped popularize the supplication of gods and goddesses for assistance in obtaining sons. The pictures also serve as a colorful record of the enduring fixation of Chinese families on the importance of sons, and the fears associated with the difficulty of raising sons to maturity. These pictures are the subject of this essay. While the essay cannot be exhaustive in its discussion of the very human tendency to appeal to the supernatural in matters of childbirth, it will examine a few specific depictions of child deliverers and protectors in Chinese art that reveal popular conceptions about where to turn for help in getting and keeping sons.

Vaiśravana

During the Tang dynasty (618–906) the Buddhist god Vaiśravana was depicted as a child-bringer in various contexts, including woodblock prints and temple wall paintings. Vaiśravana is the guardian of the North, one of four *lokapala* protecting the cardinal points at the base of Mount Sumeru, the center of the universe in both Vedic and Buddhist cosmology. In India, Vaiśravana was the Buddhist manifestation of the Hindu god of wealth, Kuvera. An early Chinese translation for "Lokapala Vaiśravana" was "Caishen Tianwang" (Heavenly King God of Wealth).[3] The Buddhist iconography for Vaiśravana that spread to East Asia was a warrior carrying reliquary treasure in the form of a pagoda. To the Chinese, no treasure was greater than a child. Thus Vaiśravana as child bearer takes only a short stretch of the imagination.

The concept of Vaiśravana as bringer of sons was strengthened by a miraculous story recorded by the renowned pilgrim Xuanzang (602–664) in *Xiyou ji* (Journey to the West), an account of his travels through Central Asia to India completed in 648. A certain Khotanese king, desperate for an heir, prayed in the temple of Vaiśravana. In answer to his prayers, the head of the central image split open and a child emerged. When the king later asked how to nourish the baby, the earth at the foot of Vaiśravana's image opened and something like a breast appeared for the infant to suckle. Xuanzang reported the story in the context of the origins of Khotan and its people:

> The [present] king is extremely courageous and warlike; he greatly venerates the law of Buddha. He says that he is of the race of Bishamen (Vaiśravana) deva. In old times this country was waste and desert, and without inhabitants. . . .
>
> . . . The [first] King [of Khotan] having built towns and settled the country, and acquired much religious merit, now had arrived at extreme old age and had no successor to the throne. Fearing lest his house should become extinct, he repaired to the temple of Vaiśravana, and prayed him to grant his desire. Forthwith the head of the image opened at the top, and there came forth a young child. Taking it, he returned to his palace. The whole country addressed congratulations to him, but as the child would not drink milk, he feared he would not live. He then returned to the temple and again asked for means to nourish him. The earth in front of the divinity then suddenly opened and offered an appearance like a pap. The divine child drank from it eagerly. Having reached supreme power in due course, he shed glory on his ancestors by his wisdom and courage, and extended far and wide the influence of his laws. Forthwith he raised to Vaiśravana a temple in honour of his ancestors. From that time till now the succession of kings has been in regular order, and the power has been lineally transmitted.[4]

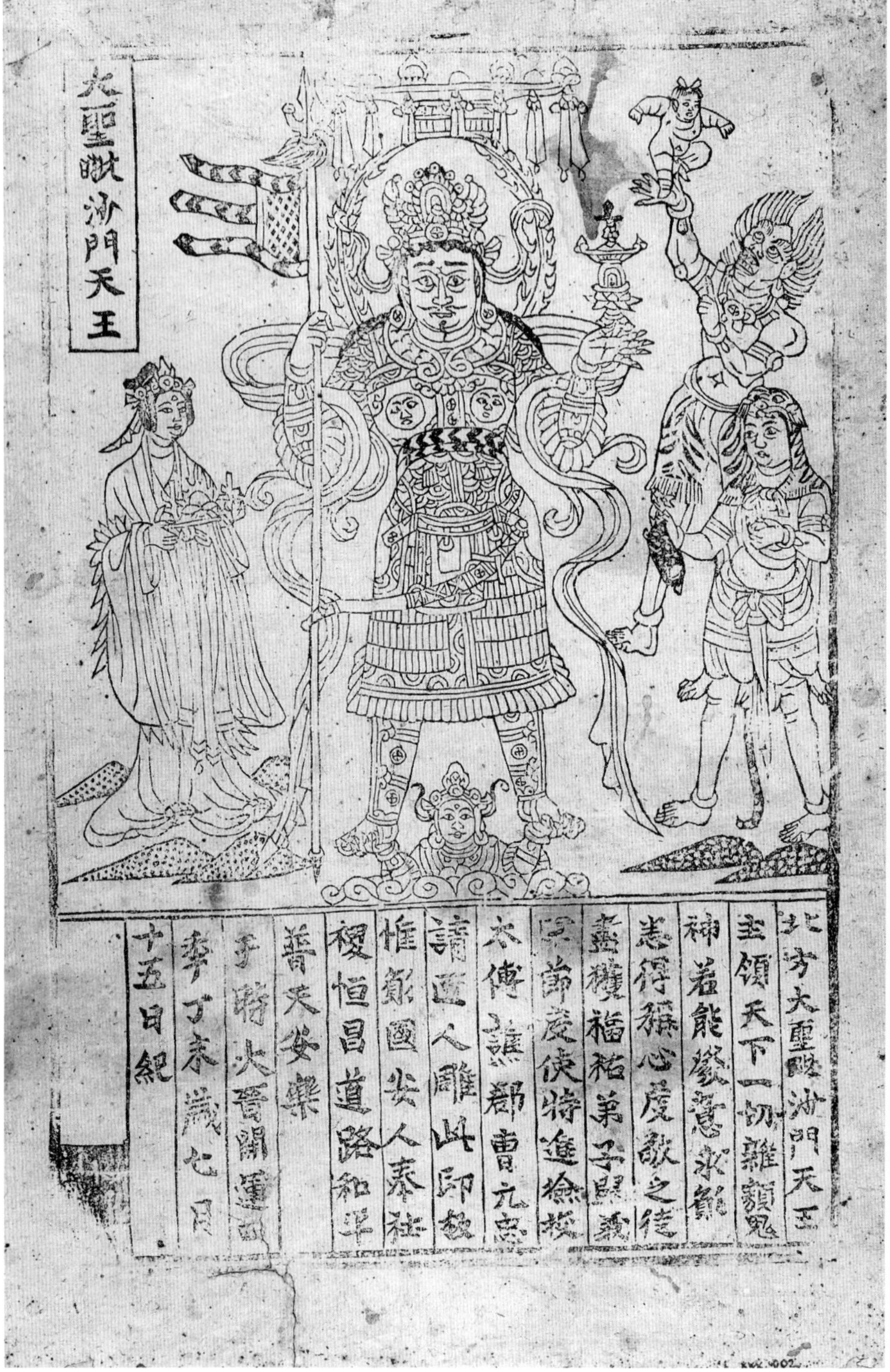

Figure 6.1 Vaiśravana with attendants. 947. Woodblock print; ink on paper; 51 x 32 cm. From Mogao cave 17, Dunhuang. © The British Library, OA 1919.1-1.0245.

The preceding account is an example of Xuanzang's ability to use traditional Chinese values to promote the Buddhist faith. He extolled the Khotanese kings for their veneration of the law of Buddha. As a result of their faith and good works, the former wasteland was civilized and a son was miraculously born to an old king. The building of a Buddhist temple in honor of the king's ancestors ensured the orderly transmission of the right to rule. Nearly every example of the sinicizing of Buddhism appeals to the Chinese sense of filial piety and the need for sons to maintain the patriline. Thus it is not surprising that on thc popular level, some Buddhist deities were transformed into providers of sons.

A single woodblock print, dated to 947, shows Vaiśravana with three attendants, one of whom lifts a baby boy high into the air with one hand (fig. 6.1). He stands under a canopy, his feet resting on the upturned palms of a female figure representing the earth goddess who nurtured the son that Vaiśravana presented to the Khotanese king. In his right hand, he holds a banner, and in his left, a pagoda, symbols common to his representation as Guardian King of the North. An attendant *gandharva* in the lower right corner of the picture holds a jewel-regurgitating mongoose, symbol of Kuvera, as well as a flaming pearl. The figure who holds the child aloft is a *yaksha*, one of twenty-eight demon generals in Vaiśravana's army. On Vaiśravana's right is a female attendant bearing fruit, symbol of fecundity. The inscription reads:

> The great Heavenly King from the North, Vaiśravana is lord of all the earth and every kind of demon and god. If one prays with determination [to Vaiśravana] he will receive all that his heart desires. [Vaiśravana will] do everything possible to give divine help to his humble and devoted followers. The Military Commissioner and Specially Promoted Grand Inspector of Guanyi Pass, Cao Jiuzhong from Qiao prefecture, commissioned an engraver to make this print so that the country would [continue to] have peace and society would prosper, that the roads would be safe and the common people would enjoy happiness. At this time the great Jin [dynasty] has good fortune in all seasons. Recorded on the fifteenth day of the seventh month of the *dingwei* year.[5]

Multiple copies of this print were found in a cache of documents sealed up sometime in the tenth century in cave 17 of the Mogao caves near Dunhuang. One is currently part of the collection of the British Library. Additional copies made from the same block are in the Bibliothèque Nationale in Paris. The print is a tribute to Vaiśravana, commissioned and distributed as a means of supplication. While the inscription invokes general blessings of local prosperity, the illustration refers specifically to Vaiśravana's power to bring children. The practice of distributing multiple copies of prayers was intended to increase one's chances of success in raising a male posterity. Private prayer was not discounted in asking for blessings, but the opportunity to praise a god in public was rarely missed. Chinese folk gods had a very human need for recognition. If one's petition to deity was publicly announced, the god could lose face if he did not respond. On the other hand, if the prayer was answered, all within the realm of the petitioner's circle would be impressed by the power of the god; their faith and contributions to his altar would increase. Through the public distribution of prayers, one could also attain recognition for filial piety. Giving out copies of illustrated words on paper, regardless of whether or not the recipient could read the words, documented the expenditure of personal resources to ensure the patriline and was an effective way to display respect and devotion to one's ancestors.

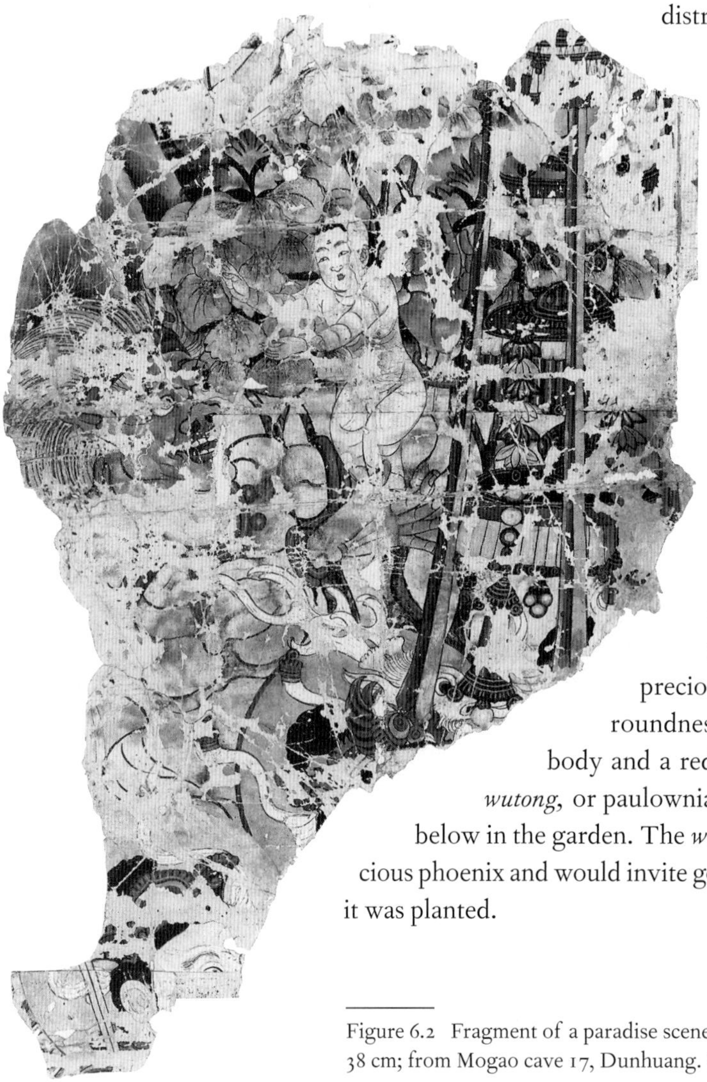

An earlier example of an infant boy held aloft by a demonic attendant to Vaiśravana is found in the fragment of an eighth- or ninth-century painting on paper, also part of the cache hidden at Dunhuang (fig. 6.2). Only the headdress of the guardian king remains, but the entire child has been preserved. The rendering is exquisite: thin, precise lines delineate the figure in the fine style of the high Tang. The child has ruddy cheeks and cinnabar lips, and his folds of precious baby fat are lightly shaded to accentuate the roundness. The *yaksha* who holds him high has a blue body and a red face. The boy is held against a background of *wutong*, or paulownia, leaves presumably growing from a tree rooted below in the garden. The *wutong* tree is the fabled resting place of the auspicious phoenix and would invite good fortune to the owners of any garden in which it was planted.

Figure 6.2 Fragment of a paradise scene. Eighth or ninth century. Ink and colors on paper; 57 x 38 cm; from Mogao cave 17, Dunhuang. © The British Museum, OA1919.1-1.0178 (Ch. 00373.a).

Songzi Guanyin

By the Song period (960–1279), the sinicized Avalokiteshvara, or Guanyin, had eclipsed Vaiśravana's role as child giver. Vaiśravana temples and child-seeking cults continued in northern China, but they played a minor role. As Chinese dominion gradually shifted to the south, indigenous southern folk deities worked their way into the identity of Guanyin. Eventually the bodhisattva assumed a decidedly female character in China that was very different from its Indian origins.[6]

The concept of Guanyin as child giver is based on the twenty-fifth chapter of the *Lotus Sutra*, which describes Guanyin as a savior with thirty-three personifications who has the power to rescue people in peril and the power to grant children. This particular chapter was often printed separately, and assumed great importance in Chinese depictions of Guanyin in art and literature. The passage that declares Guanyin's ability to provide sons is only one of the many reasons to praise the bodhisattva enumerated in the chapter. But the promise is clear and speaks so directly to the Chinese need for sons that it became the basis for the cult of Songzi Guanyin, or "Guanyin, Giver of Sons." As translated by Burton Watson, the passage reads:

> If a woman wishes to give birth to a male child, she should offer obeisance and alms to Bodhisattva Perceiver of the World's Sounds and then she will bear a son blessed with merit, virtue, and wisdom. And if she wishes to bear a daughter, she will bear one with all the marks of comeliness, one who in the past planted the roots of virtue and is loved and respected by many persons.
>
> Inexhaustible Intent, the Bodhisattva Perceiver of the World's Sounds has power to do all this. If there are living beings who pay respect and obeisance to Bodhisattva Perceiver of the World's Sounds, their good fortune will not be fleeting or vain. Therefore living beings should all accept and uphold the name of Bodhisattva Perceiver of the World's Sounds.[7]

The earliest extant depiction of Songzi Guanyin is from a ninth-century illustrated manuscript of the "Guanyin Chapter," preserved at Dunhuang and now part of the Stein collection in the British Library (fig. 6.3).[8] The pictures illustrate each of the "ten perils and two wishes of humankind" to which Guanyin responds, including the wish for a child. This early version is in narrative form, showing first a married couple kneeling before Guanyin. The second picture shows the same woman, in a squatting position, with an infant emerging from under her dress. In this rendition, the mother physically gives birth to the child in answer to prayers to Guanyin. The iconography of Songzi Guanyin established later is very different from this early picture. Ming and Qing depictions consistently show a live infant personally delivered by Guanyin. The parents cease to be included, which makes the picture more economical, and more generally applicable as well. The birth process is also comfortably euphemized by depicting the blessing, a son, without reference to the pain or danger of childbirth.

As late as the thirteenth century, a standard iconography for Songzi Guanyin was still not widespread. Woodblock pictures of Guanyin that were privately commissioned to illustrate printed charms *(dharani)* give few visual clues that the prayers address childlessness. It is only by means of the text that the purpose of the charms becomes clear. The printed prayers contain magical phrases, excerpts from esoteric works that were chanted in supplication, as well as contemporary accounts of individuals whose prayers had been answered. Similar to the tenth-century example of the Vaiśravana print (fig. 6.1), the illustrated charms were produced in multiple copies for distribution among neighbors, friends, and relatives.

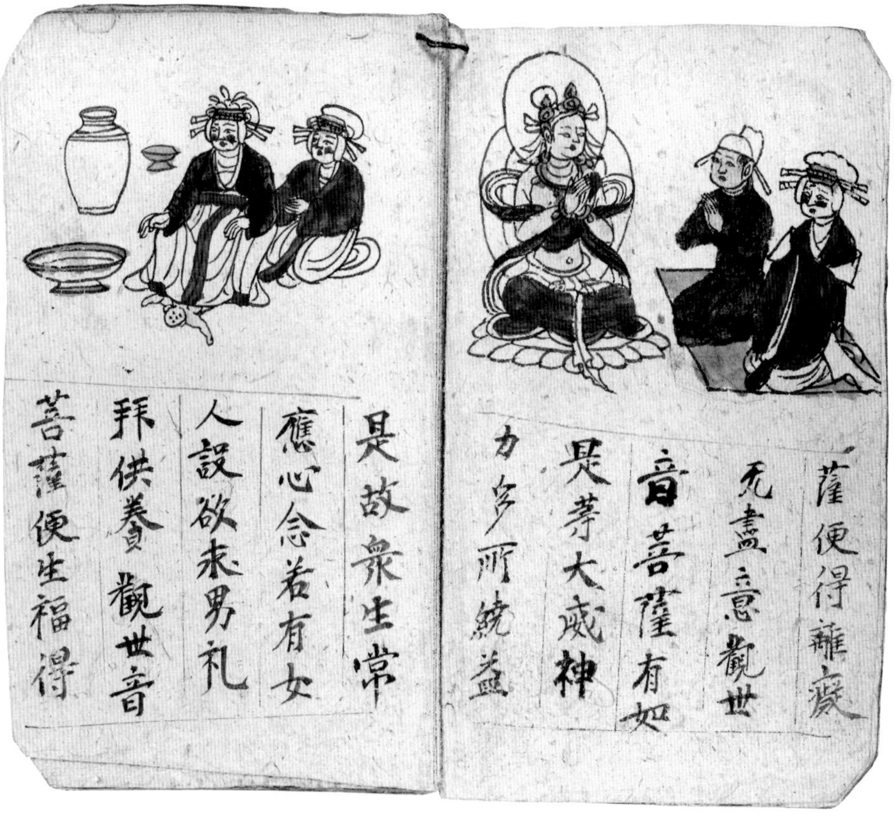

Figure 6.3 Two pages from the illuminated manuscript of the *Guanyin Sutra*, ninth century. Painting on paper; about 17.6 x 17.6 cm; from Mogao cave 17, Dunhuang. © The British Library, S6983.

A rare surviving example of this type of *dharani* illustration, now in a private collection, is shown in figure 6.4. Two *dharani* texts—*Dabeixin tuoluoni jing* (Great Compassion *dharani* sutra) and *Baiyi Dabeixin wuyinxin tuoluoni jing* (White-robed Great Compassion five-mudras *dharani* sutra)—were printed and illustrated as a set of sixteen woodblock sheets that was mounted in a folding format. The *Dabeixin tuoluoni jing* can be found among the canonical texts of the *Tripitaka*. Translated into Chinese in the eighth century, it was immensely popular during the Song period among those seeking the birth of sons. The *Baiyi Dabeixin wuyinxin tuoluoni jing*, on the other hand, is of Chinese origin, a folk document that imitates the style of the doctrinal *dharani*.[9]

The frontispiece to the *Dabeixin tuoluoni jing* (not shown) depicts a very early version of White-robed Guanyin of Putuoshan with attendants Longnü and Shancai—a celestial guardian figure and two human Chinese bureaucrats.[10] The frontispiece for the *Baiyi Dabeixin wuyinxin tuoluoni jing* shows an unusual version of Guanyin, with twelve heads, which perhaps represents a local folk variant of the more typical eleven-headed Guanyin (fig. 6.4, far right). Five human worshipers kneel in the foreground with roughly drawn symbols that presumably represent the five mudras. The inscription reads:

> This is a print of the illustrious twelve-headed bodhisattva whose five mudras mark all living beings. She has completely exorcised the demons [that prevented me from having a son]. These are true words that I wish to publish so that all living beings [will know that my wife is] pregnant.

Following the twelve-headed Guanyin, six scenes illustrate various ways one might approach Guanyin for help in gaining a son. Six different forms of Guanyin are shown in celestial suspension over temple rooms where individuals and families gather to pray. The inscriptions briefly describe the methods used to solicit blessings:

1. Praise to Heluo Dana Duoluoye![11] According to the promise in the sutras, I beseech her for an heir.
2. Praise to the Thatagata! I wholeheartedly take hold of the sutras.
3. This is Puolujie Dishuo Buoluo. To obtain a son, I will print sutras.
4. This is the female bodhisattva. If you support the sutras, she will protect you.
5. This is the great female bodhisattva. Donate sutras and your wish will be fulfilled.
6. This is the great Jialuo Nijia. Perfect the *Tripitaka*.

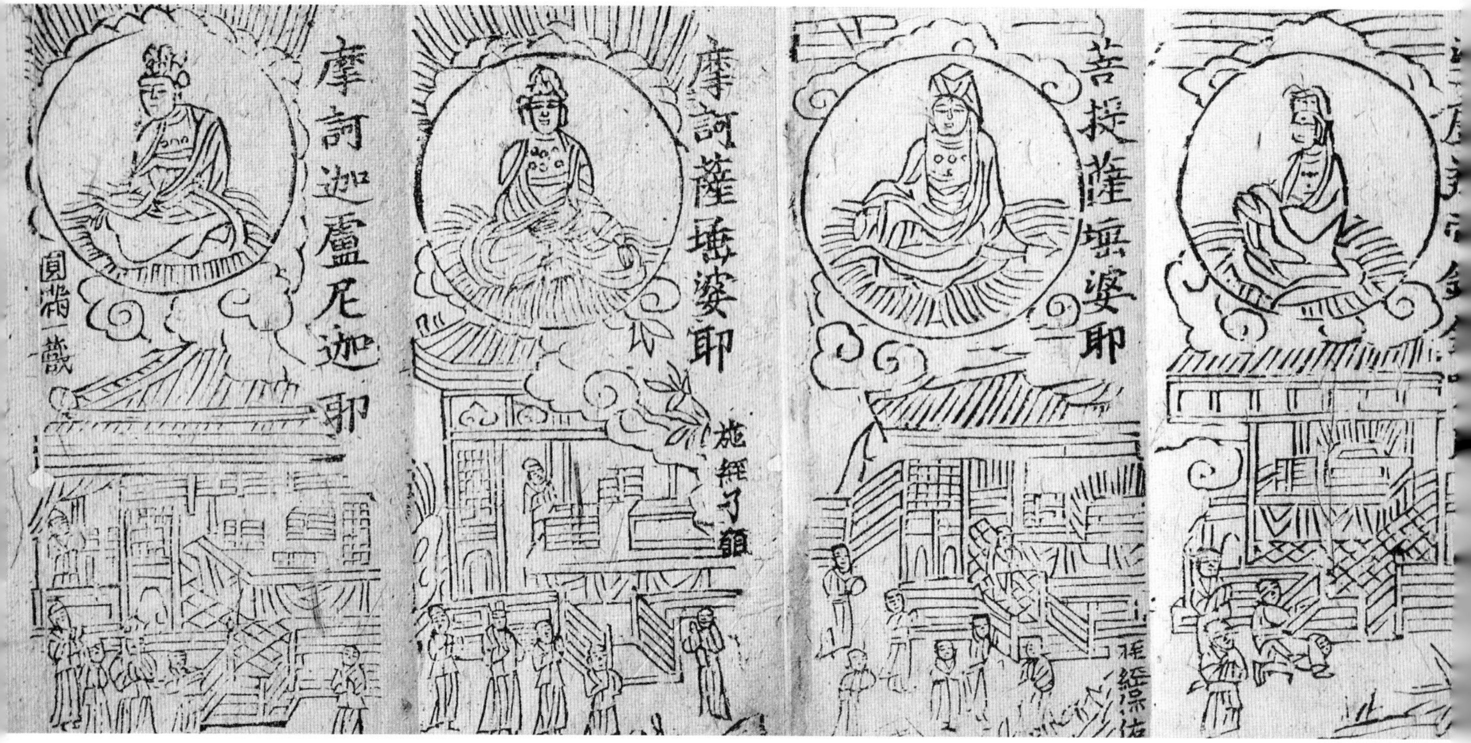

Figure 6.4 Illustrations of Guanyin, from *Dabeixin tuoluoni jing* and *Baiyi Dabeixin wuyinxin tuoluoni jing*, published incantations to get sons. Southern Song, thirteenth century. Woodblock print on hemp paper; each sheet 18.2 x 16.8 cm. Private collection.

The illustrations are crudely drawn and emphasize the faithful acts of the supplicator. There are no infants depicted, but the commentary printed at the end of this set recounts four dated examples of individuals, including Wang Xianchun (1147) and Zheng Zhili (1207), whose distribution of the *Dabeixin tuoluoni jing* resulted in the birth of sons. As translated in the catalogue entry for Sam Fogg, *Chinese Books:*

> Wang Xianchun suffered after the deaths of several of his children, so much so that in the Dingmao year of the Shaoxing reign-period [1147], he obtained this sutra and decided to chant it every day. In the next year, as expected, he had a son. Zheng Zhili, in his forties, from Pujiang county of the Wei prefecture had no heir, so in the Dingmao year of the Kaixi reign-period [1207], he vowed to print this sutra, and in the next year, as expected, he received a son.[12]

No infants are depicted in these thirteenth-century prints, and even the iconography for Guanyin is unstable (though the text indicates quite clearly that Guanyin was already conceived of as female). But by the fourteenth century, the image of a

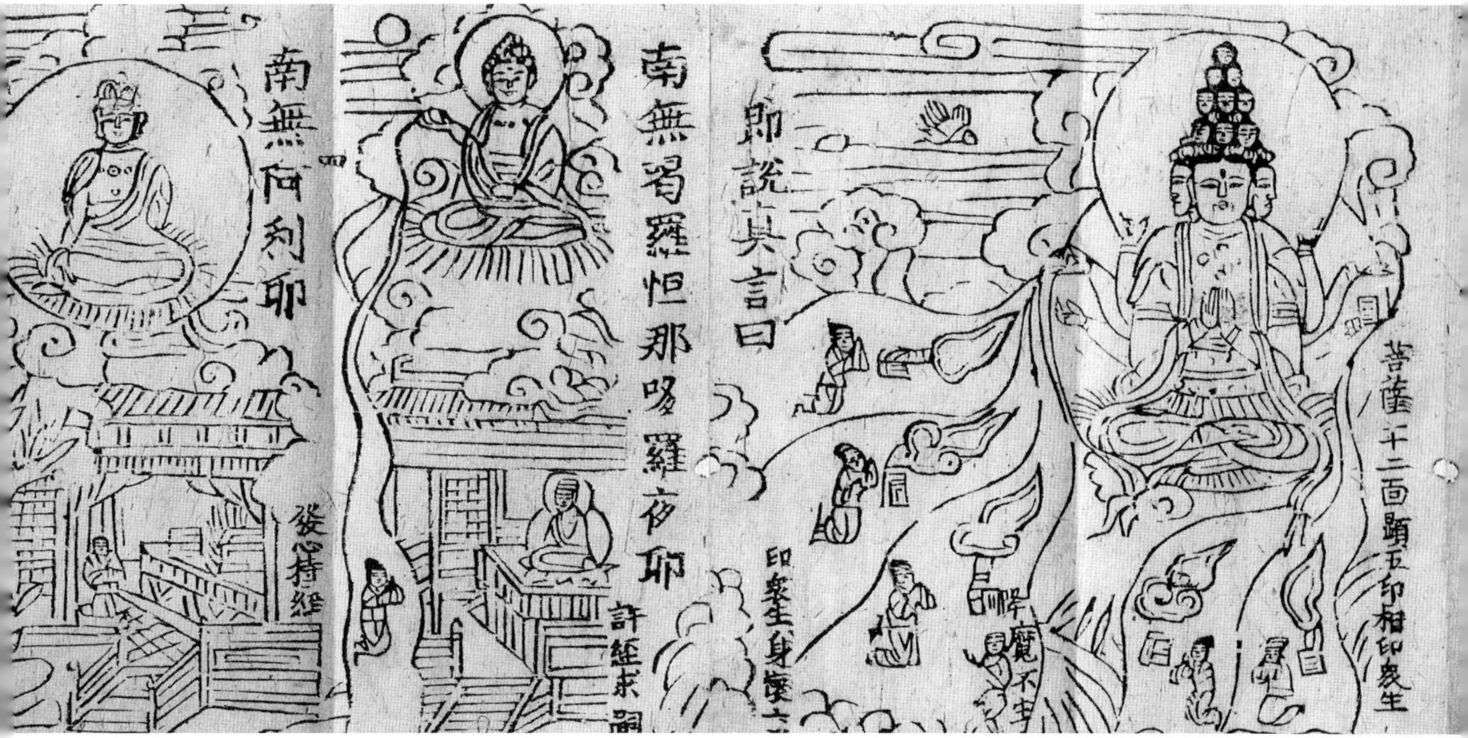

motherly Guanyin holding a precious infant boy was firmly established as the standard iconography for Songzi Guanyin. Whether or not Christian images of Mary and Jesus influenced this change is beyond the scope of this essay, but the pictorial idea that Guanyin would personally deliver the child to her supplicants was widespread in the Ming period (1368–1644). As has been pointed out recently by various authors, government-supported propaganda during the Ming focused on women's role in childbearing and the rearing of virtuous sons to the exclusion of other societal duties. It is thus not surprising that women at every level of society in the late imperial period turned to Guanyin for help. Chinese social lines are blurred in the context of the desire for sons, but the patron's class can often be distinguished by the medium of the commissioned work, if not the inscription. The court and wealthy families had access to lavish materials with which to illustrate Songzi Guanyin, while crudely cut woodblock prints were usually all that common families could afford. In the societal context of wishes for sons, however, it was the ritual action that was important, rather than the form or quality of the artwork.

An elegant court painting made during the early Ming shows a stately Guanyin seated on a royal lion, holding a beautifully jeweled infant boy on her lap (fig. 6.5).

Figure 6.5 Guanyin bestowing a son. Ming, sixteenth century. Hanging scroll; ink, color, and gold on silk; 120.3 x 60 cm. The Metropolitan Museum of Art, 1989.152. Purchase, Friends of Asian Art Gifts, 1989. All rights reserved, The Metropolitan Museum of Art.

A Central Asian youth escorts the descent of the goddess, holding a regal banner decorated with a dragon's head, gourd-shaped fruits, and jewels. Guanyin is also attended by the pilgrim Sudhana (Shancai), who is often shown in the form of a young boy as Guanyin's acolyte. Shancai's sash too is decorated with fruit and jewels. The baby wears a red apron ringed by an imperial belt and carries a large imperial seal in his hands. The seal sets him apart as an heir to the power of the throne. The painting was possibly commissioned by one or more of the imperial wives who hoped to give birth to an heir to the throne. Concern for the imperial line was especially intense at court during the Jiajing reign period (1522–1566), when this painting was most likely made, because the emperor did not produce an heir during the first ten years of his regime. The fact that the Jiajing emperor was not the son of his predecessor, a violation of the rules of succession, made the need for a legitimate heir particularly pressing. The kilns at Jingdezhen, which were under imperial patronage, responded to this concern with an abundance of ceramics decorated with playing children, and frequent representations of the hundred sons of King Wen. This Ming painting was also made for the court. But unlike the prolifically decorated ceramics, which reflect a national concern, this painting seems to embody the private desires of an individual woman for the deliverance of just one royal boy.

Qiu Zhu (second half of the sixteenth century), the daughter of Qiu Ying (ca. 1494–ca. 1552), made an opulent album of twenty-eight pictures of Guanyin in gold ink on black paper, for private consumption. Her depiction of Songzi Guanyin shows the bodhisattva seated on a cloud, playfully pushing a baby boy off the cloud toward Earth (fig. 6.6). The golden wrist and ankle bracelets of the baby, as well as the costly materials with which the images were made, indicate that the album was produced for members of the gentry class.

That the album was also made for someone of considerable intellect is indicated by the inclusion of the *Heart Sutra* as a preface, as well as enigmatic poetry written opposite each leaf that relates the various manifestations of Guanyin to the different means of enlightenment. The inscription facing Songzi Guanyin suggests multiple interpretations of this illustration. The imagery alludes to Guanyin's literal and spiritual rescue of a person in peril of falling, as described in the twenty-fifth chapter of the *Lotus Sutra:*

> Suppose you are on the peak of Mount Sumeru and someone pushes you off. Think on the power of that Perceiver of Sounds and you will hang in midair like the sun! Suppose you are pursued by evil men who wish to throw you down from a diamond mountain. Think on the power of the Perceiver of Sounds and they cannot harm a hair of you![13]

"Falling" is also a symbol for enlightenment. The falling *infant* can be interpreted positively as the pure self, free of attachments and open to enlightenment. Or it can represent casting off of the shackles of ignorance (in the form of an infant's perception of the world) as one's mind is illumined by the teachings of Buddha.

Figure 6.6 Qiu Zhu (1550–1580), copy of *Thirty-two Manifestations of Guanyin*, illustrations and poetry by Li Gonglin (1049–1106). Album leaf thirteen of twenty-eight; gold on black paper; 29.9 x 22 cm. Private collection.

Guanyin as child giver persisted in the visual arts throughout the Qing period (1644–1911), showing up in the private, intellectually oriented art of the Confucian scholars as well as in public places and among the common people. A subdued literati-style painting done by Liu Rong in 1845, shows Guanyin seated on a rock, a white robe covering her jeweled crown (fig. 6.7). The calligraphic brush, the seals, and the inscriptions set this painting apart as one made for those with literary tastes. The simplicity of White-robed Guanyin was favored by Chan Buddhists and thus appealed to Neo-Confucian intellectuals. The bamboo and rock symbolize the meditative forms of Guanyin; they are also preferred scholarly motifs. In the literati tradition, the artist has paid particular attention to the presentation of the rock and bamboo. But then Liu Rong unexpectedly placed a red-robed child in the lap of this figure meditating in nature. The child *(zi)* reaches for a branch of *osthmansus (gui)*, forming a pun for a "precious and talented son" *(guizi)*, the kind of boy who would attain officialdom. Around his neck is a *changmingsuo*, or long-life locket, worn by children to symbolically lock them to mortal life. While men of the educated class relied on themselves to provide their sons with the classical training necessary for ascension to power, they could not control the actual birth and preservation of sons. It was not beyond the scope of this powerful elite to seek the aid of Guanyin. The inscription says:

> In the 25th year of the Daoguang era (1845), in the winter month of the *yi si* cycle, I respectfully painted this ninety-fourth incarnation of Guanyin. May it be broadly disseminated in the ten directions, as an offering made to my ancestors. May there be wealth and blessings according to their wishes, through the influence of merciful Guanyin. The devoted disciple, Liu Yongzhi (*h.* Henan).

While Liu Rong's combination of the white-robed and child-giving forms of Guanyin may have been intentional, folk renditions of the goddess were almost always an unconscious amalgamation of pleasing symbols from various sources. An early-twentieth-century woodblock print is labeled *Baiyi Songzi Guanyin* (White-robed Child-giving Guanyin) (plate 12). Crudely cut and mass-produced for sale as a New Year print, the picture illustrates that the patrilineal values of the court and gentry were imitated among the lower classes. It also illustrates the delightful mixture of motifs that is common in popular art. The willow and rock are consistent with traditional iconography for the white-robed Guanyin, but the lotus seat belongs to another Buddhist genre altogether. Pine branches and bamboo, favored by the literati as longevity symbols, are arbitrarily added as well. In late imperial China, gentlemen with classical educations were highly esteemed, and the most likely to wield power and wealth. The families of these literate men counted on their sons to prolong their prominence, and schooled them accordingly. While lower-class families in reality had little chance to provide their sons with the education necessary to advance their social position, they nonetheless adopted the symbolism of the literati for use in New Year pictures. In this example in plate 12, the precious little boy held by Guanyin is even dressed in a miniature scholar's robe.

Bestowers of Children Depicted in Late-Qing New Year Prints: Three Star Gods, General Baotong, the Qilin, and Goddess of Taishan

Children are a prolific subject of New Year pictures, symbolically conveying the best possible wishes for the coming year. In late Qing woodblock prints, many pictures

Figure 6.7 Liu Rong (*h.* Yanchong), *Songzi Guanyin*. Late Qing, 1845. Hanging scroll; ink and color on paper; 69 x 29.3 cm. Shanghai Museum.

of child givers were made for the New Year. Those bringing children appear in various forms in the prints, including Three Star Gods, General Baotong, the *qilin*, and Goddess of Taishan. Three Star Gods (Sanxing)—Happiness, Wealth, and Longevity—are an obvious pictorial choice for child givers because the blessings they bestow are most easily realized through the gift of sons. Depictions of the three nearly always show them surrounded by little boys, and in some cases, they are shown actually bringing an infant son to a family. In figure 6.8, the god Happiness holds an infant in his arms, symbolizing the gift of sons as the most sure means to felicity. In this picture, as typical of many depictions of Three Star Gods, Longevity is shown as an old man with white beard and balding, extended cranium, while Happiness and Wealth are depicted as scholar-bureaucrats. In the popular mind, the power and prestige of government officials were such that their dress was suitable for deity. In fact, beginning in the twelfth century, local deities at times were actually granted official titles by human beings.[14] As judicial bureaucrats wielded the power to decide a person's fate, it was not a very big stretch of the imagination to believe them capable of presenting sons, at least in pictorial form. To pictorialize a child giver in the guise of a provincial judge sympathetic to the needs of the populace was indeed an appropriate sign of good fortune in the coming year. The wish that sons become eminent

Figure 6.8 *The Three Star Gods*. Early twentieth century. Woodblock print; ink and color on paper; 60 x 100 cm. Museum of the History of Religion, St. Petersburg. After Maria Rudova, *L'imagerie populaire chinoise* (Leningrad: Aurora Art Publishers, 1988), no. 62.

officials might also have been embodied in the representation of the child giver as scholar-official.

Another powerful human office, that of general, is represented by Baotong Jiangjun, initially a child protector. With his horse as a ready means of conveyance, the humanlike General Baotong was easily transformed from protector to deliverer. The infant boy rides in front of the general, enveloped in his bosom (plate 13).

The *qilin* is one of four mythical beasts in China that symbolize good fortune, along with the dragon, the phoenix, and the tortoise. It has been associated with progeny at least as far back as the fourth century B.C., forming the imagery of one of the songs in the *Shijing* (Book of odes) that celebrates the sons and grandsons of King Wen.[15] As discussed by Julia Murray in chapter 5 of this volume, the divine elements that magnified the importance of the birth of Confucius included the deliverance of a jade tablet to his mother by a *qilin*. The *qilin* was depicted in art as early as the Song period and became a standard subject for New Year prints in the Qing period. Often a beautiful young woman accompanies the boy and *qilin* in elaborately designed prints (fig. 6.9). The woman undoubtedly symbolizes motherhood and fertility, but she is also a fetching decorative addition, and an extension of the felicitous greetings of the New Year.

Pictures of Goddess of Taishan, whose mountain abode was visited by child-seeking pilgrims in the Qing period, are rare compared to the many versions of the child-bestowing Guanyin and are found primarily in northern China in the form of woodblock prints. Also called Tianxian Niangniang (Immortal Empress) and Bixia Yuanjun (Princess of the Dawn Clouds), the goddess of Taishan lives at the summit of Mount Tai, the most eminent of the five sacred peaks of China, located in Shandong province. She is usually considered the daughter of the god of Mount Tai, magistrate of the underworld whose temple is at the base of the mountain. Her cult began to build after the Song emperor Zhenzong, on an excursion in 1008 to Mount Tai, discovered an image of a female deity and built a temple for her. By the end of the Ming dynasty, she and her eight attendants were strongly associated with childbirth and child protection.[16] In the early Qing period, hundreds of temples built for her flourished throughout northern China. At her Mount Tai shrine alone, each spring thousands of women and couples made pilgrimages to petition the goddess for children. Women took dolls from the altars of her temples, to keep at home until a child was born. The doll, or a new one, was then returned to the temple along with thanks offerings of food and money.[17]

An early-twentieth-century New Year print (fig. 6.10) shows Goddess of Taishan as the central figure in a trinity, flanked by two of her attendants, Son-granting Goddess (Songzi or Songsheng Niangniang) and Goddess of Eyesight (Yanguang

Niangniang).[18] Each of the three wears a pigeon headdress, one of the few distinguishing iconographical symbols of the deities of this cult. Two phoenixes decorate the sleeves of the central figure's robe, and in this figure's hands is a jade memorial tablet. The characters for *moon* and *sun* on the front of her robe represent the dual aspects of Chinese cosmology, *yin* (female/moon) and *yang* (male/sun). A female holding an infant boy stands in front of the son-granting goddess. On the other side of the altar, in front of the goddess of eyesight, a male holds an eye. The man and woman are shown delivering celestial gifts—a son and healthy eyes. They also represent a filial son and daughter-in-law who pray to the goddess of Taishan for blessings for their parents. On the altar in front of the goddesses are an infant boy and an eye, placed on either side of the candles and incense burner. These represent the cloth or ceramic eyes and the dolls made of various materials including silver and

Figure 6.9 *Qilin Songzi.* Early twentieth century. Pair of woodblock prints; ink and color on paper; 108 x 61 cm. Hermitage Museum, 4947, 4948. After Maria Rudova, *L'imagerie populaire chinoise* (Leningrad: Aurora Art Publishers, 1988), nos. 35–36.

Figure 6.10 Tianxian Niangniang (Immortal Empress; Goddess of Taishan). Early twentieth century. Woodblock print; ink and color on paper; 48 x 40 cm. Hermitage Museum, 3485. After Maria Rudova, *L'imagerie populaire chinoise* (Leningrad: Aurora Art Publishers, 1988), no 11.

gold (depending on the wealth of the petitioners) that were offered at the shrines of the goddess of Taishan in gratitude for the blessings of children and healed eyes.[19]

As with Guanyin, the powers of the goddess of Taishan were not limited to granting children. Initially no Chinese god was specifically a child bringer. But as the popularity of a deity such as Guanyin or Goddess of Taishan increased, and tales of her miracles grew, she inevitably became a provider of the most sought-after commodity in China: sons. The high status of child giver evolved from an already well-established record of other impressive feats.

Child Protectors

The birth of a son is only the first step in meeting filial duties. The child must also survive and be taught to carry out familial obligations. Anxiety over the health and welfare of male children inspired a colorful array of deities assigned to protect the sons of the folk. While the educated elite relied heavily on written knowledge in the form of pharmaceutical texts and Confucian moral instruction to guide and preserve their sons, they also actively used the iconography of protective deities in their art.

An early example of the visual conception of child protectors is a set of three rectangular leaves of paper with animal-headed figures painted on both sides of each leaf, made in the ninth century and preserved at Dunhuang (fig. 6.11). The leaves were originally strung together, as indicated by a center hole cut in each leaf. One of the inscriptions, for the stag-headed figure, refers to "sixteen female spirits protecting small children," which indicates that the three leaves probably belonged to a set of eight.[20] The one feature that distinguishes each of the spirits as female is a pair of large breasts, which appear heavy with nourishment. Each figure is accompanied by a child, but that child is more often shown in a dangerous rather than a protected position. For example, the cat-headed deity holds the infant upside down, grasping it by the wrists and ankles, while the boar-headed deity stands over an infant strapped to a narrow wooden bench. Each picture is inscribed with the name of the

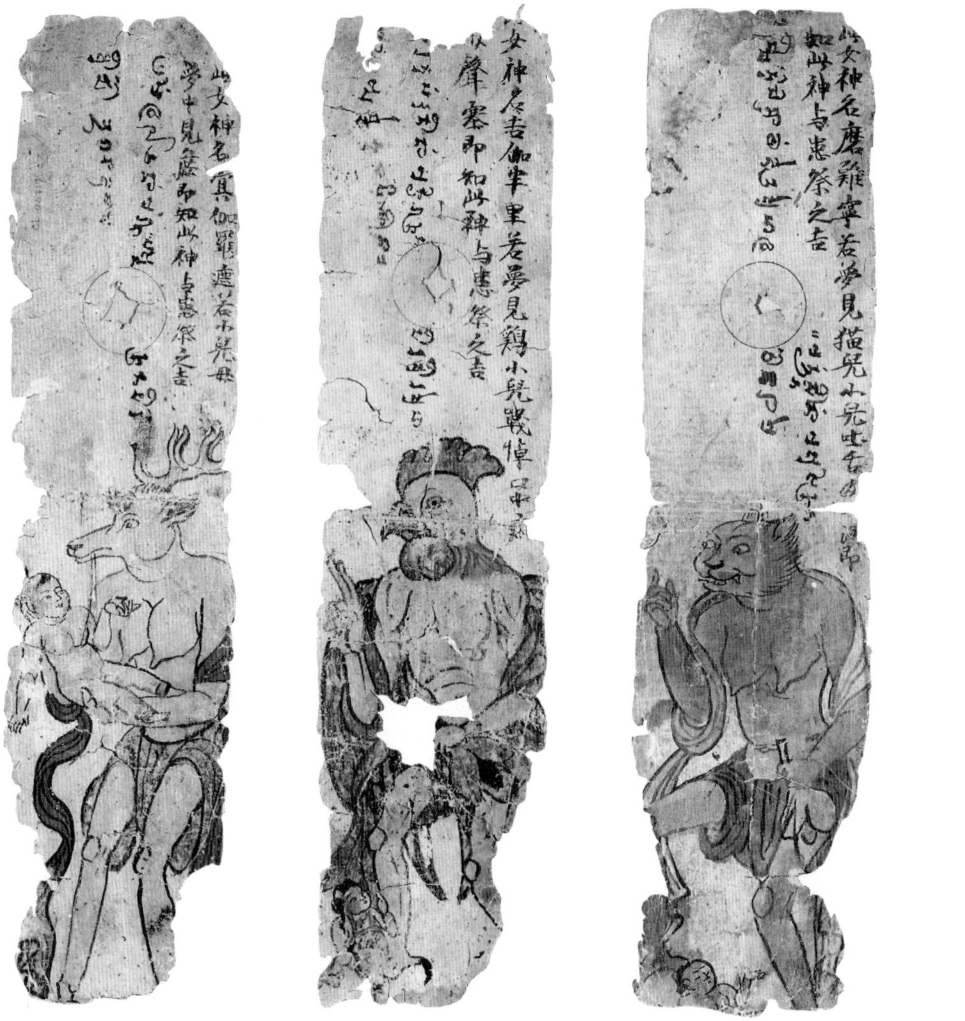

Figure 6.11 Six female spirits to protect children. Ninth century. Ink on paper; each leaf 8 x 33 cm. From Mogao cave 17, Dunhuang. © The British Museum, Stein collection, OA 1919.1-1.077.

deity and a short description of how to appease her to avoid a specific malady. Both pictures and text reveal deep fear of childhood illness, as well as strong distrust of supernatural forces.[21] The inscriptions that accompany the illustrations are translated following figure 6.11.

1. This female spirit's name is Yijialuozhe.[22] If the small son's mother sees a roe in a dream, then she will know this spirit intends harm. A sacrificial offering will restore good fortune.
2. This female spirit's name is Jijialaoli. If a chicken is seen in a dream, and if the small boy is terrified, has sores in his mouth, and is unable

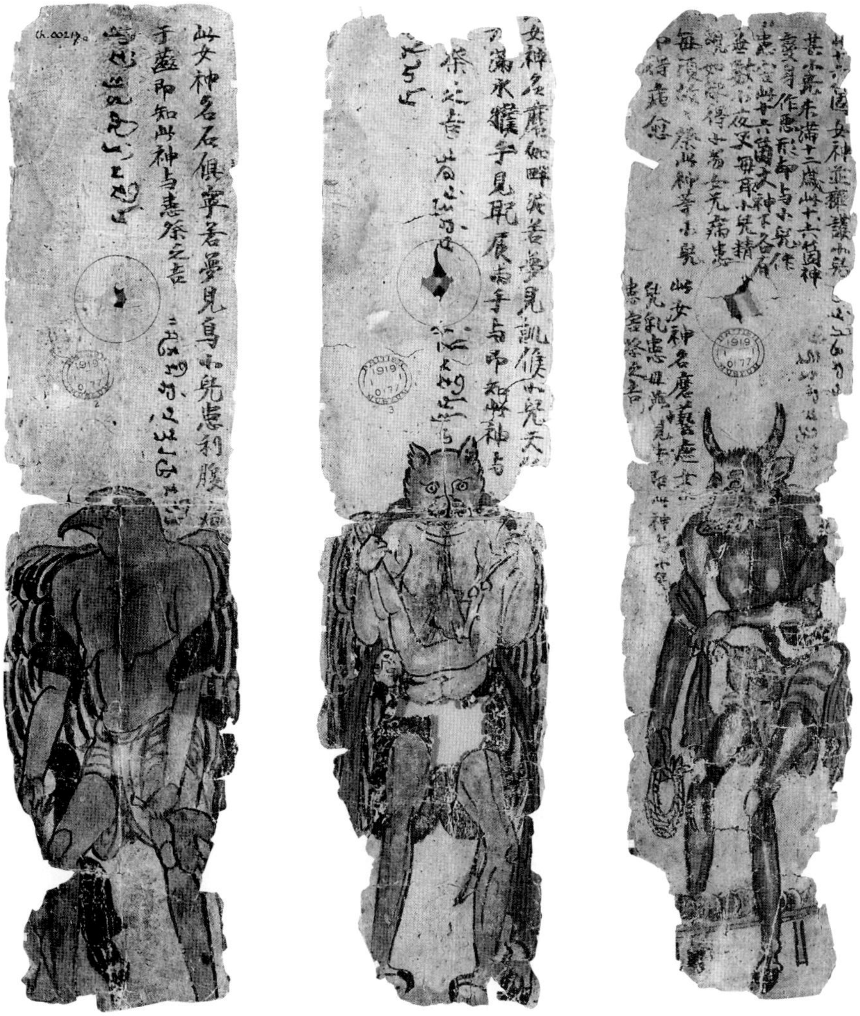

to utter a sound, then you will know this spirit caused the malady and you must sacrifice to it.

3. This female spirit's name is Monanning. If a cat is seen in a dream, and the boy's tongue is thrust out, you will know this spirit must be sacrificed to in order to overcome the malady.
4. This female spirit's name is Shizhuning. If a bird is seen in a dream, and the boy has diarrhea and abdominal pains, then you will know the malady comes from this spirit. If you sacrifice to it, all will be well.
5. This female spirit's name is Mojiabanni. If a beast is seen in a dream, the boy will contract smallpox, with sores full of pus. If you see pox on

Figure 6.12 Archer with children. Qing, eighteenth century. Hanging scroll; ink and colors on silk; 114.5 x 75 cm. Musée des Arts Asiatiques-Guimet, Paris MG20S85. © Photo RMN-Ravaux.

his neck and hands, you will know the malady comes from this spirit. If you sacrifice to it, the child will get better.

6. This female spirit's name is Moyizhinü. If the mother's breast milk is bad and she sees an ox in a dream, then this spirit will harm the small son. Sacrifice to it, and the child will be fine.

Postscript on leaf 6. These sixteen female spirits can protect small boys under the age of twelve, but they can also change their bodies into evil forms to harm them. Each heavenly spirit has countless small demons *(yakshas)* under her who frequently seize the souls of children. If a mother detects these small changes [in her child] and wants to avoid severe illness, she must frequently and conscientiously sacrifice to these spirits and pray until the child is healed.

The iconography of animal-headed figures with milk-laden breasts did not become part of the standard visual repertoire beyond the ninth century, but another source of possible danger to getting and preserving sons, introduced in the Song period in the form of Dog Star (Gou Jing), is recognizable in a variety of illustrations. The fate of families who were plagued with infertility or a high rate of infant mortality was said to be determined by this particular star. The means for reversing this fate was apparently constructed by Lady Fei, wife of the last ruler of the Later Shu state (935–965), after her husband was killed and she was added to the harem of the conquering founder of the Song dynasty, Emperor Taizu (r. 960–976). Lady Fei had retained a portrait of her beloved husband, Meng Chang, who was a renowned archer. When questioned, she claimed that it was a picture of Zhang Xian, a somewhat obscure deity prayed to by women desirous of sons. The bow and arrow were explained as tools used to divert Dog Star and change the fate of childless couples.[23]

Figure 6.13 Zhang Xian shooting Dog Star. Qing, Kangxi period, 1662–1722. Porcelain vase; 44.5 cm. Photo Copyright © Asian Art Museum of San Francisco.

This particular theme was conducive to pictorial representation—in fact, the origin of the theme itself was a picture—and there are a number of examples extant from the Ming and Qing periods. Scrolls and ceramic vases depicting the archer Zhang Xian were used to decorate the bedroom and are thus not uncommon objects. An eighteenth-century painting in the Musée Guimet is typical of the standard representation (fig. 6.12). Zhang Xian is portrayed as a Confucian scholar surrounded by seven boys of various ages. The humanization of Zhang Xian, or Immortal Zhang, is not surprising, considering the origins of the first "representation" of him in painting. But it also reinforces the Confucian idea of the moral control of the superior man over bad elements. Seven sons are an especially lucky number because of the similarity in sound between *qi* (seven) and *ji* (propitious). The inscription reads:

> Ten thousand generations to the prince. Painted three days before the Qingming Festival in the fifth year of the Yongzheng reign (1728) by Jiang Tingxi from Nansha.

The date, three days before the Qingming festival, suggests that the painting was made for presentation as a holiday gift. Festivals in general were times of exorcism in China, and the Qingming festival, held in late spring, was associated in particular with expelling disease-causing spirits prior to the arrival of summer heat.

A Kangxi-period vase in the Asian Art Museum of San Francisco is another typical example of Zhang Xian shooting Dog Star (fig. 6.13). Flanked by two boys, Zhang Xian takes aim with his bow, in the upper register of the vase. Below, a group of palace women gathered on a terrace suggest a holiday theme, again tying exorcism to state-sponsored festivals.

The spirits illustrated in the preceding examples were initially malign but brought under control through human or humanlike intervention. This is the very same theme as found in the Gan Bao tale from the third century quoted in the first paragraph of this chapter. While the supernatural was highly important in determining the source of human misfortune, the role of individual mortals was also significant. Tension in the balance of power between natural and supernatural in controlling the birth and survival of sons has been an underlying theme of Chinese stories since at least the third century, and of pictorial subject matter since at least the Tang period. The more crucial the need for sons, the more the power shifted away from human

Figure 6.14 Procession of deities. Ming, 1443. Mural painting at Fahai Temple, near Beijing, left side of north wall. After *Fahaisi bihua* (Beijing: China Travel and Tourism Press, 1993), pl. 55.

beings. The child-devouring Hariti was a menace so strong that it required the power of Shakyamuni Buddha himself to bring her under control. In India, Hariti was originally one of the demonic *yakshini*. She married Pancika, the chief of twenty-eight *yaksha* generals in the army of Vaiśravana, and gave birth to five hundred demon sons. Human parents appealed to Buddha to stop Hariti from eating their children. Buddha then hid Hariti's youngest son under Buddha's alms bowl, keeping him there until Hariti converted to Buddhism and became a vegetarian. Buddha instructed his human followers to supply food offerings for Hariti at each monastery. From that time, Hariti became both a symbol of fertility and a child protector.

When Xuanzang visited Northern India in the eighth century, he found a sculpted or painted image of Hariti with at least one child, near the dining hall door of every monastery.[24] By that time, the cult of Hariti had also become popular in China, where she was nicknamed Guizi Mu, Mother of Demon Sons. Hariti was not a child giver in China, most likely because of the Chinese proclivity to avoid *gui*. Nobody wanted a demon son. Rather, her protection was sought for sons already born. No doubt, as the mother of five hundred boys, not one of whom she was willing to give up, she was viewed as an enormously successful protectress.

Julia Murray has pointed out that Chinese artists developed an iconography for depictions of Hariti that was unique in Asia. Focusing on the dramatic confrontation between Buddha and Hariti's demon army who fought to free her imprisoned son, the forces of good appear on one side of a handscroll, opposing the forces of evil on the other, with the child under the alms bowl in the middle.[25] The love of duality in China is enough to explain this particular representation. But the lengths to which Hariti goes to recover her son are also noteworthy, and surely were another compelling reason for the popularity of this depiction. The personal concession required of Hariti—the renunciation of a favorite food—might have been one of those models of self-sacrifice that were constantly held up to women, especially during the Ming period. There is the message strongly conveyed in this subject that nothing is more important than a son.

Illustrations of Hariti's confrontation with Shakyamuni are most often in the form of handscrolls. Ming temple murals and large ritual paintings, which are far more public compositions than the handscroll, focus on a different representation of Hariti, that of a beautiful court woman in Shakyamuni's entourage (fig. 6.14). For a religious setting, the converted Hariti—one of a grand procession of lesser gods that accompanies the Buddha—is an appropriately impressive subject. In Chinese temple versions, Hariti is consistently shown with an exquisitely beautiful boy child dressed in red.[26] The focus is still on the precious son, who has now been returned to her and never leaves her side (plate 14). The child symbolizes the orthodox ideal that boys are coveted, pampered, and educated by their mothers, and protected by the gods. This ideal was continually reinforced in Ming visual culture—in public and private paintings, in illustrated books, and in the decorative arts.

Conclusion

In China, every family had access at some level to divine intervention. The paintings and prints discussed above were an important visual reminder of the power of the gods to act on behalf of human believers. The most powerful of the folk deities were envisioned as child givers. The pictures were also used to celebrate past blessings and to predict good fortune for the future. The association of children with prosperity is especially apparent in artworks of the late-imperial period, when depictions of children in the company of gods were given as gifts and greeting cards. The proliferation of child givers and child protectors illustrated in art reinforced the Confucian dogma of order in the universe. The art illustrates man's elaborate attempts to maintain control of forces only poorly understood, the forces that governed successful pregnancy, uneventful birth, and preservation of male offspring.

7

Family Pictures

Ann Barrott Wicks

The most important institutional affiliation in imperial China was the family. It was regarded as both the embodiment of civilization and the means of transcending death. Yet who among us who have studied traditional Chinese art can name more than a handful of works that depict the family as a unit? Of the pictures that do exist, none before the Qing period (1644–1911) could be considered an actual likeness of a real family. The few paintings that show a mother and father together with their children illustrate set themes. They are prototypes with strong cultural messages, including the insignificance of the emotional bond of the nuclear family when it conflicts with the interests of the extended patrilinear family.

According to Chinese mythology of the Han period (206 B.C.–A.D. 220), it was the culture-bearing deity Fuxi who introduced marriage when he united with his sister Nüwa, the independent creator-goddess in earlier Chinese myth.[1] Because of the importance in Han civilization of the marriage unit, Han artists depicted these deities as a couple initiating human life together, which strengthened the importance of marital ties. Figures carved on Han stone funerary walls show the pair as anthropomorphic beings with serpentine tails entwined to symbolize their union. While earlier accounts of Nüwa tell how she fashioned tiny clay figures that became the first human beings, giving her the role of creator, Han writers emphasized in their versions of the story the civilizing aspect of the institution of marriage and gave credit to the male god for his part in ordering society. The Eastern Han historian Ban Gu (d. A.D. 92) gave this interpretation of the legend:

> In the beginning there was yet no moral nor social order. Men knew their mothers only, not their fathers. When hungry, they searched for

food; when satisfied, they threw away the remnants. They devoured their food hide and hair, drank the blood, and clad themselves in skins and rushes. Then came Fuxi and looked upward and contemplated the images in the heavens, and looked downward and contemplated the five occurrences on earth. He united man and wife, regulated the five stages of change, and laid down the laws of humanity.[2]

Han tomb art, albeit infrequently, provides the first visual representations of the family in Chinese art. In one of the ceiling carvings at the Wu Liang shrines in Shandong province (second century A.D.), a child-sized figure clings to the sleeves of Fuxi and Nüwa (fig. 7.1). The child represents the purpose of marriage, which even before the Han period was primarily to produce offspring for the continuance of the patriline. While the parents are immortal and the child symbolizes humankind, this appears to be the first depiction in Chinese art of a "family."

Another family scene at the Wu Liang shrines illustrates the story of Zhu Ming, a man who placed his relationship to his profligate younger brother above the concerns of his wife (fig. 7.2). In one version of the story, he went so far as to divorce his wife for criticizing his brother. The carving shows Zhu Ming at the far right and his wife on the opposite far left. His younger brother stands next to him, gesturing at the woman to depart. Next to Zhu Ming's wife is their son, who clings to his mother's sleeve in an attempt to prevent her from leaving. The brother stands between Zhu Ming and his wife and child, indicating his role in the disruption of the family. Thus, ironically, the representation of a human family that survives in Han art is

Figure 7.1 Fuxi and Nüwa. Han, second century. Rubbing of stone ceiling carving from the Wu Liang shrine, Jiaxiang, Shandong. After Wu Hung, *The Wu Liang Shrine: The Ideology of Early Chinese Pictorial Art* (Stanford: Stanford University Press, 1989), 246.

Figure 7.2 The story of Zhu Ming. Han, second century. Rubbing of stone wall carving from the Wu Liang shrine. After Wu Hung, *The Wu Liang Shrine*, 293.

of a group in disharmony, despite Han rhetoric of the civilizing function of marriage.

Textual sources praise Zhu Ming's exemplary loyalty to his brother, without even mentioning children or the impact such an action might have on a child. But the artist added his own editorial views in depicting the close attachment of Zhu Ming's son to his mother. Standing aloof on the right, Zhu Ming hardly seems a heroic figure in this depiction of his story. But he is a sterling example of the Han virtue of performing one's public duty *(yi)*, despite the private love *(si ai)* that might motivate lesser men.[3] The closeness between mother and son in the picture reinforced Han ideas that the moral education of children was the responsibility of the mother and began even while the child was in the womb.[4] It is also an example of the vulnerability of and insecurity of life for Han children that Anne Kinney and Wu Hung have explained in insightful new interpretations of Han literature and art.[5] These early depictions of families serve the dual purpose of illustrating the importance of progeny for the continuation of ancestral rights (as in fig. 7.1) and teaching Confucian beliefs about public duty (fig. 7.2). But there is no indication from the art that Han people saw childhood as a specific stage of development, or that children were valued for themselves and should be nurtured accordingly.

There is a wide gap between Han tomb figures and the next example of art, in which children are seen with both parents. It is a detail of a handscroll attributed to the fourth-century painter Gu Kaizhi (ca. 345–ca. 406) that illustrates a text by Zhang Hua (232–300), *Admonitions of the Court Instructress to the Imperial Concubines* (plate 15). In contrast to Han representations of children as miniature adults, the boys in this painting are unmistakably children, their shaved heads tufted in the *zongjiao* style and their clothing distinct from the men in the painting. Unlike those in Han stories, these royal children are safely shielded from harm, by the parents who surround them. At the far right, the emperor sits with his principal wife, facing two imperial concubines and fondly gazing at his children as they tumble playfully around the knees of their mothers. This intimate and harmonious group forms the base of a pyramid of figures, adding compositional stability to the harmonious tone of the painting. At the apex, and slightly removed from the others, is an older boy with his tutor and a young female servant. His separation from the younger boys, and his elegant headgear, indicates that he is the heir apparent.

The instructions to the palace women, which accompany this scene, include the line, "Let your heart be as a swarm of locusts and your race shall multiply,"[6] which alludes to songs in praise of Lady Taisi from the *Shijing* (Book of odes). Taisi was the virtuous wife of King Wen, legendary father of the first ruler of the Zhou dynasty, King Wu (r. 1122–1115 B.C.). Her generosity and freedom from jealousy allowed her to recruit other meritorious women to join her as wives of King Wen. As a result of her example, the wives lived harmoniously together, and King Wen's progeny numbered a hundred sons.[7] Thus they were like locusts who cluster in swarms and multiply plentifully. Although the ode does not refer to Taisi or King Wen by name, Confucian commentators read the poem metaphorically as a song in her praise:

> Ye locusts, winged tribes,
> How harmoniously you collect together!
> Right is it that your descendants
> Should be multitudinous![8]

The manner in which the children are depicted in this painting reinforces Osvald Sirén's suggestion that it was not painted by Gu Kaizhi, but was a later copy, perhaps of the Tang (618–906) or early Song (960–1279) period.[9] An attribution to the Song period seems probable based on the humanistic rendering of the figures. Because they were made in the "style" of Gu Kaizhi, the *Admonitions* scroll figures have an archaic flavor, giving them the appearance of "pre-Tang." The Tang style of lovely, round, symbolic children seems to have been purposely avoided. The figures are at the same time drawn in naturalistic poses that soften the didactic symbolism of the family group, a method more characteristic of Song art than Tang. Three separate stages of male maturation are distinctively illustrated in the painting—child, adolescent, and adult. This sophisticated view of human development relates to the changing views of childhood that developed in the late Tang and Song periods, as discussed in the Barnharts' essay, chapter 2, in this volume. By that time, childhood was seen as an idyllic and separate stage of development. Song painters portrayed children as significant beings in their own right, worthy of coddling, and sources of pleasure to their parents.

The idyllic harmony of the family group portrayed in the *Admonitions* scroll foreshadowed the tone of Southern Song academy paintings, which tended to focus on small pleasures. The depiction of simple joys—family life, children, small animals, bits of nature—is characteristic of Southern Song painting and reveals a humanistic determination to enjoy what was available in a time of rapidly shrinking political grandeur. This painting may also have been a gentle propagandistic effort to convey the message that all was well at the emperor's court. By illustrating harmony in the imperial family, the artist also illustrated the Confucian concept that the emperor who first orders his own house, with every member fulfilling his or her proper role in the social hierarchy, sets a cosmic precedent for order in the state. The need for good government was especially poignant after the end of the Northern Song dynasty; the imperial painting academy played its role to impart that coveted stability. In one sense, the use of children in the *Admonitions* scroll is consistent with portrayals of children in Han-period art—to promote Confucian ideals of harmony and order in the state and to reflect the continuing concern in China that heirs are provided for the imperial patriline. But the sympathetic treatment of the figures goes beyond the symbolic aspects of the painting to show an actual interest in the child as a social being. This phenomenon does not seem to have occurred in art before the Song period, and in fact became uncommon again in later dynasties.

During the Song period, there was an increase among court artists of the illustration of classical texts, especially during the long reign of Emperor Gaozong, from 1127–1163. A nostalgic longing for the glories of the Tang, while at the same time focusing inward, characterizes much of twelfth- and thirteenth-century academy painting. The *Admonitions* scroll was an early example of this type of painting; the trend continued in earnest with illustration by Li Gonglin (ca. 1041–1106) of the *Xiaojing* (Classic of filial piety), at the Northern Song (960–1126) court under Emperor Huizong (r. 1101–1126). Following Li Gonglin's monumental work, the illustration of classical texts became increasingly popular. Emperor Gaozong contributed to the trend, commissioning illustrations for which he himself wrote the calligraphy.

Among Li's illustrations for the eighteen chapters of the *Xiaojing* are four depictions of families from the scholar-bureaucrat class.[10] Each is an intimate family scene with the parents, at center, attended by a grown son. One of the scenes (and probably two, according to an early copy) includes small grandchildren. The illustration for chapter 10 shows an older couple enjoying the entertainment of a magician, a dancer, a puppeteer, and a drummer provided by their grown children (fig. 7.3). The couple's son and his wife bring food, while the grandchildren sit in the foreground, facing their grandparents and watching the entertainment. Notice that the granddaughter is typically older than the grandson, and assigned to care for him. She holds his hand while her parents busy themselves with serving the patriarch and his wife.

A similar scene takes place in a rural setting for the illustration of the sixth chapter (missing in the surviving portion of the original scroll) by an unknown artist who copied Li Gonglin's work, probably in the fourteenth century (plate 16). This picture shows a scholar and his wife, who have retired to the country, seated on a mat in a rustic thatched-roof dwelling. Behind them is a screen of calligraphy that tastefully fits the simplicity of the scene while designating the couple as members of the educated class. A simple bamboo fence frames the courtyard, where a family of chickens scratching in the dirt—cock, hen, and chicks—reinforces the theme of family harmony. Outside the fence, two peasants and a buffalo work in the neatly partitioned fields. The couple's son kneels before them with a bowl of tea or food to serve his father. Behind him stands his bowing wife with a similar bowl for her mother-in-law. The grandchildren, an older girl and her tiny brother, stand in the

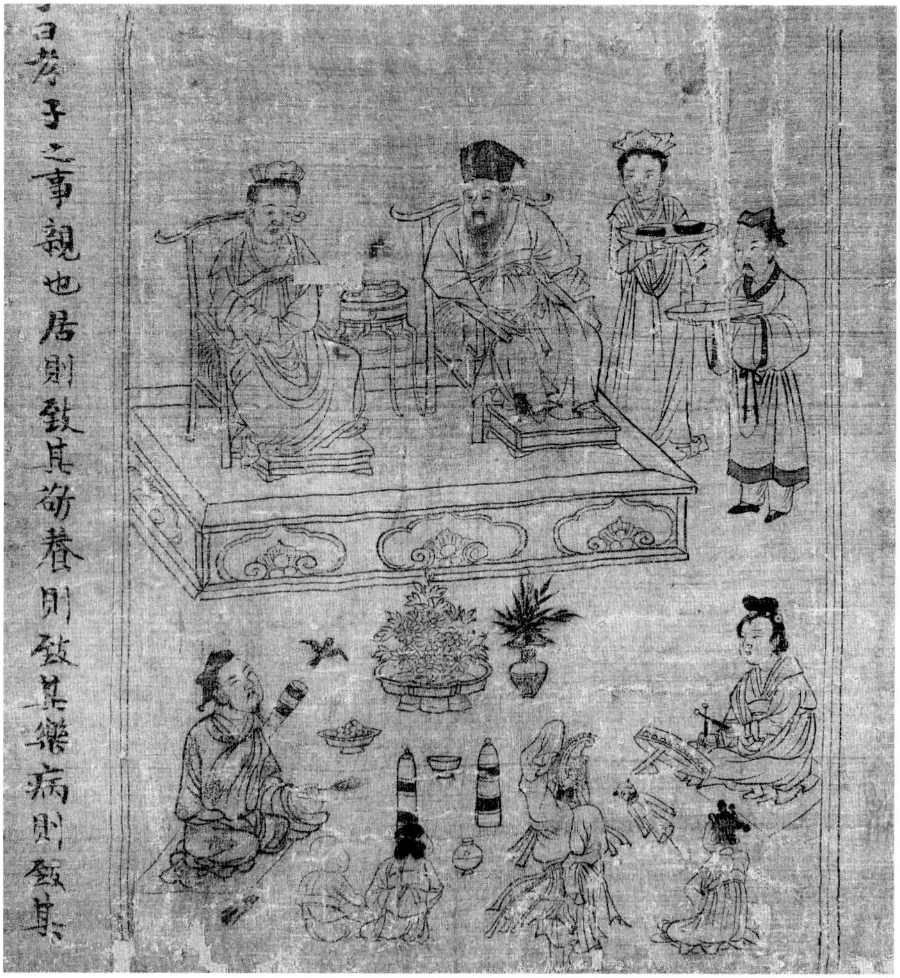

Figure 7.3 Li Gonglin (ca. 1041–1106), illustration to chapter 10 of the *Classic of Filial Piety*. Northern Song, ca. 1085. Detail of handscroll; ink on silk; 21.9 x 475 cm (entire scroll). The Metropolitan Museum of Art. From the P. Y. and Kinmay W. Tang Family Collection, Partial and Promised Gift of Oscar L. Tang Family, 1996. 1996.479a-c. All rights reserved, The Metropolitan Museum of Art.

right foreground of the picture. Both paintings represent three generations of an ideal family, with each member performing his or her expected role.

As stated earlier, after Li Gonglin's rendering of the *Classic of Filial Piety*, the popularity of illustrations of didactic literature increased at the Southern Song court. Depictions of families were occasional details in these works, but still uncommon. One Tang dynasty text that relates the story of Cai Wenji—*Eighteen Songs of a Nomad Flute*—lent itself readily to depictions of the nuclear family, but only at the point of the family's dissolution. Lady Wenji was a Han noblewoman, kidnapped by Xiongnu nomads and later ransomed by her own people. Choosing to leave her non-Chinese husband and two sons behind in order to return to China, Wenji personified both filial piety and the superiority of Chinese culture. Various sets of eighteen scenes painted to match the poems are extant, including a version in the National Palace Museum that is attributed to Li Tang, with calligraphy by Emperor Gaozong.[11] The "family" scenes in these sets are scenes of farewell, as Wenji leaves her non-Chinese husband and her sons to return to her ancestral home. Chosen for illustration here is a single album leaf in the Boston Museum that probably at one time belonged to a full set (fig. 7.4). The tender human emotions expressed in the tightly integrated group of figures is characteristic of Southern Song figure paintings. The closeness of the family seems to defy the imminent departure, and a poignant moment is beautifully portrayed. Yet Wenji's assumed cultural superiority is defined by her position at the apex of the group, and it is clear that personal feelings were not allowed to direct her choice.

Another famous family, that of the poet Tao Qian (365–427), was depicted at least once during the Song period. A twelfth-century handscroll in the Freer Gallery illustrates Tao Qian's celebrated homecoming poem, *Gui yuantian ju wushou* (On returning to my home and fields).[12] As argued by Martin Powers in a discussion of the Freer scroll, the artist's sympathetic rendering of Tao Qian's wife as she and the children welcome him home places the work securely in the humanistic realm of the Song dynasty. The artist's expression of familial and conjugal affection via the homecoming theme can be directly related to the realistic descriptions of private family life in Song poetry as discussed by Catherine and Richard Barnhart in their essay, chapter 2, in this volume. But even though a nuclear family is depicted in the homecoming scroll, it is still a symbolic, not actual, family. The ancient family of Tao Qian is used to portray a burgeoning respect during the Song period for private, more homely pleasures that could override political failures or stressful bureaucratic duties.

Another painting with a controversial date, *Riverbank*, a landscape that recently emerged from the C. C. Wang Family collection, includes a charming detail of a literatus, his wife and children in a thatched pavilion overlooking the water at the base

Figure 7.4 Wenji and her family. Southern Song, late twelfth or early thirteenth century. Formerly attributed to Gu Deqian (active second half of tenth century). Album leaf; ink and color on silk; 24.4 x 22.2 cm. Chinese and Japanese Special Fund, 1912. Courtesy, Museum of Fine Arts, Boston, 12.898.

of the mountain.[13] The figures are tiny in comparison with the landscape, but a close look reveals a seated scholar at the front of the pavilion. His preadolescent daughter stands further back in the pavilion; her mother, holding an infant boy, is even further recessed, standing just in front of a boulder that would hide her and the boy completely if she moved back a step or two. Without entering the ongoing debate over whether the painting is a genuine work of the Five Dynasties (907–960) painter Dong Yuan (active 930s–960s), it should be pointed out that the relaxed pose of the scholar, and the informal inclusion of his wife and children in an outdoor excursion, is consistent with the enjoyment of private family life that was an ideal of Song literati.

The handful of family pictures extant from the Yuan dynasty (1279–1368) are primarily landscapes with the theme of a legendary recluse moving his wife and children. The visual imagery is usually quite different from the pictures discussed above. For one thing, the families are often shown in scattered groups, and sometimes even in humorous disarray, as they make their way through the landscape. Nonetheless, the message is very similar to that of Lady Wenji's departure for China, which is the superiority of Chinese culture. The irony is that the Mongols are now rulers of China, so that "departure" from the world of the nomads must take the form of Confucian eremitism or Daoist escapism, both of which feature landscapes as worlds beyond the reach of vulgar people. Not surprisingly, these same themes reappeared in paintings of the late-Ming period, as the unstable political climate encouraged a resurgence of escapism among the literary elite.

An early-Yuan painter, He Cheng (1224–after 1315), depicted the family of Tao Qian welcoming him home in the opening section of a scroll illustrating the poet's *On Returning to My Home and Fields*.[14] Tao Qian was a natural hero for Chinese literati during the Yuan period. His life and poetry symbolized retreat among the educated class, who looked to him as a model of one able to enjoy rustic pleasures despite the poverty that accompanied his retirement from official duties. The figures in this landscape setting lack the emotional tension of those in the Song scroll. They are hierarchically placed, with Tao's wife and daughters closest to the house, and his son in the center of the composition, with hands raised in a bow to his father, who approaches from the right, standing in a boat. The family is shown in three distinct groups: patriarch, male heir, and females. Nonetheless, the rigid symmetry that is characteristic of Li Gonglin's depictions of families in *Classic of Filial Piety* is broken here by the scurrying of servants throughout the composition.

At the end of the Yuan period, Wang Meng (ca. 1308–1385) painted the family of the famous Daoist alchemist Ge Hong (283–343) as they moved to Guangzhou in search of special ingredients for Ge's elixir of immortality. In the handscroll *Ge Zhichuan Moving His Dwelling*, Ge Hong stands apart from his wife and son, looking back at them from a rustic bridge that crosses a narrow stream in the Luofu Mountains.[15] Riding a bull, his wife and son are surrounded by servants. But Ge Hong stands, without human company, next to a deer as if to symbolize his eventual status as an immortal. The tightly twisting mountains with their thick foliage form a protective barrier for the family from what Wang Meng must have perceived as a very dangerous world.

An anonymous Yuan painter emphasized the provincial manners of the recluse Yang Pu in a humorous rendition of Yang Pu's family's move back to the city after Yang had been persuaded to join the Song bureaucracy as a government official (fig. 7.5). Like a country bumpkin, he wades in the water with his garments rolled up, turning his backside to his wife as he gestures farewell to a group of rural friends with

Figure 7.5 Yang Pu moving his family. Yuan, late thirteenth century. Handscroll; ink and light color on paper; 52.7 x 231.1 cm. Art Institute of Chicago, Kate S. Buckingham Fund, 1952.9. Photograph © 2000, The Art Institute of Chicago.

their simple wives and ragged children. His own wife unabashedly nurses their son as she leads from the wide back of a water buffalo the scraggly procession of servants carrying household goods. This parody of the dignified leave-taking of a noble official could also be read as a pictorial reinforcement of the ideal of reclusion. Yang Pu's rustic life was enviable; his departure from it was humorously out of place. He maintained his individuality even when called into state service.

Another theme of both Yuan and Ming (1368–1644) paintings was the move of Xu Xun's family. The late-Ming painter Cui Zizhong (d. 1644) painted this subject in at least two hanging scrolls that show the family moving through the mountains; both scrolls are reminiscent of Wang Meng's depiction of the family of the alchemist Ge Hong.[16] Xu Xun, a Daoist adept of the Eastern Jin (317–420), was said to have been taken with his entire family into the realm of the immortals to live forever. In the Cleveland version of Cui's painting, the figures are shown high in the mountains. Xu's wife and tiny son lead the procession, seated on a water buffalo surrounded by servants. Xu Xun is mounted on a second buffalo that also pulls a cart in which his mother is seated. A group of servants carrying bundles looks up from the left foreground as the departing group moves up the mountain away from them. Though the theme is appropriately escapist, reflecting hard times for the literati in both the Yuan

and late-Ming periods, there is still an emphasis placed on the preservation of the ancestral line. Though immortality comes only through an individual's dedicated self-cultivation, Xu Xun was still able to manage to take his ancestors (mother) and descendants (son) with him.

One of the details of the murals in Yongle Palace's Chunyang Hall, part of a Daoist monastery completed in 1358, is another example of the enduring necessity of caring for one's ancestors, even in the context of celebrating the individualism of Daoist immortals. Three interior walls of the Chunyang Hall are painted with fifty-two scenes from the life of Lü Dongbin, one of the Eight Immortals of Daoism who became a cult figure in Chinese folk religion.[17] The narrative includes wonderful details of daily life, featuring children at home, in a village school, at the pharmacy. In one scene, a filial son watches as his wife administers medicine (miraculously procured from Lü Dongbin) to his blind mother (plate 17). A capable older daughter brings food for her grandmother, while her young brother stands near the old woman with his hands in her lap. The proximity of the little boy to the grandmother emphasizes his importance to her. Producing a male heir is every bit as much a filial duty as providing a cure for blindness. The son, in scholar's robes and hat, looks at his ideal family with perfect satisfaction. The Confucian hierarchy seen in

Li Gonglin's family scenes in the *Classic of Filial Piety* is preserved in this picture, but the arrangement of the figures is more informal and relaxed. One might not expect to see illustrations of filial piety in a Daoist temple; nonetheless, what seems to be the most enduring of all Chinese values—continuation of the family line—is illustrated here in thoughtful detail.

Lan Ying (1585–after 1660) and Xie Bin (active mid-seventeenth century), late-Ming professional painters with a determined literati flavor to their works, drew a rare picture of a scholar at leisure with his immediate family (fig. 7.6). The handscroll is a portrait of an actual person, referred to in Lan Ying's inscription only by his sobriquet, "the venerable Shiren." The scholar is shown in various landscape settings—walking, using a staff, on a mountain path beneath pine trees; seated, with his elbows resting on a rock, near a mountain stream and pines; gazing with an aged friend through a moon window from his study, while an adolescent boy draws water for tea from a stream; approaching a cavelike rock tunnel, accompanied by another young servant; and finally, seated in a boat with his wife and two young sons. Appropriately, his family appears in the very innermost part of the scroll, symbolizing that they belong to the most private aspects of his life. While the setting is informal, the family is still shown with great propriety. The wife and smallest son are at the back of the boat, almost hidden by a rock that juts out into the stream. The scholar and his older son sit at the front, separated from the "inner quarters" of the boat by a small

Figure 7.6 Lan Ying and Xie Bin, *Scholar in a Landscape*. Early Qing, 1648. Detail of handscroll; ink and color on paper; 11 7/16 x 167 inches. Extended loan to the University of California, Berkeley Art Museum, from the Sarah Cahill Collection. Photographed by Benjamin Blackwell.

table holding books and a bronze wine container. That the scholar is shown at leisure, enjoying a nature outing with his family, is both unusual and heartwarming.

The theme of Xie Bin and Lan Ying's portrait of Shiren appears to be the same as that of other paintings from the Yuan and late-Ming periods that include pictures of families—the escape of the literati from civil service duties. There is a possibility that the family in the boat was not meant to show a pleasure excursion but may instead be another scholar-moves-his-family scene. It is not unreasonable to suggest that, though not directly stated in the inscription, the painting may have been made as a farewell gift for Shiren.

The emphasis on escapism dwindled in the Qing dynasty (1644–1911), at least in works that picture Chinese families. Depictions of parents and small children from that period are most often found among the works of court artists. An interest in documenting daily life led to paintings that featured the families of farmers cheerfully engaged together in agricultural production. This was a type of propaganda that pleased the Manchu emperors because it expressed peace and abundance under their reign.

A Picture of Perfect Felicity (Quanqing tu) attributed to Leng Mei (active ca. 1703–1742), a painter who worked with European artists at the Kangxi (1662–1722) and Qianlong (1736–1795) courts, is a good example of the type of propaganda patronized by members of the wealthy elite, the families of the scholar-bureaucrats (fig. 7.7). Leng Mei belonged to the imperial painting academy during the last two decades of the Kangxi emperor's reign, and then again during the first few years of the Qianlong period, through which he became acquainted with European artists who served at the court. There is no record that he served as a court painter during the Yongzheng reign (1723–1736). *Quanqing tu* was most likely painted during that hiatus from court service, because the signature does not include the word *chen* (your servitor), which was standard for works done at court.[18] In the painting, elegant Chinese figures are placed in a garden setting that emphasizes the architecture—pavilions and walls with variously shaped openings. The architecture and the mountains beyond are organized according to Western devices that he learned at court, such as showing the zigzag walk and the thickness of the wall, through the moon door. The subject is a family gathered to celebrate the Lantern Festival held on the fifteenth day of the lunar year, the last festivity in the observance of the New Year. As a picture for the New Year, it is replete with symbols of good fortune. "Perfect felicity" is illustrated by a harmonious picture of a scholar with his wife, two concubines, and twelve male children playing together in a luxurious garden. Twelve boys corresponds to the number of years in a Chinese cycle, indicating that one's male progeny will continually be replenished.

園
金門畫史冷枚

Figure 7.7 *(facing page)* Leng Mei (active ca. 1703–1742), attrib., *A Picture of Perfect Felicity (Quanqing tu)*. Qing, ca. 1723–1735. Hanging scroll; ink and color on silk; 150 x 99 cm. Cincinnati Art Museum, Gift of Mrs. James L. Magrish, 1953.149.

Visual puns reinforce the message of other good wishes for the New Year. The boy holding a fish-shaped lantern symbolizes affluence, because *yu* (fish) is a homophone for "abundance." An abundance of sons is directly connected to wealth, for a family's best chance for riches and prestige was to raise a son who could pass the civil service exams and enter government service. The two boys at the left of the painting enact the return of a successful civil service candidate to his hometown, pulling a toy carriage and blowing a horn in celebration. In the foreground, four boys play with a lantern made to look like a cage holding five red bats. *Fu* (bat) sounds like the word for "good fortune." In addition, red is the color of happiness in China, and the number five suggests the "five joys," first enumerated in the *Shujing:* long life, riches, health and tranquility, love of virtue, and the ability to fulfill one's destiny.[19] Another boy plays with a *lingzhi* fungus, symbol of longevity. Two wish-granting scepters *(ruyi)*, held by one of the boys in the pavilion and a secondary wife, symbolize that all the aforementioned good fortune will occur "as you wish."

A flourishing bamboo grove can be seen through the moon door and behind the garden wall, while plum trees frame the pavilion. Both these plants are indicative of the season. Together they illustrate the saying *hongmei jieshi; lüzhu shengsun* (the red plum bears fruit; the green bamboo puts forth shoots). The saying describes early spring and reproduction in the plant world. In addition *shengsun* (put forth shoots) is a homophone for "produce grandsons," thus directly referring to human reproduction as well. All the symbols in the painting work together to illustrate that male progeny is the focus of the family's "felicity." Though its figures and setting are more naturalistic than any of the pictures discussed so far in this essay, *Quanqing tu* is still not a picture of a real family. It is the ideal family; the anonymous faces allow it to serve as a portrayal of what many of the wealthy elite supposed was representative of the best life had to offer.

It was among Qing court paintings that portraits of actual families as documents of personal appearance first began to appear. One of the earliest of these works is by Gu Ming (late seventeenth century). His only extant work, *Yunxi Teaching Buddhist Scripture*, is a portrait of an imperial son with his mother (or possibly wife).[20] In the picture, Yunxi, the twenty-first son of the Kangxi emperor, is dressed in plain garments and sits casually on a stool, one leg crossed over the other, leaning on his elbow, on a stone table next to him. He holds a scroll in one hand; antique art objects are laid on the table, and a servant boy approaches holding a few volumes of scripture. Seated opposite him, on a low stone table, is a woman, also plainly dressed, holding the hand of his red-robed little son. In the foreground an elegant young maid prepares refreshments. The boy holds a peach and gestures toward two cats in the foreground, one of which also has a peach. Both cats and peaches symbolize longevity, which is also represented by the child. In the context of this picture, having already fulfilled his filial duty by producing a grandson, Yunxi is free to expound on Buddhist scripture. It is likely that he does this at the request of his mother, who might have taken comfort in playing with her grandchild while listening to the sutras. The figures are comfortably posed, and the artist deftly and warmly individualized the faces of the three royal family members.

There is no question that court painters were influenced by Western ideas of portraiture, as a number of European artists worked alongside Chinese painters at the Manchu court. The most notable of these was the Jesuit Giuseppe Castiglione (1688–1768), an Italian who served as a court painter during the reign periods of the Kangxi, Yongzheng, and Qianlong emperors. Castiglione introduced daringly realistic portraits of the Yongzheng emperor, and catered to Qianlong's flare for drama by painting him costumed in exotic settings.[21] Castiglione's *New Year's Painting (Suichao tu)* is a picture of the Qianlong emperor with two of his wives and nine imperial sons in the midst of an informal celebration of the New Year (plate 18). The setting and composition are very similar to that of Leng Mei's *Quanqing tu*, lively figures arranged around an architectural construct. The father is framed by the pillars of the raised veranda at the far right of both compositions. Children spill out of the geometric frame conveying a sense of abundance, and a moon gate at the left of each composition leads to courtyards beyond. The big difference is the figures, which in Castiglione's work are individually identifiable by personal and highly naturalistic facial features. Castiglione introduced Western-style chiaroscuro and modeling to portraiture, creating illusionary three-dimensional effects, which intrigued the early Manchu emperors.

In the painting, Qianlong sits with the youngest son, dressed in red, on his lap, holding a New Year dumpling on a toasting stick as another son prepares a fire in the brazier at his feet. Three sons wear gold crowns that mark them as children of imperial wives. They are fittingly placed in close proximity to the emperor, with the older two standing at his side; the emperor's two consorts stand behind him, the farthest back from the open courtyard. The picture is filled with the symbols and wordplay that delighted the Qianlong emperor. Two of his children carry sheaves of grain and a bowl of fruit, symbolizing agricultural plenty. One boy carries a lantern in the shape of a fish, symbol of abundance; another son holds a halberd and chime, a rebus for good fortune. Seasonal plants and activities, such as snow-covered bamboo and plum, the lighting of firecrackers, and the making of dumplings, highlight the time of year.

The architectural settings for both Leng Mei's and Castiglione's figures are stock backgrounds, a combination of Western and Chinese elements that was used in numerous court paintings. Thus, although of the two works discussed above, Leng Mei's *Quanqing tu* was probably made a few years earlier than Castiglione's *Suichao tu*, one cannot raise the question of who influenced whom. Leng Mei learned the style at court and used it extensively in backgrounds for his lithe and slender depictions of palace women. It is known that groups of court painters assisted Castiglione in the production of his works. According to art historian Yu Hui, this portrait of Qianlong may have been made around 1738 with the help of court painters Tang Dai, Chen Mei, Sun You, Shen Yuan, and Ding Guanpeng.[22]

Once Castiglione had introduced imperial family portraiture with realistically modeled facial expressions and naturalistic poses, a few other artists used the same features to portray succeeding emperors with their immediate family members. But the daring informality and intimate realism of Castiglione's depictions of Qianlong were not widely copied. It is important to recognize the scale of these portraits of the emperor's family. The works, including the early portraits by Castiglione, were of immense proportions, obviously symbolic of the incomparable status of the "first family" of the imperial state, and examples of them are still rare. Currently all known imperial family portraits are in the collection of the Palace Museum in Beijing.

The same formula used by Leng Mei and Castiglione was used by a group of court artists a century later to paint the Daoguang emperor (r. 1821–1851) with his principal wife and three tiny children in an autumn pavilion (plate 19). Daoguang and his consort are seated at the far right of the painting, framed by the two pillars and an overhanging pine branch at the entrance to the pavilion. Within this square, Daoguang is further framed, seated in the center of a low wooden platform *(kang)* with a landscape screen behind. At the left of the picture, one sees through the window of the covered walkway to the garden and buildings beyond. In the foreground are three children, a maid, and two lesser wives. One of the palace women waters plants, and the other holds the hand of a little boy, presumably her son, who reaches out to pet a dog. The maid carries tea for the emperor and his wife, who are seated in the pavilion. Two other children also play with dogs, on the stone steps of the pavilion. One of them is a little girl! The figures are more stiffly posed than those of Castiglione's, and the faces of the women are stylized. Yet the artist has attempted a more naturalistic effect in the faces of the emperor and the three children.

Two of Daoguang's daughters are also included in *Emperor Daoguang and Family in Spring* (plate 20). The girls are preadolescent, their hair still in side bundles; their lips are cherry red and they are elegantly dressed in green and pink robes. Their names and titles are written next to them: Shou'en and Shou'an, Princesses of the Highest Rank (Shou'en Gulungongzhu; Shou'an Gulungongzhu). Five sons are in the picture, identified only by their birth order—sons four, six, seven, eight, and nine. The sons' names are omitted as a measure of protection. As writing or speaking the personal name of the emperor was taboo, it was safer not to inscribe the names of potential heirs to the throne. Five sons and two daughters were traditionally thought to represent the perfect number and gender balance of children in the ideal Chinese family. The emperor's wife is missing from this painting, so it is not a "family picture" in the same sense as most of the other works discussed in this essay.

The artist has used the same framing technique as Leng Mei and Castiglione, setting the emperor apart by himself in a raised pavilion at the right of the painting. Three small boys, sons seven, eight, and nine, playfully fly kites in the shapes of the auspicious characters *shou* (longevity) and *fu* (good fortune) at the center of the composition. The two older sons are not free to play, however. Like their father, they are seated at writing desks in a pavilion, each framed separately by the posts and lintels of the architecture. Their pavilion is at the left of the composition, lower than that of their father's shelter and connected to it by a stone path. The fourth son *(huang sizi)*, who succeeded his father to the throne, is wearing an imperial yellow robe. He looks up briefly from his painting, as though to pose for a camera shot. Son number six, in a blue gown, pauses from writing calligraphy. The emperor holds a new snuff bottle, alluding to the current fashion of sniffing tobacco. Books, a teacup, writing brushes, and ink are on the elegant tables set in his pavilion. The light green coloring of the willow tree evokes the mood of spring. Other plants include bamboo, peach blossoms, lotus, and cymbidium. The arrangement of the figures is more formal than in the painting by Castiglione, and the postures more stiff, but the artist did make a significant effort to use Castiglione's method of naturalizing and individualizing the family members' faces.

Experimentation with Western techniques to portray identifiable facial characteristics went beyond the court. By the nineteenth century Western-influenced likenesses had become widespread in portraits of men of the literati class. Family pictures were still far under-represented in the corpus of portrait paintings. In fact, group paintings of any sort were less frequently made in the late Qing than individual portraits, in spite of the long tradition of depicting gatherings of the literati. The few depictions that I have come across of two parents and their children preserve the traditional separation of men and women seen in previous pictures and use visual means to emphasize the importance of the patriarch.

A portrait of the family of Xue Chengji by Hua Guan (late eighteenth to early nineteenth centuries) shows Xue in a rustic setting, evoking the theme of retirement and simplicity (plate 21). The trees, the coloring, and the composition itself were taken from the repertoire of Wen Zhengming (1470–1559), who also made landscape "portraits" of retired scholars on their estates. The difference is of course the individualistic treatment of Xue's face. Xue looks directly out at the viewer as he pauses momentarily in the humble task of polishing the surface of a bronze mirror with a stone. His wife and young son look out from the bamboo gate of his thatched-roof country compound. The gaze of the red-robed infant and his mother, however, is not outward but is focused on Xue, who is in the center of the composition. Partially hidden behind the door to Xue's dwelling, their faces are not individualized like that of Xue, but are stylized and anonymous, no different from the stock landscape. Xue's self-cultivation, symbolized by the mirror polishing, is the theme of this picture. His focus on himself is justified by the portrayal of a young son who will attend to family duties in the future. In Chinese culture, individual enlightenment, whether Buddhist, Daoist, Confucian, or otherwise, is allowable and admired only if the patriline has first been provided with an heir.

In a portrait of Jiang Shiquan (1725–1785), Hua Guan shows the scholar with his wife, mother, and three children in a boat (plate 22). In this case, the family members all have individualized faces. They look straightforwardly out of the boat; none of them looks toward Jiang. Only the servants are anonymous; most of them turn away from the viewer and remain completely faceless. The figures are hieratically arranged, with Jiang at the front of the boat, raised slightly on a higher seat than the others and closest to the outside area of the covered boat. Each figure is individually framed and set apart. Jiang, in a relaxed pose, is framed by the arching entrance to the boat's cabin. His two sons are in the outer compartment. The older son is seated at a desk, with books and the windowsill forming a border around him. The younger son sits at the side of his brother's desk, framed against a white partition. The women are in the innermost area of the cabin, but they are not hidden from view. Jiang's wife is framed by one window; her small daughter and Jiang's mother are at the second window. The little girl is centered in the frame, while her grandmother sits behind her and to the side. On the deck, three male servants steer the boat and cook food. Two female servants accompany the women in the inner cabin. The scholar looks relaxed and expansive; he holds a rolled-up scroll in one hand. The two sons are the most crowded and confined, looking almost trapped by the desk, books, and canopied window. The women have much more room within their inner partition. No study materials are set out; instead, a dish of fruit (the ubiquitous symbol of fertility) sits untouched on the table behind them, as though foreshadowing events to come in the life of the little girl. Jiang Shiquan, a poet of some renown, inscribed the painting himself, describing the family's safe return from a mountain outing in spring. At the time the picture was painted, Jiang was thirty-nine years old and in the midst of a successful career.

Conclusion

Family pictures have naturally been idealized in all cultures. They portray what we want to see, what we want to remember about ourselves, and what we hope to project to those who follow us. Photography has extended the possibilities for family image-making, in some degree, to nearly every class of people throughout the world, so that family portraits are fairly common possessions in the twentieth century, in China and elsewhere. Each of these pictures has a story to tell, often about the individuals, but always about the time and the culture in which it was produced.

Within the long history of pre-twentieth-century China, from the time of the first portrayals of family groups in the Han period through the nineteenth century, one might expect wide variations in the ways families were painted. There are some stylistic changes that follow the development of figure painting in China. But overall there is not much diversity in Chinese depictions of the family. Compositional symmetry and stability are emphasized in most of the works. The male-female and generational hierarchies are always accentuated in the placement of figures. The only time a woman is seen in a central position is in depictions of Lady Wenji with her non-Chinese husband. Despite changes in the style of the figures, differences in the historical circumstances and material objects portrayed, or fluctuations in the degree of individualization of the persons depicted, Chinese family pictures project amazingly consistent themes. Each picture embodies the message that the purpose of the family is to produce filial sons. Many of the paintings are charming, and some reveal real warmth and personal interaction among family members. But individuality and personal relationships are not the primary focus. Each picture is entrenched in a conscious portrayal of cultural assumptions about the ideal family. The perfect family has more sons than daughters; the grown sons are filial; women and men live separate lives; girls and very young boys stay with their mothers; men lead the older boys through strictly confined roles to take their places in the outside world. These ideals are the assumptions behind the pictures, the unspoken guidelines that frame the relatively rare visual representations of the Chinese family.

Notes

Chapter 1: Introduction

1. Kinney, "Infancy and the Spirit World in Ancient China"; K. E. Brashier, "Death as Controlled Transformation," paper presented at the Annual Meeting of the Association for Asian Studies, 1995.
2. Michael J. Carr, "Personation of the Dead in Ancient China," *Computational Analyses of Asian and African Languages* 24 (March 1985), 1–108.
3. For examples, see Wu Hung, "Private Love and Public Duty"; idem, *Monumentality in Early Chinese Art and Architecture*, 192–217.
4. Translated and illustrated in Wu Hung, *Monumentality in Early Chinese Art and Architecture*, 201–203.
5. Kinney, "Dyed Silk: Han Notions of the Moral Development of Children"; idem, "Attitudes toward Child's Play in Han China," forthcoming in Kinney, *Representations of Childhood and Youth in Early China*.
6. Published in *Zhongguo meishu quanji*, vol. 8, pl. 66.
7. Isabelle Robinet, *Taoism: Growth of a Religion*, translated by Phyllis Brooks (Stanford: Stanford University Press, 1997); Livia Kohn, *The Taoist Experience: An Anthology* (Albany: State University of New York Press, 1993).
8. Robinet, *Taoism*, 135.
9. Kohn, *Taoist Experience*, 181–188.
10. Illustrated in Kohn, *Taoist Experience*, fig. 17.
11. Clunas, *Pictures and Visuality in Early Modern China*, 117–118.
12. Illustrated in Michael Gough, *The Origins of Christian Art* (New York: Praeger Publishers, 1974), fig. 70.
13. Examples are illustrated in Jessica Rawson, *Chinese Ornament: The Lotus and the Dragon* (London: British Museum, 1984), 40.
14. Translation from Ryoichi Hayashi, *The Silk Road and the Shōsō-in* (New York and Tokyo: Weatherhill/Heibonsha, 1975), 30.
15. Laing, "Auspicious Images of Children in China," 47–48.
16. Furth's contributions in this area include *A Flourishing Yin: Gender in China's Medical History*, 1998; "From Birth to Birth: The Growing Body in Chinese Medicine," 1995; "Rethinking VanGulik: Sexuality and Reproduction in Traditional Chinese Medicine," 1994; and "Concepts of Pregnancy, Childbirth, and Infancy in Ch'ing Dynasty China," 1987.
17. Furth, "From Birth to Birth: The Growing Body in Chinese Medicine,"168–169.
18. Illustrated in Shen C. Y. Fu, *Traces of the Brush: Studies in Chinese Calligraphy* (New Haven, Conn.: Yale University Press, 1980), fig. 32.
19. Translated by Patricia Berger. The painting is illustrated and discussed briefly in James Cahill, ed., *Shadows of Mount Huang: Chinese Painting and*

Printing of the Anhui School (Berkeley, Calif.: University Art Museum, 1981), 111–113.

20. See examples in Hans H. Frankel, *The Flowering Plum and the Palace Lady: Interpretations of Chinese Poetry* (New Haven, Conn., and London: Yale University Press, 1976), 95–103.
21. Ibid., 99–100.
22. Pei-yi Wu, "Childhood Remembered," 145–148.
23. Li Zhi, *Fenshu* (Book burning [Li's collectanea]), 1590. Reprint (Beijing: Zhonghua shuju, 1961), 97–99. Translation is rephrased after Pei-yi Wu, ibid., 147.
24. Scarlett Ju-yu Jang describes in depth the ox-herd metaphor used by Chan monks to explain the ten stages of enlightenment in "Ox-herding Painting in the Sung Dynasty," *Artibus Asiae* (1992), 54–93.
25. Angela Ki Che Leung, "Relief Institutions for Children in Nineteenth-century China," in Kinney, ed., *Chinese Views of Childhood*, 251–278.
26. One of the Yangzhou Eccentrics, Hua Yan (1682–1765), painted *Children's Games in Four Seasons*, 1737, an album of 12 leaves that depicts the activities of ordinary children, entertaining themselves in a rustic village setting. Several versions of the album are extant, including complete sets in the collections of Wango H. C. Weng, Dr. S. Y. Yip, and the Shanghai Museum. [Portions of the version by Wang Su (1794–1877) in Dr. Yip's collection are published in *Anthology of Chinese Art: Min Chiu Society Silver Jubilee Exhibition* (Hong Kong, 1985), no. 90; and Brown and Chou, *Transcending Turmoil*, no. 38.] Hua Yan's move away from showing well-dressed children, with expensive toys, playing in the elaborate gardens of the wealthy was a refreshing innovation, typical of his playful treatment of other traditional themes. The spontaneous play of real children is effectively conveyed by loose, whimsical brush strokes. At the same time, many of the conventions of auspicious imagery are still intact in this album. For example, five boys are included in each of the twelve scenes, the youngest of which usually wears a red jacket. The number of boys is a reference to the story of the five sons of Dou Yujun of the Song dynasty, all of whom passed the imperial examinations and entered officialdom.
27. James Cahill letter to Ann Wicks, 1996.
28. This painting is widely published. See Yang Xin, et. al., *Three Thousand Years of Chinese Painting*, fig. 73.
29. Similar pieces are also in the Metropolitan Museum of Art and I Tatti, Florence, Italy. All are copies after a work by Zhou Wenju; some of them may be parts of the same scroll. See *Eight Dynasties of Chinese Painting* (Cleveland: Cleveland Museum of Art, 1980), 27–29.
30. Illustrated in ibid., fig. 16.
31. I know of two such figures, the one portrayed here, and one in the collection of T. T. Tsui, Hong Kong.

Chapter 2: Images of Children in Song Painting and Poetry

1. The Metropolitan Museum scroll and the Freer fan are discussed in Wen Fong, *Beyond Representation*, 21–26.
2. Illustrated in Laing, "Auspicious Images of Children in China," 49.
3. Ibid., 47–52.
4. The later history of children in auspicious imagery is sketched in Bickford, "Three Rams and Three Friends."
5. Powers, "Discourses of Representation in Tenth- and Eleventh-Century China," 88–125; idem, "Humanity and 'Universals' in Sung Dynasty Painting," 135–145; idem, "Love and Marriage in Song China," 50–62.
6. We are thinking of such sympathetic depictions of foreigners as those in Li Gonglin's *Five Horses*, published in Sirén, *Chinese Painting*, vol. 3, pls. 191–192; and the handscroll in Boston attributed to Li Zanhua known as *Nomads with a Tribute Horse*, published in Wu Tung, *Masterpieces of Chinese Painting from the Museum of Fine Arts, Boston: T'ang through Yuan Dynasties* (Tokyo: Otsuka Kogeisha, 1996), no. 7. Intelligent, courageous, and admirable women are the subject of the illustrated song cycle "Eighteen Songs on a Nomad Flute," published in Robert Rorex and Wen Fong, *Eighteen Songs of a Nomad Flute* (New York: Metropolitan Museum of Art, 1974). Both women and the poor are represented with understanding in Li Gonglin's *Classic of Filial Piety* handscroll in the Metropolitan Museum; see Richard Barnhart, et. al., *Li Gonglin's "Classic of Filial Piety,"* 1993.

7. Deng Chun, *Huaji, juan* 6.
8. See Cahill's essay in Fong and Watt, *Possessing the Past*, 1996, especially p. 174.
9. Liu Fang-ju, "Su Han-ch'en's Children at Play," *National Palace Museum Bulletin* (2000).
10. See especially Powers' "Humanity and 'Universals' in Sung Painting."
11. Kojiro Yoshikawa, *An Introduction to Sung Poetry*, trans. Burton Watson (Cambridge: Harvard University Press, 1967), 17.
12. Translation by Catherine Barnhart. For another translation and discussion of the poem, see Jonathan Chaves, *Mei Yao-ch'en and the Development of Early Sung Poetry* (New York and London: Columbia University Press, 1976), 149–150. Chaves' translation is also included in Wu-chi Liu and Irving Yucheng Lo, eds., *Sunflower Splendor: Three Thousand Years of Chinese Poetry* (Garden City, N.Y.: Anchor Press/Doubleday, 1975), 316. The Chinese text is in *K'uei Yeh Chi* (Bloomington and London: Indiana University Press, 1976), 138.
13. Wu Hung, "Private Love and Public Duty," 79–81.
14. Ibid., 138–140.
15. Pei-yi Wu, "Childhood Remembered," 137–138.
16. Chaves, *Mei Yao-ch'en*, 149; 160–161.
17. Ibid.
18. Wu, "Childhood Remembered," 138–140.
19. Charles Hartman, *Han Yü and the Tang Search for Unity* (Princeton: Princeton University Press, 1986), 101.
20. Wu, "Childhood Remembered," 139.
21. Ibid., 141.
22. Ibid.
23. Ibid., 142.
24. Ibid., 144.
25. Ibid., 141.
26. Yoshikawa, *An Introduction to Sung Poetry*, 66–67.
27. Chaves, *Mei Yao-ch'en*, 24.
28. Burton Watson, *The Columbia Book of Chinese Poetry: From Early Times to the Thirteenth Century* (New York: Columbia University Press, 1984), 136.
29. Ibid., 288–290.
30. Translation by Catherine Barnhart from Chinese text in *K'uei Yeh Chi*, 136–137.
31. Chaves, *Mei Yao-ch'en*, 192.
32. Frederick W. Mote, *The Poet Kao Ch'i* (Princeton: Princeton University Press, 1962), 136–137.
33. Translation by Catherine Barnhart from Chinese text in the Sibu beiyao edition of *Qingqiu shiji zhu* (Shanghai: Zhongua Book Company, n.d.).
34. Tang Hou, *Huajian*, 26.
35. Susan Bush, *The Chinese Literati on Painting* (Cambridge: Harvard University Press, 1971), p. 69, modified.
36. Burton Watson, *The Columbia Book of Chinese Poetry*, 308–309. An interesting discussion of this poem and the theme is found in Powers, "Humanity and 'Universals' in Sung Painting."
37. For a selection of references see James Cahill, *An Index of Chinese Painters and Paintings* (Berkeley: University of California Press, 1980), 228–229.
38. See, for example, the massive pair of herd-boy and buffalo paintings in the Freer Gallery of Art, each measuring about 180 x 150 cm, one of which is reproduced in Richard M. Barnhart, "An Imaginary Exhibition of Chinese Paintings from the Freer Gallery," *Orientations* (March, 1993), fig. 5; and see the introductory essay in this volume, by Wicks and Avril, fig. 1.19.
39. Jang, "Ox-herding Painting in the Song Dynasty."
40. Laing, "Li Sung and Some Aspects of Sung Figure Painting." See also Laing, "Auspicious Images of Children in China," and Powers, "Humanity and 'Universals' in Sung Dynasty Painting."
41. Powers, "Humanity and 'Universals' in Sung Painting," 142.

Chapter 3: One Hundred Children

1. The baby was named Leizhenzi, after the thunder. He developed wings and a beaklike nose, resembling Garuda of Hindu mythology.
2. Liu Fang-ju, *"Zhuse xianrun tidi rusheng,"* 22.
3. Ibid., 20.
4. Ibid., 19.
5. Ibid., 92; Du Shuhua, *"Guhua zhong di ertong tiandi,"* 5.
6. See the discussion by Ellen Avril and Ann Wicks in the introduction to this volume.
7. Yutaka Mino, *Freedom of Clay and Brush through Seven*

Centuries in Northern China: Tz'u-chou Type Wares, A.D. 960–1600 (Bloomington: Indiana University Press, 1981), figs. 138, 140.

8. Fighting with crickets was a favorite pastime at court as well as among commoners. It was especially popular during the Song dynasty.
9. Meng Yuanlao, *Dongjing menghua lu zhu* (Memoirs of the Eastern Capital), annotated by Deng Zhicheng. Reprint (Hong Kong: Hong Kong Commercial Press, 1961), 215; James C. Y. Watt, *Chinese Jades from Han to Ch'ing* (New York: The Asia Society in association with John Weatherhill, Inc., 1980), 110–111.
10. Xiong Liao, ed., *Zhongguo lidai qinghua huadian* (A pictorial dictionary of blue-and-white decorations) (Hangzhou: Zhongguo meishu xueyuan, 1995), vol. 1, pp. 82.3, 84.1, 86.1.
11. James C. Y. Watt and Anne E. Wardwell, *When Silk Was Gold* (New York: Harry N. Abrams, Inc., 1997), 194–195.
12. Peter Y. K. Lam, ed., *2000 Years of Chinese Lacquer* (Hong Kong: Oriental Ceramic Society of Hong Kong and Art Gallery of the Chinese University of Hong Kong, 1993), 138, fig. 70.
13. Ibid., cat. no. 57; Wang Shixiang, *Zhongguo gudai qiqi* (Ancient lacquer vessels of China) (Beijing: Wenwu Press, 1987), no. 63.
14. The Institute of Archaeology, CASS; Museum of Ding Ling; and the Archaeological Team of the City of Beijing, *Ding Ling* (The imperial tomb of the Ming dynasty at Ding Ling) (Beijing: Wenwu Press, 1990), vol. 1, 136–140.
15. *Zhongguo meishu quanji,* vol.8 (Lacquer), pl. 66.
16. Yang Yinshen, *Zhongguo youyi yanjiu,* 18.
17. Ibid., 13.
18. This is also called "to jump the hundred wheels," or *tiao baisuo.* The *bai* in this case is "hundred" instead of "white."
19. Zheng Chuanyin, Zhang Jianzhu, eds., *Zhongguo minsu cidian* (Dictionary of folk customs) (Hong Kong: Commercial Press, 1987), 345.
20. *Ding Ling*, vol. 1, 234.
21. Wang Lianhai, *Zhongguo minjian wanju jianshi,* 181.
22. Liulichang is now a tourist area of Beijing, with shops selling books and antiques.
23. Dun Lichen, *Annual Customs and Festivals in Peking,* 77–78; Wang Lianhai, *Zhongguo minjian wanju jianshi,* 171–174.
24. Wang Lianhai, *Zhongguo minjian wanju jianshi,* 168.
25. Du Shuhua, *"Guhua zhong di ertong tiandi,"* 10.
26. Bartholomew, "Botanical Puns in Chinese Art," 32.
27. Soren Edgren, *Chinese Rare Books in American Collections* (New York: China House Gallery, 1984), 104–105.
28. Ibid., cat. no. 30a.
29. Luan Baoqun and Wang Jing, ed., *Chengshi moyuan* (Mr. Cheng's ink compendium) (Hebei: Hebei meishu chubanshe, 1996), 162. A Ding Yunpeng seal on the woodcut indicates that the nine-sons ink cake was his design.
30. Li Zhongyuan, *Wenshi diangu* (Decorative motifs and allusions) (Shenyang: Liaoning Education Press, 1990), 142.
31. A good description of *doucao* is found in chapter 62 of *Honglou meng* (Red chamber dream), by Cao Xueqin. For a translation, see Yang Hsien-yi and Gladys Yang, *A Dream of Red Mansions* (Beijing: Foreign Language Press, 1978), 2: 369–370.
32. Christie's auction catalogue, *The Jingguantang Collection*, part 2, New York, March 20, 1997. Similar pieces are found in the Philadelphia Museum of Art and the Metropolitan Museum of Art. See *Ming Porcelains* (New York: China House Gallery, 1970), cat. no. 58. For a woodblock illustration of this game see Soren Edgren, *Chinese Rare Books in American Collections,* cat. no. 34 (see note 27).
33. Jacqueline Simcox, *Chinese Textiles* (London: Spink and Sons Ltd., December 5–23, 1994), sales cat. no. 43.
34. *Chinese Textile Masterpieces: Sung, Yuan and Ming Dynasties* (Hong Kong: Plum Blossom International, Ltd., 1988), no. 13.
35. *Gui* refers to the phrase *"changong zhegui* (plucking osmanthus from the Moon Palace)," or passing the civil service examination for the *jinshi* degree.
36. See Julia Murray's essay, chapter 5, in this volume.
37. Wang Shixiang, *Zhongguo gudai qiqi* (Lacquers of ancient China) (Beijing: Wenwu Press, 1987), pls. 75–77.

38. Found as decorations on porcelains and as themes in paintings, these rebuses included *sanyang kaitai* (three male lines begin the *tai* hexagram [the hexagram that represents the first month of the year], symbolizing prosperity in the New Year); *zhiri gaosheng* (a man pointing at the sun, representing an imminent rise in rank); and *qiaolu fenghou* (a bird, deer, wasp, and monkey that form a pun for *juelu fenghou*, or wealth and rank).
39. Zhang Rong, "Carved Lacquers of the Qing Dynasty with the Hundred Children Design," *Wenwu tiandi* 5 (1991): 49; Wang Shixiang, *Zhongguo gudai qiqi*, cat. no. 89.
40. Yang, *A Dream of Red Mansions*, 1:26.
41. Zhang Rong, "Carved Lacquers of the Qing Dynasty," 48–49.
42. Yang Yinshen, *Zhongguo youyi yanjiu*, 46–51.
43. Ibid., 49.
44. National Palace Museum, *Special Exhibition of Ch'ing Dynasty Enamelled Porcelains of the Imperial Ateliers* (Taipei: National Palace Museum, 1992), no. 146.
45. Peter Lam, ed., *Imperial Porcelain of the Late Qing from the Kwan Collection* (Hong Kong: Art Gallery, the Chinese University of Hong Kong, 1983), 43, fig. 8.
46. Maria Rudova, *Chinese Popular Prints*, pls. 58–61.

Chapter 4: Representations of Children in Three Stories from Biographies of Exemplary Women

1. Clunas, *Pictures and Visuality in Early Modern China*, 1997; and Vinograd, *Boundaries of the Self: Chinese Portraiture 1000–1600*, 1992.
2. The most nuanced discussion of this distinction occurs in Dorothy Ko, *Teachers of the Inner Chambers: Women and Culture in Seventeenth-Century China*, 12–14 and *passim;* and Francesca Bray, *Technology and Gender: Fabrics of Power in Late Imperial China*, esp. 139–147.
3. T'ien Ju-k'ang, *Male Anxiety and Female Chastity: A Comparative Study of Ethical Values in Ming-Ching Times* (Leiden: E. J. Brill, 1988), 39.
4. Lisa Raphals, *Sharing the Light: Representations of Women and Virtue in Early China*, 116–117. She also suggests that the importance of illustrations in the late-Ming editions favors lurid tales of virtue over what she refers to as tales of "intellectual virtue."
5. On Lü Kun, see particularly Joanna Handlin, "Lü Kun's New Audience: The Influence of Women's Literacy on Sixteenth-Century Thought," in Wolf and Witke, eds., *Women in Chinese Society*, 13–38.
6. Pei-yi Wu has noted a similar phenomenon in the autobiographical writings of men in the Ming and Qing periods: In accounts of childhood, mothers loom large but fathers are by and large absent. See his "Childhood Remembered," in Kinney, ed., *Chinese Views of Childhood*, 131–133. Charlotte Furth has noted a parallel absence in family instructions. There is very little attention in that genre to children per se; what is of all-consuming interest is adult sons. See Charlotte Furth, "The Patriarch's Legacy: Household Instructions and the Transmission of Orthodox Values," in K. C. Liu, ed., *Orthodoxy in Late Imperial China* (Berkeley and Los Angeles: University of California Press, 1990), 196.
7. Prefatory comments to Huang Shangwen text, cited in Katherine Carlitz, "The Social Uses of Female Virtue in Late Ming Editions of *Lienü zhuan*," *Late Imperial China* (1991), 133.
8. Hegel, *Reading Illustrated Fiction in Late Imperial China*, 164.
9. Hillis Miller, *Illustration* (Cambridge: Harvard University Press, 1992), 102–103.
10. Anne S. Farrer, *The* Shui-Hu Chuan*: A Study in the Development of Late Ming Woodblock Illustration* (Ph.D. diss., Harvard University, 1984), 99. The Chinese term for this style is *"shangtu xiawen,"* which literally means "illustration on top, text on bottom." Robert Hegel writes that this style of illustration first appeared in this particular text (Hegel, *Reading Illustrated Fiction*, 139).
11. Raphals, *Sharing the Light*, 116–117.
12. Carlitz, "The Social Uses of Female Virtue," 128. See also *Zengbu chuanxiang binglin gujin lienü zhuan* (Taipei: Guangwen, 1981).
13. Shih Hsio-yen, "On Ming Dynasty Book Illustration" (M.A. thesis, University of Chicago, 1958), 47–48.
14. Yao Dajuin in Stephen West and Wilt Idema, trans., *The Moon and the Zither: The Story of the Western*

Wing (Hsi Hsiang chi) (Berkeley: University of California Press, 1991).

15. Hegel, *Reading Illustrated Fiction*, 317.
16. There are several translations of this story. See Patricia Ebrey, *Chinese Civilization: A Sourcebook* (New York: the Free Press, 1993), 72–74, and Albert O'Hara, *The Position of Women in Early China*, 40. My translation differs slightly from both of these. The story was illustrated at least as early as the Song period. See Guo Zhongshu (active mid-tenth century), *The Three Moves of Mencius' Mother*, album leaf, ink and light colors on silk, National Palace Museum, Taipei. The *Lienü zhuan* seems to be the earliest extant textual account of the story of Mencius' mother. The brief biography of Mencius in *juan* 74 of the *Shiji* does not discuss his childhood.
17. Lü Kun, *Guifan*, in *Zhongguo gudai banhua xongkan di er pian* (Shanghai: Guji chuban she, 1994) *juan* 4, p. 7a (564). Liu Xiang's text says "When Mencius grew up, he studied the six arts." Lü Kun truncates the passage so that it seems as if the adult Mencius is being reprimanded.
18. I.e., the *Book of Poetry* (*Shijing*) and the *Book of Rites (Liji)*, two of the fundamental texts of the Confucian canon.
19. Lü Kun, *Guifan* (1994), 566.
20. Examples are too numerous to recount. Note however the half tables in *Huitu Lienüzhuan* (Zhibuzuzhai edition, 1779) *juan* 1, pp. 46b–47a and again at *juan* 3, pp. 25b–26a.
21. It is not clear where Tushan is. Some commentators say that it is the name of an ancient state. Three places in China with the name of Tushan claim to be the place where Yu married: one in Anhui, one in Zhejiang, and one in Sichuan. The intriguing possibility exists that the Tushan woman is non-Han, though it seems impossible to verify. At any rate, all the places that claim to be the place where Yu married are rather far afield from the bend of the Yellow River, where the Han state was located. Thus to the mind of the Han recorder of these legends, she may well have carried an exoticism bordering on the foreign. Deborah Porter suggests that Tu refers to a place located in the heavens, in the area between Scorpius and Corona Australis. See Porter, *From Deluge to Discourse: Myth, History, and the Generation of Chinese Fiction* (Albany: State University of New York Press, 1996), 49.
22. *Shiben*, "Dixi," 4.3a, cited in Porter, *From Deluge to Discourse*, 198, n. 77.
23. Arthur Waley, *The Book of Songs* (Boston: Houghton Mifflin, 1937), 215, no. 202.
24. *Lun xu*, which is glossed as *zhi wei* (to support). See Zhang Jing, ed., *Lienüzhuan jinzhu jinshi* (Lienüzhuan: Modern notes and interpretations) (Taipei: Shangau Yingshuguan, 1994), 10.
25. O'Hara, *Position of Women in Early China*, 20–21.
26. Deborah Porter points out a further significance of these four days. In addition to referring to specific days, the terms refer to broadly calendrical time: *Xin* refers to the time period from the autumnal equinox to the first month of winter; *ren* is the period from the first month of winter to the solstice; *gui* begins with the solstice and ends with the first month of spring; and *jia* begins with the first month of spring and ends with the vernal equinox. [Porter cites Léopold de Saussure, *Origines de l'astronomie chinoise* (Paris: Librarie Orientale et Americaine, 1930), 294.] Her interpretation of this has to do with her identification of Yu with Antares, and the disappearance and reappearance of Antares in the sky. She suggests that the winter solstice is connected with marriage, conception, and regeneration, and hence these four days are an appropriate time for Yu to devote himself to domestic work, especially because he is not busy in the skies. See Porter, *From Deluge to Discourse*, 50.
27. For a discussion of the principles of heredity and merit and the ways in which they are mediated in Chinese mythology, see Sarah Allan, *The Heir and the Sage: Dynastic Legend in Early China* (San Francisco: Chinese Materials Center, 1981). See in particular the analysis of Yu and Qi in chapter three.
28. James Legge, *The Chinese Classics* (Hong Kong: Hong Kong University Press, 1960), 3:85.
29. *Lüshi chunqiu*, cited in Lin Geng, *Tianwen lunjian* (Beijing: Renmin wenxue chuban she, 1983), 28–29.
30. *Shiji* (Beijing: Zhonghua shuzhu, 1979) *juan* 2, pp. 80–81. Translated by William Nienhauser, et. al., *The Grand Scribe's Records Volume I: The Basic Annals*

of Pre-Han China (Bloomington: Indiana University Press, 1994), 35.

31. Some scholars read this to be a three-legged turtle. See *Shiben* (*Baibucongshu jicheng*) "Dixi," cited in Porter, 178, n. 198.
32. This passage has aroused some commentarial perplexity. Rémi Mathieu has suggested that it may refer to a shamanistic dance. See Rémi Mathieu, *Anthologie des mythes et légendes de la Chine ancienne* (Paris: Gallimard, 1989), 126.
33. *Han shu* (Beijing: Zhonghua shuju, 1962) *juan* 1, p. 6 (190). See the discussion in Jing Wang, *The Story of Stone* (Durham, N.C.: Duke University Press, 1992), 54; and in Anne Birrell, *Chinese Mythology*, 122–123. Both Wang and Birrell translated the passage. Although I benefited from both translations, my own differs slightly from either. It is worth noting here that Qi literally means "to open up." Yan Shigu's commentary is reproduced in many editions of the *Han shu*. See for example the Sibu beiyao edition, *juan* 6, p. 15b. The ability to turn into a bear, reflecting ancient shamanistic practices, was apparently a family trait. When Gun, Yu's father, turned into a bear, he was returned to human form by a shaman. See "Tian wen," in David Hawkes, *Songs of the South: An Ancient Chinese Anthology of Poems by Qu Yuan and Other Poets* (New York: Penguin, 1985), 129. See also the discussion in Bernhard Karlgren, "Legends and Cults in Ancient China," *Bulletin of the Museum of Far Eastern Antiquities* 18 (1946), 250–251. The misstep onto the stone is attributed by some scholars as the cause of Yu's lameness.
34. Bernhard Karlgren has suggested that the story of the birth of Qi is probably a late one. As Karlgren points out, when Yan Shigu makes a direct quotation, he normally uses the phrase "the text says *(yue)*." In this case, Yan writes "for the affair, see *Huainanzi (shi jian)*." Karlgren interprets this as referring to the laconic mention of Qi's birth from a stone. Karlgren further adduces as evidence for his theory that the story is late because it is not recounted by Han sources such as Wang Chong or Huangfu Mi. His final piece of evidence that the story is late is that the *Lienü zhuan* version makes it quite clear that not only is Qi's mother not transformed into a stone but she raises him to proud adulthood. (Karlgren, ibid., 250–251) The fact that the text is missing from the extant versions of the *Huainanzi* need not concern us overly here. The point that it is repeated in Yan Shigu's authoritative commentary to the Han dynastic history means that it is a version of the story that would have been known to Ming readers. See *A Concordance to the Huainanzi* (Hong Kong: Commercial Press, 1992), 19:205.
35. For a discussion of this text, in addition to the discussion in Hawkes, 1985, see Liu Xiaofeng, "Will Heaven Ever Reply: Qu Yuan and the 'Heavenly Questions,'" translated by Nancy Liu and Lawrence R. Sullivan in *Chinese Studies in Philosophy* 26:4 (summer, 1995). See also the translation and discussion in Victor Mair, *The Columbia Anthology of Traditional Chinese Literature* (New York: Columbia University Press, 1994), 371–381.
36. David Hawkes, *Ch'u Tz'u: The Songs of the South, An Ancient Chinese Anthology* (Oxford: Clarendon Press, 1959), 129. The last line, though lovely English, presents something of a perplexity, and not all commentators would endorse Hawkes' reading. Lin Geng's translation into modern Chinese is something like this: "Why did the sad Tushan lady take up with Yu, who had so little regard for her feelings?" (Lin Geng, *Tianwen lunjian*, p. 30). Victor Mair translated the lines as follows: "Yu's energy was devoted to his work / Having descended to inspect the land below. / How did he get that Tu mountain maid / And unite with her midst the terraced mulberries? / Yearning for a consort, he mated with her / From whose body was born a successor. / Why did he crave different tastes / And feel satisfied with a morning's delight?" (Mair, *Columbia Anthology*, 376). Cheng Jiazhe glosses the phrase "crave different tastes" as indicating that Yu and Tushan came from different ethnic groups *(zulei)*. See Cheng Jiazhe, *Tianwen xinzhu* (Chengdu: Sichuan renmin chubanshe, 1984), 79. Deborah Porter, in a recent reading of the early myths that stresses the spatial and astronomical dimensions, reads the passage as follows: "Yu's ability enabled him to contribute benefits; he descended to survey the land below.

Where did he obtain that girl from Tu mountain, with whom he was man and wife at Taisang?" (*Deluge to Discourse*, 78).

37. Hawkes, *Ch'u Tz'u*, 129.
38. Classical ritual texts stipulated that a man should marry at the age of thirty.
39. Cited in Yuan Ke, *Shenhua xuanshi baiti* (Shanghai: Guji, 1980), 188–189.
40. *Shiji* 49:1947; cited in Raphals, *Sharing the Light*, 17.
41. The text uses the word *xiong*, which literally means "elder brother," to refer to her brother-in-law. The Aunt of Lu is referred to as *gujie*, which normally means "father's sister." The caption refers to the nephew as *zhi*, which means "brother's child."
42. Translation slightly modified from O'Hara, *The Position of Women*, 137. The story was illustrated as early as the Han dynasty in stone tomb reliefs. See Wu Hung, *The Wu-liang Shrine*, 256–257; 160, fig. 121. See also the discussion by Wu Hung in "Private Love and Public Duty," in Kinney, ed., *Chinese Views of Childhood*, 87–88.
43. O'Hara, *Position of Women*, 137.
44. *Lienü zhuan, juan* 5. See the discussion in Chuhui Judy Lai, "The Han Representation of Exemplary Women: Context and Interpretation" (Ph.D. diss., University of Michigan, 1991), 57–59.
45. This radical intervention is characteristic of Lü Kun as an editor. Liu Xiang begins by introducing the virtuous aunt to the reader. Lü Kun simply begins by saying "Qi attacked Lu." The texts continue more or less parallel, with some minor differences. Liu Xiang has the Qi general ask the child, "Is the fleeing woman your mother?" and Lü Kun has him ask, "Who is the fleeing woman?" In a perplexing and poignant interchange that Lü Kun omits, Liu Xiang has the general ask, "Who is the child in your mother's arms?" and the child replies, "I don't know." Another vivid interchange omitted by Lü Kun is the direct threat from the general to the public-spirited aunt. The general raises his bow and cries out, "Stop! If you don't stop I'll shoot you!" The dramatic details that Lü Kun has omitted perhaps limit the empathy that the reader feels for the aunt and her children, but they are generally consonant with the editorial need to shorten.
46. Lü Kun, *Guifan* (1927 reprint), *juan* 4, p. 2. Cited in Lai, "Exemplary Women," 121.
47. Hsu Pi-ching, "Celebrating the Emotional Self: Feng Meng-long and Late Ming Ethics and Aesthetics" (Ph.D. diss., University of Minnesota, 1994).
48. See for example the soldiers in *juan* 3, p. 2b; *juan* 5, p. 12b; *juan* 5, p. 17b; *juan* 6, p. 29a; and Bozong's wife *juan* 2, p. 6a.
49. Margery Wolf, *Women and the Family in Rural Taiwan*, 32–41.
50. Yao and Shun are both sage kings of antiquity who had sons of no particular merit and thus passed the throne on to more virtuous men. For amplification of this theme, see Sarah Allan, *The Heir and the Sage: Dynastic Legend in Early China* (San Francisco: Chinese Materials Center, 1981).
51. Sherry Jenq-yunn Mou, "Gentlemen's Prescriptions for Women's Lives: Liu Hsiang's *The Biographies of Women* and its Influence on the *Biographies of Women*" (Ph.D. diss., Ohio State University, 1994); Carlitz, "Social Uses of Female Virtue," and Katherine Carlitz, "Desire, Danger and the Body: Stories of Women's Virtue in Late Imperial China," in Gilmartin, et. al., eds., *Engendering China*, 101–124.
52. Raphals, *Sharing the Light*, 9. Note that this is the question Raphals brings to the text; she is not asserting that it is intrinsic to the text. Nonetheless, she does pose this text as one that can answer the question.
53. Carlitz, "Desire, Danger, and the Body," 102.

Chapter 5: The Childhood of Gods and Sages

1. A general discussion of this topic is provided in Kinney, "The Theme of the Precocious Child in Early Chinese Literature."
2. For a summary of the portents associated with Jesus' birth, see Belting, *Likeness and Presence*, 279.
3. For a convenient introduction to the textual sources and iconography, see Karetzky, *Life of the Buddha*.
4. Illustrated in Sherman E. Lee, *A History of Far Eastern Art*, 5th ed. (New York: Harry N. Abrams, Inc., 1994), fig. 114.
5. See Ching, "Who Were the Ancient Sages?" Western conceptions of "human" and "divine" do not corre-

spond completely to Chinese ideas about relationships between earthly and heavenly (cosmic) realms.

6. See DeWoskin, "Famous Chinese Childhoods." Zongli Lü further discusses Han ideas that established unusual birth as one sign of the "culture hero," in an unpublished paper, "Miraculous Birth in the Han Texts," for the Association for Asian Studies annual meeting, Boston, 1999.
7. For extended discussion and further sources concerning the complex organization of the religious landscape in late imperial China, see Shahar and Weller, eds., *Unruly Gods*, 1–36; and Romeyn Taylor, "Official Altars, Temples, and Shrines Mandated for All Counties in Ming and Qing," *T'oung Pao* 83 nos. 1–3 (1997): 93–125.
8. Shahar and Weller, *Unruly Gods*, 1.
9. For explicit discussions of competing conceptions of a single deity, see James Watson, "Standardizing the Gods," Duara, "Superscribing Symbols," and Katz, "Enlightened Alchemist or Immoral Immortal?" All of these studies indicate that attempts to "superscribe" certain cults by incorporating them into the official pantheon met with mixed success.
10. The poem is in the "greater odes" *(da ya)* section (Mao no. 245). Its account of Houji is extensively discussed in Kinney, "Theme of the Precocious Child."
11. The purpose of the sacrifice is dramatically changed in Liu Xiang's rendition of Jiang Yuan's life in *Lienü zhuan*, where she is presented as an exemplary mother; translated in O'Hara, *Position of Women in Early China*, 17–19. Liu Xiang states that Jiang Yuan made the sacrifice after conception because she did *not* want to bear the child.
12. Kinney, "Theme of the Precocious Child."
13. These temples have been studied by Ling-en Lu, who discusses the Houji images of one of them in an unpublished paper, "Ming Images of Divine Females in the Mural Paintings at the Jiyi Temple," Association for Asian Studies annual meeting, Washington, D.C., 1998.
14. Wei Xie (active fourth century) is the earliest artist recorded as illustrating the complete *Odes*, which he did for Eastern Jin emperor Mingdi (r. 323–325). Illustrations of individual poems attributed to earlier artists do not include "Birth of the People." For further discussion and references, see Murray, *Ma Hezhi and the Illustration of the Book of Odes*, 8–9.
15. I base this suggestion on the surviving illustration of a thematically comparable poem, "Multitude of the People" ("Zhengmin," Mao no. 260) in the "Tang" chapter of the *da ya;* see reproduction in Murray, *Ma Hezhi and the Illustration of the Book of Odes*, pl. 40. The poem describes the many exemplary accomplishments of the early Zhou minister Zhongshan Fu, which the illustration symbolizes with an idealized portrait of the protagonist, in the posture and clothing of an exemplary Confucian official.
16. These scenes appear on the east wall and are briefly discussed by Ling-en Lu (as in note 13). For black-and-white details, see *Jiyimiao bihua*, compiled by Wang Zeqing and Liang Ziming (Beijing: Renmin meishu chubanshe, 1982), 8–10. A color detail of the abandoned infant is reproduced in *Shanxi gu jianzhu tonglan* [A panorama of ancient Chinese architecture in Shanxi] (Taiyuan: Shanxi renmin chubanshe, 1986), 247; and in *Zhongguo meishu quanji*, vol. 13:155.
17. Ling-en Lu (note 13) reproduces two early-seventeenth-century examples, one that shows birds covering Houji with their wings as he lies on an icy pond (Lu's fig. 10, from *Huitu Lienü zhuan*), the other including motifs from all three of his abandonments (Lu's fig. 11, from *Gu Lienü zhuan*). Lu suggests that even though Jiang Yuan had tried hard to get rid of her newborn baby, Liu Xiang included her as a model mother because once she realized that Houji was divinely protected, Jiang Yuan took him back and raised him well. Alternatively, Anne Behnke Kinney suggests that Jiang Yuan was a good mother for behaving responsibly by trying to get rid of an ill-omened child as a threat to the community; see Kinney, "Infant Abandonment in Early China," 122–123.
18. Murray, "Buddhism and Early Narrative Illustration in China," 17–31; idem, "Evolution of Pictorial Hagiography in Chinese Art," 81–97.
19. Reproduced and discussed in Nagahiro Toshio, *Rikuchō jidai bijutsu no kenkyū* (Research on the arts of the Six Dynasties period) (Tokyo: Bijutsu shuppansha, 1969), English summary, chap. 3, and pl. 10.

20. Reproduced in *Zhongguo meishu quanji,* vol. 19, no. 2. The front of the stele, which features a seated Maitreya in high relief, is reproduced in Katherine R. Tsiang, "Chinese Images of the Dharma: Regional Formulations and National Revisualizations," *Orientations* 29, 2 (February 1998): 71, fig. 1. The zigzag sequence from bottom to top remained an option in much later pictorial biographies, for example in the individual panels of Ming murals illustrating the life of the Buddha at the Jueyuansi in Sichuan (see discussion below). Such an arrangement is also described by Grootaers as a feature of a Yuan or Ming mural in a temple near Xuanhua, Hebei (in the region called "Chahar" when he wrote his account), depicting the life of the god Zhenwu, the "Dark Warrior"; see Grootaers, "Hagiography of the Chinese God Chen-Wu," 167, Dv133a.
21. The stele is reproduced in Tsiang, "Chinese Images of the Dharma," 74, figs. 6a–6b.
22. Fully reproduced and discussed in compilation by Dunhuang Research Institute, *Chūgoku sekkutsu: Tonkō bakukō kutsu,* vol. 1, pls. 174–177; also in *Zhongguo meishu quanji,* vol. 14, pls. 126–131.
23. For extensive reproductions and description, see *Fanzhi Yanshansi.*
24. Baocheng, a native of Siming (Ningbo), was a monk at the Baoensi monastery in Nanjing, the early Ming capital. His compilation was first published in 1425 and subsequently reprinted several times. My discussion is based on an example in the National Central Library (Rare Book no. 8967).
25. The Chinese text gives his name as Pishoujiemotian, which is identified as "all-doer or maker . . . patron of artisans . . . minister of Indra and his director of works"; see Soothill and Hodous, comp., *Dictionary of Chinese Buddhist Terms,* 307b–308a.
26. See Mu Xueyong, ed., *Jian'ge Jueyuansi Mingdai fozhuan bihua,* 2.
27. See ibid., 44. Another seeming discrepancy actually is not; Mu Xueyong inexplicably counted as two scenes the single illustration in which Siddhartha displays his extraordinary strength by shooting an arrow through a row of iron targets and by hurling an elephant. Ibid., 52.
28. The temple was built in 1383 by the first prince of Jin, Zhu Kang, a son of the Ming founder. The hagiographical wall paintings originally occupied the walls of a gallery connected to the Daxiongbaodian, one of six major halls. The reduced-size copies were made during major renovations in the 1470s and 1480s and were probably intended for reference in future repairs. For detailed information and reproductions, see Zhang Jizhong and An Ji, eds., *Taiyuan Chongshansi wenwu tulu* (Taiyuan: Shanxi renmin chubanshe, 1987). No artists' names are recorded for the original murals or the copies, which were given the title *Shijia shizun yinghua shiji tu* (Pictures of the traces of the transformations of the venerable Shakya). There are altogether eighty-four separate pictures, which is fewer than in *Shishi yuanliu* because the latter also illustrates the post-nirvana development of the religion.
29. *Taiyuan Chongshansi wenwu tulu,* 7–10.
30. These connections are discussed by many scholars; see particularly Shahar, "Vernacular Fiction and the Transmission of Gods' Cults," in *Unruly Gods,* 184–211; idem, *Crazy Ji;* Cedzich, "Cult of the Wu-t'ung/Wu-hsien," 137–218; Johnson, ed., *Ritual Opera, Operatic Ritual;* and Grootaers, "Hagiography of the Chinese God Chen-Wu."
31. Katz, "Enlightened Alchemist or Immoral Immortal?" 85–91; idem, *Images of the Immortal.*
32. My understanding of the Yonglegong murals is particularly indebted to Katz, "Enlightened Alchemist or Immoral Immortal?"; and Anning Jing, "A Pictorial Hagiography of Lü Dongbin," unpublished paper for the conference "State and Ritual in East Asia," Paris, 1995. The paintings were done in 1358 by the workshop of Zhu Haogu on the walls of the Chunyangdian (Hall of Purified Yang). See reproductions in *Yonglegong bihua quanji.*
33. Nonetheless, there is some difference between being bathed by human attendants and being showered by nine dragons in the sky. The latter treatment may have been reserved for gods of the highest status. In this regard, it seems significant that illustrations of the "eighty-one transformations" of the Daoist patriarch Laozi include one in which nine dragons shower his

dais with water; see Reiter, *Leben und Wirken Lao Tzu's in Schrift und Bild*, pl. 16b.

34. Grootaers, "Hagiography of the Chinese God Chen-Wu," 145.
35. Shahar, *Crazy Ji*, 59.
36. Kleeman, *A God's Own Tale*, 90–91.
37. *"Tianhou shengmu shiji tuzhi," "Tianjin Tianhou gonghui tu" heji*, notes to pl. 1.
38. See Ching, "Who Were the Ancient Sages?"; idem, *Mysticism and Kingship in China*.
39. Zongli Lü, "Miraculous Birth," and Zhu Pingyi, "Why Were the Sages so Ugly?" unpublished papers for the Association for Asian Studies annual meeting, Boston, 1999.
40. Sima Qian, *Shiji*, *juan* 47, pp. 1905–1947.
41. Although Sima's text is ambiguous (p. 1905), the third-century compilation *Kongzi jia yu* (Sayings of Confucius' family) clearly states that Confucius' mother offered the prayer alone; see *Kongzi jia yu*, *juan* 9, p. 39 (93). Most versions of Confucius' pictorial biography show only Confucius' mother conducting the sacrifice, attended by a couple of maids. However, Ming moralists were obsessed with the idea that women who went out of their homes to participate in religious rituals threatened the social order. Accordingly, a variant composition for this episode in some versions of the pictorial biography shows Confucius' father leading the sacrifice, attended by his wife and servants. For further discussion of the versions with the variant scenes (i.e., the anonymous mid-sixteenth-century third recension known as *Shengji quantu;* Wu Jiamo's *Kongsheng jiayu tu* of 1589; and a *chuanqi* play, ca. early seventeenth century, called *Xinbian Kongfuzi zhouyou lieguo dacheng qilin ji* [Newly compiled record of Master Kong making the rounds of the states and fulfilling the unicorn]), see Murray, "Illustrations of the Life of Confucius."
42. For examples of apocryphal stories about Confucius collected in the Eastern Jin period, see Wang Jia, *Shi yi ji*, *juan* 3, pp. 4–5. Two influential Kong family genealogies that include the miraculous elements are Kong Chuan, *Dongjia zaji* (Miscellaneous records of the Eastern house), 1134, and Kong Yuancuo, *Kongshi zuting guangji* (An expanded record of the Kong lineage), 1227. Both are from Linlang bishi congshu, ser. 65 (Taipei: Guangwen shuju, 1967). See also Jensen, "Wise Man of the Wilds," idem, *Manufacturing Confucianism*.
43. The same versions of the pictorial biography that show Confucius' father sacrificing on Mount Ni (note 41) also include him in this scene. It is he who takes the jade tablet from the *qilin*, not his wife.
44. The classic study of the state cult of Confucius is Shryock, *Origin and Development of the State Cult of Confucius*. For useful updating, see Wilson, *Genealogy of the Way*.
45. For detailed discussion, see Murray, "Temple of Confucius and Pictorial Biographies of the Sage," and "Illustrations of the Life of Confucius."
46. Ching, *Mysticism and Kingship in China*, chap. 2.
47. Ibid., 53. In this regard, it is worth noting that Tang Minghuang (r. 712–756) officially designated Confucius a king in 739. Until abolished in the Jiajing ritual reforms of 1530, the phrase "culture-propagating king" *("wenxuan wang")* was part of Confucius' official title.
48. Kinney, "Theme of the Precocious Child," 19. More often seen is the claim that a distant ancestor of a dynastic house was the incarnation of some god. For example, in 1012, Song Zhenzong announced that the Yellow Emperor had appeared to him in a dream and revealed that he had taken human form as Shengzu (Holy Ancestor), the progenitor of the Zhao family. Tang emperors claimed that Laozi was their Holy Ancestor. See Ebrey, "Portrait Sculptures in Imperial Ancestral Rites in Song China," 53.
49. The accounts were composed by Cao Xun (1098–1174), who was briefly in captivity with Gaozong's mother until he escaped to the south in 1127, and they were illustrated by a court painter or painters. Of the twelve scenes, only seven appear to have survived in some form. The project is described in detail in Murray, "Ts'ao Hsun and Two Southern Sung History Scrolls," 1–7.
50. E.g., see Bian Yongyu, *Shigutang shuhua huikao*, painting section, *juan* 14, pp. 8a–3b; Wu Sheng, *Da guan lu*, *juan* 14, pp. 18a–22b.
51. Kinney, "Theme of the Precocious Child"; idem,

"Dyed Silk: Han Notions of the Moral Development of Children," 17–56. Kenneth DeWoskin points out that auspicious anomalies connected with conception, gestation, and birth are common in informal histories, and especially in fictionalized biographies, by contrast to those in official histories; see DeWoskin, "Famous Chinese Childhoods," 67–68.

52. Liu Xiang originally compiled and illustrated the *Lienü zhuan* as an admonition to the Han emperor Chengdi (33–7 B.C.), perhaps to guide his selection of appropriate consorts. By the Period of Disunion, the stories were understood as directed to women. In *Jingfudian fu* (Rhapsody on the Palace of Luminous Prosperity), the poet He Yan (d. 249) refers to images of exemplary women painted on the walls of the Wei palace for the edification of the palace ladies; see translation and notes, Knechtges in *Wen xuan or, Selections of Refined Literature*, vol. 2 (Princeton: Princeton University Press, 1982), 292–293.
53. Kinney, "Theme of the Precocious Child," 13.
54. Chou, *Scent of Ink*, no. 35.

Chapter 6: The Art of Deliverance and Protection

1. Gan Bao, *Soushen ji*, *juan* 16, p. 376, translated by Kenneth J. DeWoskin and J. I. Crump, Jr., in *In Search of the Supernatural: The Written Record* (Stanford: Stanford University Press, 1996), 183.
2. Hsu Chin-hsiung, "The Life Cycle: Birth, Education, Marriage, and Death," chapter 13 of an unpublished manuscript for the revision of Hsu Chin-hsiung and Alfred H. C. Ward, *Ancient Chinese Society* (San Francisco: Yen Wen Publishing Company, 1984).
3. Alice Getty, *The Gods of Northern Buddhism: Their History and Iconography* (New York: Dover Publications, 1988), 156–168. Other translations of Vaiśravana into Chinese are "Duowen" and "Bishamen."
4. Samuel Beal, trans., *Si-Yu-Ki: Buddhist Records of the Western World*, vol. 4 (Delhi: Bharatiya Publishing House, 1980), 489–490.
5. I am grateful to Dr. Liang Shi, Assistant Professor of Chinese Language and Literature at Miami University; Mr. Wenyi Wu of Oxford, Ohio; and Mr. Yang Qianfu, for reviewing and suggesting improvements to my translations of this and other inscriptions used in this essay.
6. Chün-fang Yü, "*Guanyin:* The Chinese Transformation of Avalokiteshvara," in Weidner, ed., *Latter-Days of the Law*, 151–181.
7. Burton Watson, trans., *The Lotus Sutra* (New York: Columbia University Press, 1993), 300.
8. Miyeko Murase, "Kuan-yin as Savior of Men: Illustration of the Twenty-fifth Chapter of the Lotus Sūtra in Chinese Painting," *Artibus Asiae* 33 (1971), 39–74.
9. Bob Miller, Meher McArthur, Wei Chen-hsuan, and Sam Fogg, *1998 Sam Fogg Rare Books and Manuscripts Catalogue* (London: Sam Fogg, 1998), 12–13, no. 6; and Sam Fogg, *Chinese Books*, catalogue 23 (London: Sam Fogg, 2000), 22–23, no. 11.
10. Illustrated in Fogg, et. al., *1998 Sam Fogg*, 13.
11. *Heluo dana duoluoye*, *Puolujie dishuo buoluo*, and *Jialuo nijia* are variant forms of address for Guanyin that I was unable to translate. The Chinese characters are included in the glossary.
12. Fogg, *Chinese Books*, 22.
13. Burton Watson, trans., *Lotus Sutra*, 304.
14. Hansen, *Changing Gods in Medieval China*, chap. 4, 79–104.
15. *"Lin zhi chi," Book of Odes*, *juan* 1, p. 11, translated by James Legge in *The Chinese Classics* (Hong Kong: Hong Kong University Press, 1960), 4:19.
16. For more information on the goddess of Taishan, see Ken Pomeranz, "Power, Gender and Pluralism in the Cult of the Goddess of Taishan," in Theodore Huters, et. al., *Culture and State in Chinese History: Conventions, Accommodations, and Critiques* (Stanford: Stanford University Press, 1997), 182–206; Edouard Chavannes, *Le T'ai Chan: Essai de monographie d'un culte chinois* (Paris: Leroux, reprint ed., Peking, 1941); Anne Swann Goodrich, *The Peking Temple of the Eastern Peak: The Tung-yueh Miao in Peking and Its Lore* (Nagoya: Monumenta Serica, 1964), 53–76; idem, *Peking Paper Gods: A Look at Home Worship*, Monumenta Serica Monographs Series 23 (1991), 105–132; Naquin and Yü, eds., *Pilgrims and Sacred Sites in China*, 334–338.
17. The dolls at Goddess of Taishan temples are similar in concept to the magic dolls, *mohele*, mentioned in con-

nection with the Qixi festival, in Terese Bartholomew's essay, chapter 3, and in the introduction, chapter 1, in this volume. *Mohele* are also discussed in Bickford, "Three Rams and Three Friends"; and Laing, "Auspicious Images of Children in China."

18. The six additional deities are Zisun Niangniang (Goddess of Sons and Grandsons), Cuisheng Niangniang (Goddess of Swift Delivery), Naimu Niangniang (Goddess of Maternal Milk), Yinmeng Niangniang (Goddess Who Guides Young Children), Douzhen Niangniang (Goddess of Smallpox), and Peigu Niangniang (Goddess Who Strengthens Young Girls [so that they are able to leave their natal home and bear children]).
19. Pomeranz, "Power, Gender and Pluralism in the Cult of the Goddess of Taishan."
20. Whitfield and Farrer, *Caves of the Thousand Buddhas*, 88.
21. These female spirits may be distant ancestors of the *wangye*, plague gods in modern Taiwan who have the power to do evil or good. See Paul Katz, "Demons or Deities? The Wangye of Taiwan," *Asian Folklore Studies* (1987) 46:197–215.
22. I am unable to translate the names of these deities; it is likely that they are Chinese transliterations of Central Asian names.
23. As would be expected, there are varied accounts of the origin of Zhang Xian, but there do not seem to be any accounts that pre-date the Song period. Ten versions are noted by E. T. C. Werner in *A Dictionary of Chinese Mythology* (New York: Julian Press, 1969), 34–35.
24. Getty, *Gods of Northern Buddhism*, 85.
25. Murray, "Representations of Hariti."
26. Red is of course the color of good fortune in China, traditionally worn by brides and children. For additional published examples of Hariti and her son in Ming processional art, see Shanxi Provincial Museum, *Baoningsi Mingdai shuilu hua* (Beijing: Wenwu Press), fig. 84; and Mu Jiaqi, "The Pilu Temple Murals," *Chinese Literature* (June 1982), 90–95.

Chapter 7: Family Pictures

1. Birrell, *Chinese Mythology*, 33–35, 44–47.
2. This translation was done by Richard Wilhelm and taken from Wu Hung, *Wu-liang Shrine*, 247. Wilhelm's sources were Ban Gu, *Baihu Tong* (Proceedings from the White Tiger Hall) 21, in *Congshu jicheng* [Collected collectanea] (Changsha: Shangwu Press, 1937), nos. 238–239; and Wilhelm, *The I Ching*, 3rd ed. (Princeton, N.J.: Princeton University Press, 1967), 329.
3. See Wu Hung, "Private Love and Public Duty" and idem, *Monumentality in Early Chinese Art and Architecture*.
4. See Kinney, "Dyed Silk: Han Notions of the Moral Development of Children."
5. Wu Hung, op. cit.; forthcoming in Kinney, *Representations of Childhood and Youth in Early China*.
6. Translation from Sirén, *Chinese Painting*, 1:32.
7. Terese Bartholomew's essay, chapter 3, in this volume, traces the origin of *baizitu* to the legendary hundred sons of King Wen.
8. From "Lessons from the States: The Odes of Zhou and the South," *juan* 1, p. 5, *The Book of Odes*, trans. James Legge, *The Chinese Classics* (Hong Kong: Hong Kong University Press, 1960), 4:11. The saying *Zhongsi yanqing* (May your offspring be as numerous as locusts), used to congratulate families on the birth of a son, is derived from this ode.
9. Sirén, *Chinese Painting*, 1:30.
10. The scenes illustrate chapters 5, 6, 10, and 13 of the text. See Barnhart, et. al., *Li Gonglin's "Classic of Filial Piety,"* plates 3, 7, 10; fig. 44.
11. The poems exist in several versions, including a version attributed to Cai Wenji herself. See Robert A. Rorex and Wen Fong, *Eighteen Songs of a Nomad Flute: The Story of Lady Wen-chi* (New York: Metropolitan Museum of Art, 1974), 1–2, nn. 3, 4.
12. *Tao Yuanming* [Tiao Qian] *Returning to Seclusion*, twelfth-century handscroll, Freer Gallery of Art, 19.119; illustrated in Powers, "Love and Marriage in Song China," 50, 55, 57, 59.
13. The hanging scroll is extensively illustrated and discussed in Hearn and Fong, *Along the Riverbank*.
14. He Cheng (1224–after 1315), *Tao Yuanming's Homecoming Ode*, handscroll, ink on paper, Jilin Provincial Museum, Changchun. Illustrated in Yang Xin, et. al., *Three Thousand Years of Chinese Painting*, fig. 137.

15. Yang Xin, et. al., *Three Thousand Years of Chinese Painting*, figs. 163–164.
16. The paintings are in the National Palace Museum, Taipei, Taiwan, and the Cleveland Museum of Art. The Cleveland work is illustrated in Yang Xin, et. al., *Three Thousand Years of Chinese Painting*, fig. 225.
17. The Yongle Palace is located in Ruicheng county, Shanxi province, the traditional birthplace of Lü Dongbin. See Julia Murray's essay, chapter 5, in this volume; also, Paul R. Katz, *Images of the Immortal;* and idem, "Enlightened Alchemist or Immoral Immortal?".
18. See Avril, *Chinese Art in the Cincinnati Art Museum*, 80.
19. James Legge, trans., *The Chinese Classics* (Hong Kong: Hong Kong University Press, 1960), 3:5.
20. Illustrated in Yang Xin, et. al., *Three Thousand Years of Chinese Painting*, fig. 251.
21. Yu Hui, "Naturalism in Qing Imperial Group Portraiture," *Orientations* 26:7 (July/August, 1995), 42–50; Wu Hung, "Emperor's Masquerade—'Costume Portraits' of Yongzheng and Qianlong," ibid., 25–41.
22. Yu Hui, op. cit., 44–45.

Glossary of Chinese Characters

Antu shenyin (Identifying the music by reading the notation) 按圖審音

baimiao (line drawing in plain black ink) 白描

Baiyi Dabeixin wuyinxin tuoluoni jing (White-robed Great Compassion five-mudras *dharani* sutra) 白衣大悲心五印心陀羅尼經

Baiyi Songzi Guanyin (White-robed Son-giving Guanyin) 白衣送子觀音

baizitu (hundred-boy picture) 百子圖

Ban Gu (d. A.D. 92) 班固

Baocheng (fourteenth-century monk) 寶成

Baoensi (Baoen Temple) 寶恩寺

baoping (precious vase) 寶瓶

Baotong Jiangjun (General Baotong) 保童將軍

Beiji qianjin yaofang (Prescriptions worth a thousand, for every emergency) 備急千金藥方

Bishamen (Vaiśravana) 比沙門

Bixia Yuanjun (Princess of the Dawn Clouds) 碧霞元君

bolanggu (rattle drum) 撥浪鼓

bubudeng (gourd-shaped glass toy) 布布噔

bucai (without talent) 不才

caiquan (guessing game) 猜拳

Caishen Tianwang (Heavenly King God of Wealth) 財神天王

Cao Xun (1098–1174) 曹勛

changmingsuo (long-life locket) 長命鎖

changong zhegui (to pluck a branch of sweet olive from the moon; i.e., to become a successful candidate in the imperial exam) 蟾宮折桂

chen (your servitor) 臣

Chen Hongshou (1598–1652) 陳洪綬

Chen Mei (active ca. 1730–1742) 陳枚

Cheng Dayue (*zi* Junfang, 1541–ca. 1616) 程大約 (程君房)

Cheng Sui (1605–1691) 程邃

Chengshi moyuan (Mr. Cheng's ink compendium) 程氏墨苑

Chongshansi (Chongshan Temple) 崇善寺

Chuci (Songs of Chu) 楚辭

Chunyangdian (Chunyang Hall) 純陽殿

cong yuan huan cheng ([Shakyamuni] returning from the garden to the palace) 從園還城

Cui Bai (active ca. 1050–1080) 崔白

cuju (football) 蹴鞠

Cui Zizhong (d. 1644) 崔子忠

Cuisheng Niangniang (Goddess of Swift Delivery) 催生娘娘
Da ya (Greater odes) 大雅
Dabeixin tuoluoni jing (Great Compassion *dharani* sutra) 大悲心陀羅尼經
Dai Quheng (1755–1811) 戴衢亨
dao (true way) 道
daotong (transmission of the sagely way) 道通
Dijing jingwu lue (Scenes of the capital) 帝京景物略
Ding Guanpeng (active ca. 1750–1760) 丁觀鵬
Ding Ling 定陵
Ding Yunpeng (1547–1621) 丁雲鵬
Dou Yujun (Dou Yanshan, tenth century) 竇燕山 (竇禹鈞)
doubaicao or *doucao* (competitive game played with "a hundred" herbs) 鬭百草 or 鬭草
Douzhen Niangniang (Goddess of Smallpox) 痘疹娘娘
Du Fu (712–770) 杜甫
Du Hai'er (active 1111–1117) 杜孩兒
Duanwu (Double Five festival; Dragon Boat festival) 端午
Dun Lichen (1853–1911) 敦禮臣
Duowen (Vaiśravana) 多聞
Fang Ruhao (seventeenth century) 方汝浩
Fang Yulu (fl. 1570–1619) 方于魯
fanxie ("flipping shoes" game) 翻鞋
fenben (preparatory sketches) 粉本
Fenshu (Burning the books [collectanea]) 焚書
fu (bat) 蝠, a pun for *fu* (blessing) 福
Fuchuntang 富春堂
Fulushou San Xian (Three Immortals of Happiness, Wealth, and Longevity) 福祿壽三仙
furong (peony) 芙蓉, a pun for *furong* (glorious blessings) 福榮
Fuxi (creator god, husband of Nüwa) 伏羲
Gao Qi (1336–1374) 高啓
Ge Hong (Ge Zhichuan, 283–343) 葛紅(葛稚川)
gong (public) 公
gong yi (public-minded; the public good) 公義
gong zheng cheng xin (public-spirited, upright, sincere, and trustworthy) 公正誠信
Gongzhong tu (Women of the court) 宮中圖
Gou Jing (Dog Star) 狗精
Gu Jianlong (1606–after 1686) 顧見龍
Gu Kaizhi (ca. 345–ca. 406) 顧愷之
Gu Ming (late seventeenth century) 顧銘
guadie mianmian (endless generations of descendants) 瓜瓞綿綿
guan dai chuan liu (official headdress, jade belt, boat, pomegranate) 冠帶船榴, a pun for *guandai chuanliu* (official rank passed down to descendants) 冠帶傳流
Guanyin (Bodhisattva of Mercy and Compassion) 觀音
Gui yuantian ju wushou (On returning to my home and fields) 歸園田居五首
Guifan (Female exemplars) 閨範
Guifan tushuo (Female exemplars, illustrated and explicated) 閨範圖說
guihua (sweet olive; *osmanthus fragrans*) 桂花
guizi (sweet-olive branch) 桂子, a pun for *guizi* (noble sons) 貴子
Guizi Mu (Hariti) 鬼子母
gujie or *guzi* (father's sister) 姑姐 or 姑姊
Gujin lienü zhuan (Biographies of exemplary women in history) 古今列女傳
Gujin tushu jicheng (Imperial collection of books of all ages) 古今圖書集成
Guo Xi (ca. 1001–ca. 1090) 郭熙
Guo Xu (1456–after 1526) 郭詡
Guo Zhongshu (active ca. mid-tenth century) 郭忠恕
Han Yü (768–824) 韓愈
he (box) 盒, a pun for *he* (harmony) 合
he (lotus plant) 荷, a pun for *he* (peace) 和
He Cheng (1224–after 1315) 何澄

He Yan (d. 249) 何晏
Hehe Erxian (Twin Genii of Harmony and Mirth) 和合二仙
Heluo Danna Duoluoye (untranslatable name; refers to Guanyin) 喝羅怛那哆羅夜
Honglou meng (Red chamber dream) 紅樓夢
hongmei jieshi; lüzhu shengsun [shengsun] (the red plum bears fruit; the green bamboo puts forth shoots [produces grandsons]) 紅梅結實; 綠竹生筍 [生孫]
Houji (God of Agriculture) 后稷
Hua Guan (active late eighteenth and early nineteenth centuries) 華冠
Hua Yan (1682–1765) 華喦
huagun (fencing pole used in martial arts) 花棍
Huainanzi (Essays by the Sage of Huainan) 淮南子
Huang Jiayu (fl. 1617) 黃嘉育
Huang Shangwen (fl. 1603) 黃尚文
huang sizi (the fourth imperial son) 皇四子
Huang Tingjian (1045–1105) 黃庭堅
Huang Yingtai (fl. 1603) 黃應泰
Huangting waijing jing (Outer radiance scripture of the yellow court) 黃庭外景經
Huitu lienü zhuan (Illustrated biographies of exemplary women) 繪圖列女傳
huiyuan (first-place candidate in the provincial civil service exam) 會元
ji (halberd) 戟, pun for *ji* (propitious) 吉
Jialuo Nijia (name of an ancient female spirit) 迦盧尼迦
Jiang Shinong (nineteenth century) 姜石農
Jiang Shiquan (1725–1785) 蔣士銓
Jiang Yuan (mother of Houji) 姜原
jianzi (shuttlecock) 毽子, a pun for *jianzi* (see sons) 見子
jieyuan (first-place graduate of the local civil service exam) 解元
Jijialaoli (name of an ancient female spirit) 吉伽牢里
Jingfudian fu (Rhapsody on the Palace of Luminous Prosperity) 景福殿賦
jinjue (promoted to a higher rank) 進爵
jinshi (graduate of the imperial civil service exam) 進士
jiqing (halberd and stone chime) 戟磬, pun for *jiqing* (joyful occasion) 吉慶
jiqing youyu (an abundance of joyful occasions) 吉慶有余
jiuzi mo (nine-sons ink cake) 九子墨
jiwen (requiem) 祭文
jixiang (propitious) 吉祥
Jiyimiao (Jiyi Temple) 稷益廟
jue (bronze ritual vessel) 爵, symbol for *jinjue* (promoted to a higher rank) 進爵
Jueyuansi (Jueyuan Temple) 覺苑寺
junzi (superior man) 君子
juren (graduate of the provincial civil service exam) 舉人
kesi (woven silk tapestry) 緙絲
kongzhong or *kongzhu* (diabolo) 空鐘 or 空竹
Kongzi (Confucius, ca. 551–479 B.C.) 孔子
Kongzi jia yu (Sayings of Confucius' family) 孔子家語
kuangzhi (grave notice) 壙誌
kui (military helmet) 盔, pun for *kui* (first place in imperial exams) 魁
Kuixing (God of Literature) 魁星
Lan Ying (1585–after 1660) 藍瑛
Lanting (Orchid pavilion) 蘭亭
Leizhenzi (Son of Thunder and Lightning) 雷震子
Leng Mei (active ca. 1703–1742) 冷枚
Li Bai (701–762) 李白
Li Gonglin (ca. 1041–1106) 李公麟
Li Shangyin (ca. 813–858) 李商隱
Li Song (active 1190–1230) 李嵩
Li Tang (ca. 1050–after 1130) 李唐
Li Zhaodao (ca. 675–741) 李昭道

Li Zhi (1527–1602) 李贄
liansheng guizi (lotus, mouth organ, sweet olive branch) 蓮笙桂子, a pun for *liansheng guizi* (continuous birth of noble sons) 連生貴子
lianzhong san yuan (to hit three oranges in a row) 連中三橼, a pun for *lianzhong sanyuan* (to take three successive firsts; i.e., first-place candidate in all three imperial exams) 連中三元
Lienü zhuan (Biographies of exemplary women) 列女傳
Liji (Book of rites) 禮記
lingzhi (purple fungus; longevity mushroom) 靈芝
Liu Cai (d. after 1123) 劉寀
Liu Hai (Daoist immortal) 劉海
Liu Rong (active mid-nineteenth century) 劉容 (*zi* Yongzhi 泳之; *hao* Yanchong 彥沖; *hao* Henan 和南)
Liu Songnian (ca. 1150–after 1225) 劉松年
Liu Tong (d. 1637) 劉桐
Liu Xiang (80–9 B.C.) 劉向
Liu Xiang gu Lienü zhuan (Liu Xiang's ancient biographies of exemplary women) 劉向古列女傳
Liu Zongdao (active 1111–1117) 劉宗道
liuli laba (glass trumpet) 琉璃喇叭
Liulichang 琉璃廠
Longnü (Dragon King's daughter) 龍女
Lu, State of 魯
Lü Dongbin (Daoist immortal) 呂洞賓
Lü Kun (1536–1618) 呂坤
Lü Xinwu xiansheng Guifan tushuo (Mr. Lü Xinwu's female exemplars, illustrated and explicated) 呂新吾先生閨範圖說
lunxu (right order and precedence) 倫徐
Lüshi chunqiu (The spring and autumn annals of Mr. Lü) 呂氏春秋
Mao Kun (1512–1601) 茅坤
Mazu (Tianhou, Empress of Heaven, and protector of sailors) 媽祖(天后)
Mei Yaochen (1002–1060) 梅堯臣
Miankai, Prince (1795–1839) 綿愷
min (common people) 民
Mingkan huapu mopu xuanji (Ming collection of painting and ink-cake designs) 明刊畫譜墨譜選集
mohele or *mohouluo* (clay fertility figure in the shape of boy with lotus) 磨喝樂 or 摩候羅
Mojiabanni (name of an ancient female spirit) 磨伽粁泥
Monanning (name of an ancient female spirit) 磨難寧
moxiayu ("finding the fish" game) 摸瞎魚
Moyizhinü (name of an ancient female spirit) 磨醫摭女
muyu (wooden fish) 木魚
Naimu Niangniang (Goddess of Maternal Milk) 奶母娘娘
Nanhai Guanyin (South Seas Guanyin) 南海觀音
nei (inner) 內
Neiguan jing (Scripture of inner observation) 內關經
Neijing tu (Chart of the world in the body) 內經圖
Ni, Mount 尼山
Nüwa (creator goddess; wife of Fuxi) 女媧
Ouyang Xiu (1007–1072) 歐陽修
Peigu Niangniang (Goddess Who Strengthens Young Girls) 培姑娘娘
ping (vase) 瓶, a pun for *ping* (peace) 平
ping'an ruyi (may peace be with you, and all your wishes granted) 平安如意
pipa (four-string guitar; balloon guitar) 琵琶
Pishoujiemotian (Visvakarman) 毘首羯磨天
Puolujie Dishuo Buoluo (untranslatable name; refers to Guanyin) 婆盧羯帝鑠鉢羅
qi (breath, vitality) 氣
Qi (son of Yu) 啓
qiao lu feng hou (bird, deer, wasp, monkey) 雀鹿蜂猴, pun for *juelu fenghou* (wealth and rank) 爵祿封侯
qilin (mythical beast) 麒麟

qilin songzi (the *qilin* brings sons) 麒麟送子
qin (Chinese lute) 琴
qing (emotions) 情
qing (lithophone) 磬, a pun for *qing* (celebration) 慶
Qinyoutang 勤有堂
Qiu (hillock; Confucius) 丘
Qiu Ying (early sixteenth century) 仇英
Qixi (Double Seven festival) 七夕
Quanqing tu (A picture of perfect felicity) 全慶圖
Ren Bonian (1840–1895) 任伯年
renqing (human feeling) 人情
Renri (People's Day festival) 人日
rensheng (ornament made for the Renri festival) 人繩
ruyi (as you wish) 如意
Santaiguan 三臺館
Sanxing (Three Stars; the three star gods; also called Fulushou San Xian) 三星
sanyang kaitai (prosperity in the New Year) 三陽開泰
Shancai (Sudhana) 善才
Shang Di (Lord on High) 上帝
Shangqing (Supreme Purity sect of Daoism) 上清
shangtu xiawen (illustrated text, with the illustrations above the text throughout) 上圖下文
She Yongning (fl. 1618) 佘永寧
shen (god) 神
Shen Bang (fl. 1550–1596) 沈榜
Shen Yuan (active ca. 1745) 沈源
Shen Zhou (1427–1509) 沈周
sheng (sage) 聖
sheng (mouth organ) 笙, a pun for *sheng* (to give birth) 生
"Shengmin" ("Birth of the People") 生民
Shiji (Book of history) 史記
Shijia shizun yinghua shiji tu (Pictures of the traces of the transformations of the venerable Shakya) 釋迦世尊應化事跡圖
Shijiarulai chengdao yinghua shiji ji (Record of Shakyamuni Buddha's attainment of the way and transformation of his life's traces) 釋迦如來成道應化事跡記
Shijing (Book of odes) 詩經
shishi ruyi (pomegranates and scepter) 柿柿如意, pun for *shishi ruyi* (may everything be as you wish) 事事如意
Shishi yuanliu (Origins and evolution of the Shakya clan) 釋氏源流
Shizhuning (name of an ancient female spirit) 石俱寧
shou (longevity) 壽
Shou'en Gulungongzhu; Shou'an Gulungongzhu (Shou'en and Shou'an, Princesses of the Highest Rank) 壽恩固倫公主;壽安固倫公主
shu yuan (schoolroom) 書院
Shui jing zi ji shuai Zhou er wei su wang (The child of the essence of water will succeed the declining Zhou and become an uncrowned king) 水精子繼衰周而為素王
Shujing (Book of documents) 書經
Shuliang He (Confucius' father, late seventh to mid-sixth centuries B.C.) 叔梁紇
Shun (legendary sage king) 舜
si (private) 私
si ai (private love) 私愛
Siling (Four Supernatural Creatures) 四靈
Sima Qian (145–86 B.C.) 司馬遷
Songsheng Niangniang (Goddess of Childbirth) 送生娘娘
Songzi Guanyin (Son-giving Guanyin) 送子觀音
Songzi Niangniang (Son-giving Goddess) 送子娘娘
Soushen ji (Tales of the supernatural) 搜神記
Su Hanchen (twelfth century) 蘇漢臣
Su Shi (1037–1101) 蘇軾
sui (Chinese years of age) 歲
Suichao tu (New Year picture) 歲朝圖
suipan (tray used at the one-year ceremony for a son) 晬盤

Sun Simiao (581–682) 孫思邈
Taihu (Lake Tai) 太湖
Taiyi (sovereign of the interior gods) 太一
Tang Dai (active ca. 1708–1750) 唐岱
Tang Hou (active ca. 1320–1330) 湯后
Tangzi (Tang boy) 唐子
Tao Qian (Tao Yuanming, 365–427) 陶潛(陶淵明)
"Tianwen" ("Heavenly questions") 天問
Tianxian Niangniang (Immortal Empress) 天仙娘娘
tiao baisuo (jump rope game, called "jump the white wheel" or "jump the hundred years") 跳白索 or 跳百索
tong (to bore a hole) 通
tongxin (childlike heart) 童心
Tongxin shuo (On the infant's heart) 童心説
tui zaomo (spinning-date game) 推棗磨
Tushan, woman of 塗山
wai (outer) 外
wanshou (ten thousand years' longevity) 萬壽
Wanshu zaji (Scattered notes of an obliging official) 宛署雜記
Wang Ao (1384–1467) 王翺
Wang Chengpei (d. 1805) 汪承霈
Wang Meng (ca. 1308–1385) 王蒙
Wang Shimin (1592–1680) 王時敏
Wang Su (third century B.C.) 王肅
Wang Wei (699–759) 王維
Wang Yangming (Wang Shouren, 1472–1529) 王陽明(王守仁)
Wangye (Plague Gods) 王爺
Wei Xie (fl. fourth century B.C.) 衛協
Wenchang (Lord of Zitong) 文昌(梓潼帝君)
Wenxuan Wang (Culture-propagating King; Confucius) 文宣王
Wu Daozi (active ca. 710–760) 吳道子
Wu Yue chunqiu (History of Wu and Yue) 吳越春秋
wufeng (martial arts) 武風
wugu fengdeng (the "five grains," lantern) 五谷風燈, a pun for *wugu fengdeng* (a bumper harvest of all crops) 五谷豐登
Wugui (Five Osmanthus Flowers; i.e., the five sons of Dou Yanshan) 五桂
wujing kui (one who finishes first in all five sections of the imperial exam) 五經魁
wushu (martial arts) 武術
wutong (paulownia tree) 梧桐
wuzi duokui (five sons all take first place) 五子奪魁
Xia Yu (legendary king, the subduer of floods) 夏禹
Xiang Yuanbian (1525–1590) 項元忭
Xiaojing, Empress (d. 1612) 孝靖
Xiaojing (Classic of filial piety) 孝經
Xie Bin (*zi* Wenhou, active ca. 1650) 謝彬(文侯)
xin, ren, gui, jia (cyclical markers for days eight, nine, ten, and one in the ten-day week) 辛, 壬, 癸, 甲
xiong (elder brother) 兄
Xixiangji (Romance of the Western chamber) 西廂記
xiyang (playing with goats) 戲羊, a pun for *jixiang* (propitious) 吉祥
Xiyi qiuting (Enjoying the autumn) 喜溢秋庭
Xiyou ji (Journey to the West) 西遊記
xu (to succor) 蓄
Xu Wei (1521–1593) 徐渭
Xu Xun (Xu Zhengyang, Qing) 許峋(許徵陽)
Xue Chengji (mid-eighteenth and early nineteenth centuries) 薛承基
xuri dongsheng (the sun rising in the eastern sky) 旭日東升
Yanguang Niangniang (Goddess of Eyesight) 眼光娘娘
Yanjing suishi ji (Record of a year's time at Beijing) 燕京歲時記
Yan Shigu (581–645) 顏師古
yang (goat) 羊, a pun for *yang* (male principle) 陽 and *yang* (to bear children) 養
yang (nourish) 養
Yangliuqing 楊柳青

Yanshan Wulong (Five Dragons of Yanshan; i.e., the sons of Dou Yanshan) 燕山五龍
Yanshansi (Yanshan Temple) 岩山寺
Yao (legendary sage king) 堯
yehe (union in the wild) 野合
yi (righteousness) 義
Yi Yuanji (eleventh century) 易元吉
Yijialuozhe (name of an ancient female spirit) [宜]伽羅遮
yingxitu (boys-at-play picture) 嬰戲圖
Yinmeng Niangniang (Goddess Who Guides Young Children) 引蒙娘娘
Yonglegong (Yongle Palace) 永樂宮
yu (fish) 魚, a pun for *yu* (abundance) 余
Yu (see Xia Yu) 禹
Yu Xiangdou (fl. 1588–1609) 余象斗
yuan (orange) 櫞
yunluo (cloud gong) 雲鑼
Yunxi (1711–1758) 允禧
zaozi (date) 棗子, a pun for *zaozi* (early arrival of sons) 早子
Zengbu quan xiang pinglin gujin lienüzhuan (Expanded, fully illustrated and explicated biographies of notable women) 增補全相評林古今列女傳
Zhang Hong (1577–after 1660) 張宏
Zhang Kai (1398–1460) 張楷
Zhang Xian (Immortal Zhang) 張仙
Zhang Xuan (active 714–742) 張萱
Zhenwu (the perfected warrior; also called the dark warrior [Xuanwu], and guardian of the North) 真武(玄武)
zhi (brother's child) 姪
Zhi Dun (Zhi Daolin, 314–366) 支遁(支道林)
Zhibuzuzhai 知不足齋
zhi zuo ding shi fu (created to stabilize the world) 製作定世符
zhiri gaosheng (an imminent rise in rank) 指日高升
Zhong Ni (Confucius) 仲尼
Zhongli Quan (Daoist immortal) 鍾離權
zhongsi yanqing (offspring as numerous as locusts) 螽斯衍慶
Zhou Chen (active ca. 1472–1535) 周臣
Zhou Fang (ca. 730–ca. 800) 週昉
Zhou Wenju (active 961–975) 周文矩
Zhou Wen Wang (King Wen, legendary father of Zhou dynasty founder King Wu) 周文王
Zhu Kang, Prince of Jin (1358–1398) 朱康(晉王)
zhuangyuan (first-place graduate of the imperial civil service exam) 狀元
zisun hehe (harmony among descendants) 子孫和合
Zisun Niangniang (Goddess of Sons and Grandsons) 子孫娘娘
zisun ping'an (peace among sons and grandsons) 子孫平安
zongjiao (tufted hair style) 鬃繳

Select Bibliography

Ariès, Philippe. *Centuries of Childhood: A Social History of Family Life*. Translated by Robert Baldick. New York: Vintage Books, 1962.

Avril, Ellen B. *Chinese Art in the Cincinnati Art Museum*. Cincinnati: Cincinnati Art Museum, 1997.

Ayscough, Florence. *Chinese Women: Yesterday and Today*. Boston: Houghton Mifflin Company, 1937.

Baba Harukichi. *Kō Mō Seiseki zukan*. Tokyo: Zendō bunka kenkyūkai, 1940.

Barnhart, Richard M., et. al. *Li Gonglin's "Classic of Filial Piety."* New York: Metropolitan Museum of Art, 1993.

———. *Painters of the Great Ming: The Imperial Court and the Zhe School*. Dallas: Dallas Museum of Art, 1993.

Bartholomew, Terese T. "Botanical Puns in Chinese Art from the Collection of the Asian Art Museum of San Francisco." *Orientations* 16 (9) (September 1985): 18–34.

Belting, Hans. *Likeness and Presence: A History of the Image Before the Era of Art*. Translated by Edmund Jephcott. Chicago and London: University of Chicago Press, 1994.

Berthier, Brigitte. "Enfant de divination, voyageur du déstin." *L'Homme* (1984).

———. *La Dame-du-Bord-de-l'Eau*. Nanterre: Société d'Ethnologie, 1988.

Bian Yongyu. *Shigutang shuhua huikao* (Collected investigations on calligraphy and painting in Model-the-Past Hall), 1682. Wuxing: facsimile reprint of original edition, 1921.

Bickford, Maggie. "Three Rams and Three Friends: The Working Lives of Chinese Auspicious Motifs." *Asia Major* 12 (1) (1999): 127–158.

Birrell, Anne. *Chinese Mythology: An Introduction*. Baltimore: The Johns Hopkins University Press, 1993.

Bonnefoy, Yves. *Asian Mythologies*. Translated by Wendy Doniger. Chicago: University of Chicago Press, 1993.

Bray, Francesca. *Technology and Gender: Fabrics of Power in Late Imperial China*. Berkeley and Los Angeles: University of California Press, 1997.

Brown, Claudia, and Ju-hsi Chou. *Transcending Turmoil: Painting at the Close of China's Empire 1796–1911*. Phoenix: Phoenix Art Museum, 1992.

Burn, Barbara. *Metropolitan Children*. New York: Metropolitan Museum of Art, 1984.

Calvert, Karin. *Children in the House: The Material Culture of Early Childhood, 1600–1900*. Boston: Northeastern University Press, 1992.

Cammann, Schuyler. "Types of Symbols in Chinese Art." In *Studies in Chinese Thought*, edited by Arthur F. Wright. Chicago: University of Chicago Press (1953): 195–231.

Carlitz, Katherine. "The Social Uses of Female Virtue in Late Ming Editions of *Lienü zhuan*." *Late Imperial China* 12 (2) (December 1991): 117–152.

Cedzich, Ursula-Angelika. "The Cult of the Wu-t'ung/

Wu-hsien in History and Fiction." In *Ritual and Scripture in Chinese Popular Religion*, edited by David Johnson. Berkeley: Chinese Popular Culture Project, 1995, 137–218.

Chavannes, Edouard. *The Five Happinesses: Symbolism in Chinese Popular Art*. New York: Weatherhill, 1973.

Children of the Gods: Dress and Symbolism in China. Chinese Children's Dress from the Collection of Valery M. Garrett. Hong Kong: Hong Kong Museum of History, 1990.

Chin, Ann-ping. *Children of China: Voices from Recent Years*. Ithaca: Cornell University Press, 1988.

Ching, Julia. *Mysticism and Kingship in China: The Heart of Chinese Wisdom*. Cambridge Studies in Religious Traditions. Cambridge: Cambridge University Press, 1997.

———. "Who Were the Ancient Sages?" In *Sages and Filial Sons: Mythology and Archaeology in Ancient China*, edited by Julia Ching and R. W. L. Guisso. Hong Kong: The Chinese University Press, 1991, 1–22.

Chou, Ju-hsi. *The Scent of Ink: The Roy and Marilyn Papp Collection of Chinese Painting*. Phoenix: Phoenix Art Museum, 1994.

Chow Tse-tsung. "The Childbirth Myth and Ancient Chinese Medicine: A Study of Aspects of the *Wu* Tradition." In *Ancient China: Studies in Early Civilization*, edited by David T. Roy and Tsien Tsuen-hsuin. Hong Kong: Chinese University Press, 1978, 43–90.

Chūgoku sekkutsu: Tonkō bakukō kutsu (Stone cave temples of China: the Mogao caves of Dunhuang), vol. 1. Compiled by Dunhuang Research Institute. Tokyo: Heibonsha, 1980.

Clunas, Craig. *Pictures and Visuality in Early Modern China*. Princeton: Princeton University Press, 1997.

———. *Superfluous Things: Material Culture and Social Status in Early Modern China*. Cambridge: Oxford University Press, 1991.

Dardess, John. "Children in Premodern China." In *Children in Historical and Comparative Perspective: An International Handbook and Research Guide*, edited by Joseph M. Hawes and N. Ray Hines. New York: Greenwood Press, 1991, 71–94.

Day, Clarence Burton. *Chinese Peasant Cults: Being a Study of Chinese Paper Gods*. Shanghai: Kelly and Walsh, Ltd., 1940.

Deng Chun. *Huaji* (Record of paintings), preface 1167. Reprint. Beijing: Renmin meishu chubanshe, 1963.

Despeux, Catherine. *Immortelles de la Chine ancienne: Taoisme et alchemie feminine*. Paris: Pardés, 1990.

Deval, Jean. "Chinese Tiger Magic." *Threads* 30 (August/September 1990), 62–63.

DeWoskin, Kenneth J. "Famous Chinese Childhoods." In *Chinese Views of Childhood*, edited by Anne Behnke Kinney. Honolulu: University of Hawai'i Press, 1995, 57–78.

Doré, Henry. *Chinese Customs*. Translated and annotated by M. Kennelly. Singapore: Graham Brash Publishers, 1987.

Du Shuhua. "*Guhua zhong di ertong tiandi* (The world of children in ancient Chinese paintings)." *Gugong wenwu yuehkan* 4 (1) (April 1986).

Duara, Prasenjit. "Superscribing Symbols: The Myth of Guandi, Chinese God of War." *Journal of Asian Studies* 47 (1988): 778–795.

Dudbridge, Glen. *The Legend of Miao-shan*. London: Ithaca Press for the Board of the Faculty of Oriental Studies, Oxford University, 1978.

Dun Lichen. *Annual Customs and Festivals in Peking*. Translated and annotated by Derk Bodde. Hong Kong: Hong Kong University Press, 1965.

Eastlake, F. Warrington. "Cantonese Superstitions about Infants." *China Review* 9 (1880), 301–306.

Eberhard, Wolfram. *A Dictionary of Chinese Symbols: Hidden Symbols in Chinese Life and Thought*. Translated by G. L. Campbell. London and New York: Routledge, 1983.

———. *Chinese Festivals*. New York: Henry Schuman, 1952.

———. *The Local Cultures of South and East Asia*. Translated by Alide Eberhard. Leiden: E. J. Brill, 1968.

Ebrey, Patricia Buckley. *The Aristocratic Families of Early Imperial China*. Cambridge: Cambridge University Press, 1978.

———. *Chu Hsi's Family Rituals: A Twelfth-Century Chinese Manual for the Performance of Cappings, Weddings, Funerals, and Ancestral Rites*. Princeton: Princeton University Press, 1991.

———. "Conceptions of the Family in the Sung Dynasty." *Journal of Asian Studies* 43 (2) (1984), 219–243.

———. *Confucianism and Family Rituals in Imperial China: A Social History of Writing about Rites*. Princeton: Princeton University Press, 1991.

———. *Family and Property in Sung China*. Princeton: Princeton University Press, 1984.

———. *The Inner Quarters: Marriage and the Lives of Chinese Women in the Sung Period*. Berkeley: University of California Press, 1993.

———. "Portrait Sculptures in Imperial Ancestral Rites in Song China." *T'oung Pao* 83 (1–3) (1997): 42–92.

———. "Women, Marriage, and the Family in Chinese History." In *The Heritage of China*, edited by Paul Ropp. Berkeley: University of California Press, 1990.

Ebrey, Patricia Buckley, and James L. Watson, eds. *Kinship Organization in Late Imperial China*. Berkeley: University of California Press, 1986.

Fanzhi Yanshansi (The Yanshan temple in Fanzhi). Beijing: Wenwu chubanshe, 1990.

Fong, Mary H. "The Iconography of the Popular Gods of Happiness, Emolument, and Longevity (Fu Lu Shou)." *Artibus Asiae* 44 (2–3) (1983): 159–199.

———. "Wu Daozi's Legacy in the Popular Door Gods *(menshen)* Qin Shubao and Yuchi Gong." *Archives of Asian Art* 42 (1989): 6–24.

Fong, Wen C. *Beyond Representation: Chinese Painting and Calligraphy Eighth–Fourteenth Century*. New York: Metropolitan Museum of Art; New Haven: Yale University Press, 1992.

Fong, Wen C., and James J. Y. Watt. *Possessing the Past: Treasures from the National Palace Museum, Taipei*. New York: Metropolitan Museum of Art, 1996; distributed by Harry N. Abrams, Inc.

Fontein, Jan. *The Pilgrimage of Sudhana: A Study of Gandavyūha Illustrations in China, Japan, and Java*. The Hague; Paris: Mouton, 1967.

Freedman, Maurice. "The Chinese Domestic Family: Models." In *The Study of Chinese Society: Essays*. Stanford: Stanford University Press, 1979.

Furth, Charlotte. "Concepts of Pregnancy, Childbirth, and Infancy in Ch'ing Dynasty China." *Journal of Asian Studies* 46 (1) (1987): 7–35.

———. *A Flourishing Yin: Gender in China's Medical History, 960–1665*. Berkeley: University of California Press, 1998.

———. "From Birth to Birth: The Growing Body in Chinese Medicine," in *Chinese Views of Childhood*, edited by Anne Behnke Kinney. Honolulu: University of Hawai'i Press, 1995, 168–169.

———. "Rethinking Van Gulik: Sexuality and Reproduction in Traditional Chinese Medicine," in *Engendering China: Women, Culture and the State*, edited by Christina K. Gilmartin, et. al. Cambridge: Harvard University Press, 1994, 125–146.

Garrett, Valery M. *Chinese Clothing: An Illustrated Guide*. Hong Kong, New York, and Oxford: Oxford University Press, 1994.

Gernet, Jacques. *Daily Life in China on the Eve of the Mongol Invasion, 1250–1276*. Translated by H. M. Wright. Stanford: Stanford University Press, 1962.

Gilmartin, Christina K., Gail Hershatter, Lisa Rofel, and Tyrene White, eds. *Engendering China: Women, Culture, and the State*. Cambridge: Harvard University Press, 1994.

Grootaers, Willem A. "The Hagiography of the Chinese God Chen-Wu," *Folklore Studies* 11 (2) (1952): 139–181.

Gunter, Ann C. "The Art of Playing." *Asian Art* 4 (1) (winter 1991): 2–5.

Guth, Christine M. E. "The Divine Boy in Japanese Art." *Monumenta Nipponica* 42 (1) (1987): 1–24.

Hansen, Valerie. *Changing Gods in Medieval China: 1127–1276*. Princeton: Princeton University Press, 1990.

Hawes, Joseph M., and N. Ray Hines. *Children in Historical and Comparative Perspective*. New York: Greenwood Press, 1991.

Hawley, W. M. *Chinese Folk Designs*. Reprint. New York: Dover Publications, Inc., 1971.

Hay, John. *Kernels of Energy, Bones of Earth: The Rock in Chinese Art*. New York: China House Gallery, 1985.

Headland, Isaac Taylor. *Home Life in China*. New York: Macmillan Company, 1914.

Hearn, Maxwell K., and Wen C. Fong. *Along the Riverbank: Chinese Paintings from the C. C. Wang Family*

Collection. New York: Metropolitan Museum of Art and Harry N. Abrams, 1999.
Hegel, Robert. *Reading Illustrated Fiction in Late Imperial China*. Stanford: Stanford University Press, 1998.
Houdous, Lewis. *Folkways in China*. London: Arthur Probsthain, 1929.
Hsieh Jih-chang, and Chuang Ying-chang, eds. *The Chinese Family and Its Ritual Behavior*. Taipei: Academia Sinica, 1985.
Hsu, Chin-hsiung, and Alfred H. C. Ward. *Ancient Chinese Society*. San Francisco: Yen Wen Publishing Co., 1984.
Huizinga, Johan. *Homo Ludens: A Study of the Play Element in Culture*, 1938. Reprint. Boston: Beacon Press, 1955.
Imahari Seiji. "A Study of the Protective Institutions for Babies in the Sung Period." *Hiroshima Daigaku, Bungaku-bu kiyo* 8 (October 1955): 127–151.
Jang, Scarlett Ju-yu. "Ox-herding Painting in the Sung Dynasty." *Artibus Asiae* 52 (1992): 54–93.
Jensen, Lionel M. *Manufacturing Confucianism: Chinese Traditions and Universal Civilization*. Durham, N.C.: Duke University Press, 1997.
———. "Wise Man of the Wilds: Fatherlessness, Fertility, and the Mythic Exemplar, Kongzi." *Early China* 20 (1995): 408–37.
Johnson, David, ed. *Ritual Opera, Operatic Ritual*. Berkeley: Chinese Popular Culture Project, 1989.
Johnson, David, Andrew J. Nathan, and Evelyn S. Rawski, eds. *Popular Culture in Late Imperial China*. Berkeley: University of California Press, 1985.
Karetzky, Patricia Eichenbaum. *The Life of the Buddha: Ancient Scriptural and Pictorial Traditions*. Lanham, Md.: University Press of America, 1992.
Katz, Paul R. "Enlightened Alchemist or Immoral Immortal?: The Growth of Lü Dongbin's Cult in Late Imperial China." In *Unruly Gods: Divinity and Society in China*, edited by Meir Shahar and Robert P. Weller. Honolulu: University of Hawai'i Press, 1996, 70–104.
———. "The Function of Temple Murals in Imperial China: The Case of the Yung-lo Kung." *Journal of Chinese Religions* 21 (fall 1993): 45–68.
———. *Images of the Immortal: The Cult of Lü Dongbin at the Palace of Eternal Joy*. Honolulu: University of Hawai'i Press, 1999.
Kinney, Anne Behnke. "Dyed Silk: Han Notions of the Moral Development of Children." In *Chinese Views of Childhood*, edited by Anne Behnke Kinney. Honolulu: University of Hawai'i Press, 1995, 17–56.
———. "Infancy and the Spirit World in Ancient China." *Archaeology Today* (September/October, 1995): 49–52.
———. "Infant Abandonment in Early China." *Early China* 18 (1993): 107–138.
———. "The Theme of the Precocious Child in Early Chinese Literature." *T'oung Pao* 81: facs. 1–3 (1995): 1–24.
Kinney, Anne Behnke, ed. *Chinese Views of Childhood*. Honolulu: University of Hawai'i Press, 1995.
Kleeman, Terry F. *A God's Own Tale: The Book of Transformations of Wenchang, the Divine Lord of Zitong*. Albany: State University of New York Press, 1994.
Knechtges, David R. *Wen xuan or, Selections of Refined Literature*, vol. 2. Princeton: Princeton University Press, 1982.
Ko, Dorothy. "The Complicity of Women in the Qing Good Woman Cult." In *Family Process and Political Process in Modern Chinese History*. Taipei: Academia Sinica, 1992, 451–488.
———. "Pursuing Talent and Virtue: Education and Women's Culture in Seventeenth- and Eighteenth-Century China." *Later Imperial China* 13 (1) (June 1992): 9–39.
———. *Teachers of the Inner Chambers: Women and Culture in Seventeenth-Century China*. Stanford: Stanford University Press, 1993.
Kongzi jia yu (Sayings of Confucius' family). Compiled by Wang Su, third century. Reprint. Taipei: Shijie shuju, 1962.
Kroll, Paul. "In the Halls of the Azure Lad." *Journal of American Oriental Society* 105 (1) (1985): 26–77.
Kulp, Daniel H. *Country Life in South China: The Sociology of Familism*. New York: Columbia University Press, 1925.
Kwok Man Ho, and Joanne O'brien. *The Eight Immortals of Taoism: Legends and Fables of Popular Taoism*. New York: Meridian (Penguin Books), 1991.
Laing, Ellen Johnston. "Auspicious Images of Children in

China: Ninth to Thirteenth Century." *Orientations* (January 1996): 47–52.
———. "Li Sung and Some Aspects of Sung Figure Painting." *Artibus Asiae* 37 (1975): 1–38.
Lee, Thomas, H. C. "The Discovery of Childhood: Children and Education in Sung China (960–1279)." In *Kultur: Begrif und Wort in China und Japan*, edited by Sigrid Paul. Berlin: Dietrich Reimer, 1984, 159–202.
Leung, Angela Ki Che. "Relief Institutions for Children in Nineteenth-century China," in *Chinese Views of Childhood*, edited by Anne Behnke Kinney. Honolulu: University of Hawai'i Press, 1995, 251–278.
———. "Autour de la naissance: la mère et l'enfant en Chine aux xiv et xvii siecles." *Cahiers internationaux de Sociologie* 76: 51–69.
Levering, Miriam L. "The Dragon Girl and the Abbess of Mao-shan: Gender and Status in the Ch'an Buddhist Tradition." *The Journal of the International Association of Buddhist Studies* 5 (1) (1982): 19–35.
Liu Fang-ju. "Su Han-ch'en's Children at Play: Aspects of Style, Court, and Society in Paintings from the National Palace Museum." Translated and adapted by Donald E. Brix. *National Palace Museum Bulletin* 35 (1–2) (2000), 1–48.
———. "*Zhuse xianrun tidu rusheng: Su Hanchen yingxitu shixi* (An analysis of the paintings of children at play by Su Hanchen)." *Gugong wenwu yuekan*, 205 (April 2000), 4–17; 206 (May 2000), 68–82; 207 (June 2000), 61–29.
Macgowan, J. *Sidelights on Chinese Life*. London: Kegan Paul, Trench, Trübner and Co., 1907.
Mann, Susan, and Yu-Yin Cheng, eds. *Under Confucian Eyes: Writings on Gender in Chinese History*. Berkeley: University of California Press, 2001.
Mu Xueyong, ed. *Jian'ge Jueyuansi Mingdai fozhuan bihua* (Ming dynasty mural paintings of the life of the Buddha in the Jueyuan temple, Jian'ge). Beijing: Wenwu chubanshe, 1993.
Murase, Miyeko. "Kuan-yin as Savior of Men: Illustration of the Twenty-fifth Chapter of the Lotus Sutra in Chinese Painting." *Artibus Asiae* 33 (1971): 39–74.
Murray, Julia K. "Buddhism and Early Narrative Illustration in China." *Archives of Asian Art* 48 (1995): 17–31.
———. "The Evolution of Pictorial Hagiography in Chinese Art: Common Themes and Forms," *Arts Asiatiques* 55 (2000): 81–97.
———. "Illustrations of the Life of Confucius: Their Evolution, Functions, and Significance in Late Ming China." *Artibus Asiae* 57 (1–2) (1997): 73–134.
———. *Last of the Mandarins: Chinese Calligraphy and Painting from the F. Y. Chang Collection*. Cambridge: Harvard University Art Museums, 1987.
———. *Ma Hezhi and the Illustration of the Book of Odes*. Cambridge: Cambridge University Press, 1993.
———. "Representations of Hariti, the Mother of Demons, and the Theme of 'Raising the Alms-Bowl' in Chinese Painting." *Artibus Asiae* 43 (4) (1982): 253–284.
———. "The Temple of Confucius and Pictorial Biographies of the Sage." *Journal of Asian Studies* 55 (2) (May 1996): 269–300.
———. "Ts'ao Hsun and Two Southern Sung History Scrolls." *Ars Orientalis* 15 (1985): 1–29.
Nagahiro Toshio. *Rikuchō jidai bijutsu no kenkyū* (Research on the arts of the Six Dynasties period). Tokyo: Bijutsu shuppansha, 1969.
Naquin, Susan, and Evelyn S. Rawski. *Chinese Society in the Eighteenth Century*. New Haven: Yale University Press, 1987.
Naquin, Susan, and Chün-Fang Yü, eds. *Pilgrims and Sacred Sites in China*. Berkeley: University of California Press, 1992.
O'Hara, Albert. *The Position of Women in Early China*. Taipei: Meiya Publications, 1971; Westport, Conn.: Hyperion Press, 1981.
Powers, Martin J. "Discourses of Representation in Tenth- and Eleventh-Century China." In *The Art of Interpreting*, edited by Susan C. Scott. University Park: Pennsylvania State University, 1995, 88–128.
———. "Humanity and 'Universals' in Sung Dynasty Painting." In *Arts of the Sung and Yuan*, edited by Maxwell K. Hearn and Judith G. Smith. New York: Metropolitan Museum of Art, 1996, 135–145.
———. "Love and Marriage in Song China: Tao Yuanming Comes Home." *Ars Orientalis* 28 (1998), 50–62.
Raphals, Lisa. *Sharing the Light: Representations of Women and Virtue in Early China*. Albany: State University of New York Press, 1998.

Rawson, Jessica. "The Lotus and the Dragon: Sources of Chinese Ornament." *Orientations* (November 1984): 22–36.

Reiter, Florian C. *Leben und Wirken Lao Tzu's in Schrift und Bild: Lao-chün pa-shih-i hua t'u-shuo.* Würzburg: Königshausen and Neumann, 1990.

Rudova, Maria. *Chinese Popular Prints.* Leningrad: Aurora Art Publishers, 1988.

Saari, Jon L. *Legacies of Childhood: Growing up Chinese in a Time of Crisis, 1890–1920.* Cambridge: Harvard University Press, 1990.

The Scent of Ink: The Roy and Marilyn Papp Collection of Chinese Painting. Catalogue by Ju-shi Chou. Phoenix: Phoenix Art Museum, 1994.

Shahar, Meir. *Crazy Ji: Chinese Religion and Popular Literature.* Harvard-Yenching Monograph Series, 48. Cambridge: Harvard University Asia Center, 1998.

Shahar, Meir, and Robert P. Weller. *Unruly Gods: Divinity and Society in China.* Honolulu: University of Hawai'i Press, 1996.

Shishi yuanliu (The origins and evolution of the Shakya clan). Compiled by monk Baocheng. Nanjing, 1425.

Shryock, John. *The Origin and Development of the State Cult of Confucius,* 1932. Reprint. New York: Paragon Books, 1966.

Sima Qian. *Shiji* (Records of the historian). Beijing University punctuated and annotated second edition. Beijing: Zhonghua shuju, 1982.

Sirén, Osvald. *Chinese Painting: Leading Masters and Principles.* 7 vols. New York: Ronald Press Company; London: Lund Humphries, 1956.

Snow, Edward. "Meaning in *Children's Games:* On the Limitations of the Iconographic Approach to Bruegel." *Representations* 1 (2) (spring 1983): 26–60.

Soothill, William Edward, and Lewis Hodous, comps. *A Dictionary of Chinese Buddhist Terms.* London: Kegan Paul, et. al., 1934. Reprint. Taipei: Chengwen Publishing Co., 1969.

Spiro, Audrey. *Contemplating the Ancients: Aesthetic and Social Issues in Early Chinese Portraiture.* Berkeley: University of California Press, 1990.

Taiyuan Chongshansi wenwu tulu (An illustrated catalogue of the cultural artifacts of the Chongshan temple in Taiyuan). Edited by Zhang Jizhong and An Ji. Taiyuan: Shanxi renmin chubanshe, 1987.

Tang Hou. *Gujin Huajian* (Evaluation of ancient and modern paintings), ca. 1325. Reprint. Beijing: Renmin meishu chubanshe, 1962.

Taylor, Romeyn. "Official Altars, Temples, and Shrines Mandated for All Counties in Ming and Qing." *T'oung Pao* 83 (1–3) (1997): 93–125.

T'ien Ju-k'ang. *Male Anxiety and Female Chastity: A Comparative Study of Ethical Values in Ming-Ching Times.* Leiden: E. J. Brill, 1988.

"Tianhou shengmu shiji tuzhi," "Tianjin Tianhou gonghui tu" heji (Pictorial annals of the traces of the Holy Mother Empress of Heaven), late Qing. Reprint. Hong Kong: Heping tushu youxian gongsi, 1991.

Tomita Kojiro. "Two Chinese Paintings Depicting the Infant Buddha and Mahaprajapati." *Boston Museum of Fine Arts Bulletin* 42 (1944): 13–20.

Tsiang, Katherine R. "Chinese Images of the Dharma: Regional Formulations and National Revisualizations." *Orientations* 29 (2) (February 1998): 71–82.

Vinograd, Richard. *Boundaries of the Self: Chinese Portraiture 1000–1600.* Cambridge: Cambridge University Press, 1992.

Waltner, Ann. *Getting an Heir: Adoption and the Construction of Kinship in Late Imperial China.* Honolulu: University of Hawai'i Press, 1990.

———. "Kinship between the Lines: The Patriline, the Concubine and the Adopted Son in Late Imperial China." In *Gender, Kinship, Power: A Comparative and Interdisciplinary History,* edited by Mary Jo Maynes, Ann Waltner, Birgitte Soland, and Ulrike Strasser. New York: Routledge, 1996.

———. "The Moral Status of the Child in Traditional China: Childhood in Ritual and Law." *Social Research* 54 (3) (1986): 667–687.

Wang Jia. *Shi yi ji* (Collection of remaining anomalies), third century. Reprinted in *Baibu congshu jicheng,* ser. 9. Taipei: Yiwen yinshu guan, 1966.

Wang Lianhai. *Zhongguo minjian wanju jianshi* (A concise history of Chinese folk toys). Beijing: Beijing gongyi meishu chubanshe, 1991.

Watson, James L. "Standardizing the Gods: The Promotion of T'ien Hou (Empress of Heaven) along the South China Coast, 960–1960." In *Popular Culture in Late Imperial China,* edited by David Johnson,

Andrew J. Nathan, and Evelyn S. Rawski. Berkeley: University of California Press, 1985, 292–324.
Watson, Rubie S., and Patricia Buckley Ebrey, eds. *Marriage and Inequality in Chinese Society*. Berkeley: University of California Press, 1991.
Watson, William. *Tang and Liao Ceramics*. New York: Rizzoli International Publications, 1984.
Wei Dong. *Zhongguo gudai ertong ticun huihua* (Ancient Chinese paintings of children). Beijing: Palace Museum, 1987.
Weidner, Marsha, ed. *Latter-Days of the Law: Images of Chinese Buddhism 850–1850*. Honolulu: University of Hawai'i Press, 1994.
Whitfield, Roderick, and Anne Farrer. *Caves of the Thousand Buddhas: Chinese Art from the Silk Route*. New York: George Braziller, 1990.
Williams, C. A. S. *Outlines of Chinese Symbolism and Art Motives*. New York: Dover Publications, 1976.
Wilson, Thomas A. *Genealogy of the Way: The Construction and Uses of the Confucian Tradition in Late Imperial China*. Stanford: Stanford University Press, 1995.
Wolf, Arthur P. *Marriage and Adoption in China, 1845–1945*. Stanford: Stanford University Press, 1980.
Wolf, Margery. "Child Training and the Chinese Family." In *Studies in Chinese Society*, edited by Arthur Wolf. Stanford: Stanford University Press, 1978.
———. *The House of Lim: A Study of a Chinese Farm Family*. New York: Appleton-Century-Crofts, 1974.
———. *Women and the Family in Rural Taiwan*. Stanford: Stanford University Press, 1972.
Wolf, Margery, and Roxane Witke, eds. *Women in Chinese Society*. Stanford: Stanford University Press, 1975.
Wu Hung. *Monumentality in Early Chinese Art and Architecture*. Stanford: Stanford University Press, 1995.
———. "Private Love and Public Duty: Images of Children in Early Chinese Art." In *Chinese Views of Childhood*, edited by Anne Behnke Kinney. Honolulu: University of Hawai'i Press, 1995, 79–110.
———. *The Wu-liang Shrine: The Ideology of Early Chinese Pictorial Art*. Stanford: Stanford University Press, 1989.
Wu, Pei-yi. "Childhood Remembered: Parents and Children in China, 800–1700." In *Chinese Views of Childhood*, edited by Anne Behnke Kinney. Honolulu: University of Hawai'i Press, 1995, 129–156.
———. "Education of Children in the Sung." In *Neo-Confucian Education: The Formative Stage*, edited by William Theodore deBary and John W. Chaffee. Berkeley: University of California Press, 1989.
Wu Sheng. *Da guan lu* (Record of extensive looking), 1712. Collated and reprinted by Li Zunian. Wujin, 1920.
Yang Xin, Richard M. Barnhart, Nie Chongzheng, James Cahill, Lang Shaojun, and Wu Hung. *Three Thousand Years of Chinese Painting*. New Haven and London: Yale University Press; Beijing: Foreign Languages Press, 1997.
Yang, C. K. *The Chinese Family in the Communist Revolution*. Westport, Ct.: Greenwood Press, 1984.
Yang Yinshen. *Zhongguo youyi yanjiu* (A study of Chinese games), 1935. Reprint. Shanghai: Shanghai wenyi chubanshe, 1990.
Yanshansi Jindai bihua (Jin dynasty mural paintings in the Yanshan temple). Beijing: Wenwu chubanshe, 1983.
Ying-hsi-t'u: Paintings of Children at Play. Exhibition catalog. Taipei: National Palace Museum, n.d.
The Yongle Palace Murals. Beijing: Foreign Languages Press, 1985.
Yonglegong bihua quanji (Complete collection of mural paintings in the Palace of Eternal Joy). Tianjin: Renmin meishu chubanshe, 1997.
Young, Marilyn B. "Virtuous Wives and Good Mothers: Women in Chinese Society." In *Tradition and Creativity: Essays on East Asian Civilization*, edited by Ching-I Tu. New Brunswick: Rutgers East Asian Studies University Publications, 1987.
Yü, Chün-fang. "Images of Kuan-yin in Chinese Folk Literature." *Han-hsueh yen-chiu* (Chinese folk studies) 8 (1) (June 1990): 221–286.
Yuan Tian. *Chinese Folk Toys and Ornaments*. Beijing: Foreign Language Press, 1980.
Zhang Rong. "Carved Lacquers of the Qing Dynasty with the Hundred Children Design." *Wenwu tiandi*, 1991: 5.
Zhongguo gudai banhua congkan (Compilation of traditional Chinese woodblock printing). Compiled by Zheng Zhenduo. Shanghai: Gudian wenxue chubanshe, 1958.
Zhongguo meishu quanji (Complete collection of Chinese art), 20 vols. Beijing: Wenwu chubanshe, 1988.

Contributors

Ellen B. Avril is Curator of Asian Art at the Herbert F. Johnson Museum of Art, Cornell University. Previously she served as Associate Curator for Far Eastern Art at the Cincinnati Art Museum. She holds an M.A. in art history from the University of Kansas, and is the author of *Chinese Art in the Cincinnati Art Museum*, 1997.

Catherine E. Pease Barnhart is the director of the China Teaching Program at Western Washington University, where she has also taught Chinese language and literature. She holds a Ph.D. in modern Chinese literature from Stanford University and has published articles on childhood in China and on the novelist Wu Zuxiang.

Richard Barnhart is the John M. Schiff Professor Emeritus of art history at Yale University. His numerous books and articles have centered on Chinese landscape painting. Currently he is studying the man-made landscape of early China and its connection to the rest of the ancient world.

Terese Tse Bartholomew is Curator of Himalayan Art and Chinese Decorative Art at the Asian Art Museum of San Francisco. She graduated from the University of California at Los Angeles with an M.A. in the History of Chinese Art in 1968. She has published in the areas of Chinese ceramics, visual puns in the decorative arts, and Himalayan art. Her exhibitions include *Mongolia: The Legacy of Chinggis Khan* (1995), for which she coauthored the catalogue with Patricia Berger.

Julia K. Murray received a Ph.D. in Chinese Art and Archaeology from Princeton University in 1981 and B.A. and M.A. degrees in East Asian Studies from Yale

University in 1974. Currently Professor of Art History at the University of Wisconsin, she previously taught at Harvard University and Mt. Holyoke College. She has also been a curator at the Harvard University Art Museums and held research positions at the Freer Gallery of Art and Metropolitan Museum of Art. Her books include *Ma Hezhi and the Illustration of the Book of Odes* (Cambridge University Press, 1993) and *Last of the Mandarins* (Harvard University Art Museums, 1987). Her most recent work is on narrative illustration and pictorial biography.

ANN WALTNER is Professor of History at the University of Minnesota and editor of the *Journal of Asian Studies*. She received a Ph.D. in history from the University of California at Berkeley in 1981, and an M.A. in Asian Studies from Yale University in 1973. Her work is in Ming history, concentrating on gender, kinship, and religion. Publications include *Getting an Heir: Adoption and the Construction of Kinship in Late Imperial China* (University of Hawai'i Press, 1990); a co-edited volume (with Mary Jo Maynes, Birgitte Soland, and Ulrike Strasser), *Gender, Kinship, Power: A Comparative and Interdisciplinary History* (Routledge, 1996); and *The World of a Late Ming Mystic: Tanyangzi and her Followers* (University of California Press, forthcoming).

ANN BARROTT WICKS is Professor of Asian Art History at Miami University in Oxford, Ohio. She received a Ph.D. in Oriental Art History from Cornell University in 1982, and an M.A. in Asian Studies in 1977 from Cornell University. She has published in the areas of Qing and modern Chinese painting, including *Painting Paradise: The Art of Ting Shao Kuang* (China Books and Periodicals, 1998).

Index

Amitabha, Buddha, 6, 8
apsaras, 6–8, 121

Baiyi Dabeixin wuyinxin tuoluoni jing (White-robed Great Compassion five-mudras *dharani* sutra), 141, 193
baizi (hundred-boys), 16, 57–59, 63–64, 72, 74–76, 193; pictures of, 19 fig. 1.14, 34, 62 fig. 3.4, 63 fig. 3.5
Ban Gu (d. A.D. 92), 159–160, 193
Baocheng (fourteenth-century monk), 120, 188n. 24, 193
Baotong Jiangjun (General Baotong), 149, plate 13, 193
Beiji qianjin yaofang (Prescriptions worth a thousand, for every emergency) by Sun Simiao, 12, 193
Bishamen. *See* Vaiśravana
Bixia Yuanjun (Princess of the Dawn Clouds). *See* Taishan, Goddess of
Book of Odes (*Shijing*), 110, 113, 149, 162, 197
Buddha, childhood of. *See* Shakyamuni, Buddha

Caishen Tianwang (Heavenly King God of Wealth; Vaiśravana), 135, 193. *See also* Vaiśravana
Cai Wenji (Lady Wenji, second century), 165; picture of, 166 fig. 7.4
Castiglione, Giuseppe (1688–1766), 174–175, 176, plate 18
Chardin, Jean Baptiste Siméon (1699–1779), 38
Cheng Dayue (*zi* Junfang, 1541–ca. 1616), 68, 69, 71, 71 fig. 3.19, 193
Chengshi moyuan (Mr. Cheng's ink compendium) by Cheng Dayue, 69, 193
Cheng Sui (1605–1691), 20, 21 fig. 1.16, 193
Chen Hongshou (1598–1652), 18, 193, plate 2
Chen Mei (active ca. 1730–1742), 175, 193
childbirth, of emperors, 130; of gods, 108–109, 110, 116, 117, 121–123, 126, 129, 134; of literati, 131–132; pictures of, 113 fig. 5.2, 122–124 figs. 5.9–5.11, 129 fig. 5.14; of sages, 109
child development, fetal, 12; stages of life, 17, 21, 23, 162; theories of, 11–12, 24
childlikeness, 4, 23; naturalness, 49, 53–54; spontaneity, 23, 24; *tongxin* (childlike heart), 23, 198
Chongshansi (Chongshan Temple) murals, Taiyuan, Shanxi, 121–123, 124 fig. 5.10, 188n. 28, 193
Chuci (Songs of Chu), 96, 193
civil service exams, symbols of passing the, 19–20, 78–79, 81–83
Classic of Filial Piety (*Xiaojing*), 163–165, 164 fig. 7.3, 167, plate 16, 198
conception, miraculous, 108, 110, 119, 126, 127, 128, 132
Confucius (ca. 551–479 B.C.), 4, 99, 110; birth of, 128–129,